Trois Etoiles

The Member for Paris a Tale of the Second Empire

Vol. 2

Trois Etoiles

The Member for Paris a Tale of the Second Empire
Vol. 2

ISBN/EAN: 9783742817327

Manufactured in Europe, USA, Canada, Australia, Japa

Cover: Foto ©Thomas Meinert / pixelio.de

Manufactured and distributed by brebook publishing software
(www.brebook.com)

Trois Etoiles

The Member for Paris a Tale of the Second Empire

COLLECTION

OF

BRITISH AUTHORS

TAUCHNITZ EDITION.

VOL. 1184.

THE MEMBER FOR PARIS BY TROIS-ETOILES. (*Murray*)

IN TWO VOLUMES.

VOL. II.

THE MEMBER FOR PARIS:

A TALE OF THE SECOND EMPIRE.

BY

TROIS-ETOILES.

COPYRIGHT EDITION.

IN TWO VOLUMES.—VOL. II.

LEIPZIG

BERNHARD TAUCHNITZ

1871.

CONTENTS

OF VOLUME II.

THE MEMBER FOR PARIS.

THE presence of the Prince of Arcola in M. Poche-molle's shop—a novel incident on the day when Horace first beheld that nobleman there—had gradually become an event of daily occurrence. M. Macrobe knew what he was about when he brought the Prince to see Mdlle. Georgette. The Prince, to his weakness for horses and heraldry, added a third more artistic weakness for women. It was not the weakness of a debauchee, but the highly-cultivated and epicurean worship for what he deemed the fairer and incomparably better half of creation.

The Prince of Arcola was one of those gentlemen who would be all the happier for having some object to their lives. To be sure, he cherished an ambition, which was to win the French Derby, and when he had accomplished that, then the English Derby—but this dream, for the fulfilment of which he relied much more on his trainer's indomitable efforts than on his own, only engrossed his energies in a partial manner, and left him time enough on his hands to feel that the world was occasionally wearisome. He would have liked to possess a large estate had that been practicable; but it was not according to his notions. If he were to begin forming a vast domain, it must be split up at his death and allotted in equal portions to his heirs, whoever they might be: and if there were half-a-dozen of these heirs, the portion of each would be about the size of an English yeoman's farm. This was beggarly. Had aliens been permitted to hold land in England, he would have got out of his difficulties by emigrating there and founding an estate under the tutelary auspices of primogeniture. As it was, he had more than once turned over the project of getting himself naturalized, only it was the probationary residence under some roof, not his own, which balked him.

Very correct in his attire, cut by an English tailor, shaved *à l'Anglaise*—that is, sporting moustache and whiskers, but no beard, and irreproachably gloved, he had adopted the habit of driving down to the Rue Ste. Geneviève in his phaeton to see Horace. But somehow he generally came at hours when his friend was absent: and this furnished a pretext for stepping into the shop below and staying sometimes half-an-hour, sometimes more. The visit of a prince might be a rather appalling circumstance in the life of a British haberdasher: especially if that prince had a prancing equipage and a groom in livery waiting for him at the street corner; but the shoulders of Frenchmen are equal to any weight of honour. After the first interview or two, M. Pochemolle set down the frequent calls to the pleasure M. d'Arcola probably took in his, M. Pochemolle's conversation. There would be nothing strange in that. M. le Prince and he held, he had observed, identical views on most points. When talking politics, M. Pochemolle said:

"We men of order"—implying the solidarity existing between all persons of conservative mind—such as the Prince and himself—as against the disorderly or *canaille*.

That Georgette was not so blind need hardly be said. As she plied her needle in seeming unconsciousness, the motives of the Prince of Arcola's frequent visits could not quite escape her. At first they importuned her, these visits, and she scarcely opened her lips. But women who have been slighted are wounded in their self-love as well as in their deeper affections, and there was nothing unnatural in the fact that a homage which raised her in her own eyes by proving that all men were not as disdainful of her as Horace had been, should come to be regarded, not with pleasure indeed, but with something approaching to a mild sense of gratitude. She now and then hazarded a timid answer to some of the Prince's remarks, and her mother said she was beginning to look better.

"I am not more fortunate than usual," said the Prince, walking into the shop with a smile, after inquiring uselessly for Horace one afternoon, some five weeks after M. Macrobe's fête. "Madame Pochemolle and Mademoiselle, your servant. M. Pochemolle, why this is seditious literature: are you, too, on our friend's committee?"

"Why, no, mon prince; I was just reading one of the addresses M. Gerold has circulated," responded M. Pochemolle, ruefully, and he displayed an enormous yellow poster, headed: "*Dixième Circonscription Electorale de la Seine. Candidature de l'Opposition. Circulaire à MM. les Electeurs.*"

"I hear the candidature is progressing remarkably well," said the Prince, accepting the seat which the draper hastened to offer him. "M. Gerold has a capital list of names on his committee, all the Orleanist phalanx, Baron Margauld at the head of them."

"And yourself, M. le Prince?" asked Mdme. Poche-molle.

"No, I am not on it, being no free agent; from father to son we must be Bonapartists in our family. But I give good wishes, and anonymous subscrip-tions."

"Which is what M. Macrobe does too, I hear," said M. Pochemolle, sighing. "Dear me, M. le Prince, this is a most awkward predicament; I never voted for a Republican in my life, except when they were in power, yet I could never bring myself to vote against M. Gerold."

"Providence has left a door of escape out of every human dilemma, M. Pochemolle. A cold in the head or an attack of gout are never-failing excuses. M. Macrobe, too, was in a difficulty. As Chairman of the Crédit Parisien, and newly-appointed Knight of the Legion, he could not decently have taken open part against the Government. So he labours under the rose, and is most indefatigable. If Gerold gets through it will be mainly owing to him."

"He is a most honest man, M. Macrobe, and the shares of the Crédit Parisien continue to rise every day," said M. Pochemolle.

"I shall be glad to see M. Horace deputy," re-marked his wife; "though there will be no reading his speeches in the paper now that the Government pro-hibits parliamentary reports. He will have a silver-laced uniform, with a sword, and twelve thousand francs a year."

"Supposing he be elected," added the Prince, doubtfully, "but I am afraid it is not so sure. You see how the Radicals are treating him: they have refused to support his candidature; and that new paper of theirs, *Le Tocsin*, assaults him in a most scoundrelly way."

"Yes, I brought a copy of it home yesterday," grinned M. Alcibiade Pochemolle, who was measuring enough calico to make a petticoat. "They blackguarded him like good 'uns—said he only wanted to get into the House to finger the salary and then turn his coat and betray the party. I never read anything like it. M. Horace killed that other journalist for much less than that."

"Why should not the *Tocsin* say all this if it be true?" said Georgette calmly, without raising her eyes from her work. "It is a newspaper's duty to enlighten the public."

This was the first time Georgette had spoken, and her remark was so unexpected, so utterly at variance with the habitual gentleness of her speech, that everybody remained silent-struck. The Prince, who was seated close to the counter behind which she worked, examined her rapidly, and noticed that her lips were set, that her eyes gleamed, and that her needle-hand, as it stitched with feverish haste, trembled, and often missed the point. She looked up and repeated quietly: "M. Horace Gerold has given no proof that he is better than other men. It seems to me that gold is the only thing for which people care nowadays. For that they would sell their bodies and their souls."

"Georgette!" exclaimed M. Pochemolle, scandalized and frightened; and Mdme. Pochemolle, letting fall her work on the floor, grew red and white by turns.

The Prince, divining some emotion which had found its vent in the impulse of a wild moment, and which doubtless was already repenting having betrayed itself, came quickly to Georgette's relief.

"Mademoiselle speaks in a general way," he said. "She means that electors are so often imposed upon that they may be excused for being a little suspicious. I agree with her, and think that under existing circumstances we may perhaps make special allowances for our Radical friends. They have not a single representative in the House, and they are naturally anxious to get a member who will reflect their peculiar views better than M. Gerold, who, as Mademoiselle says, is as fond as we all are of the comforts and refinements which money procures."

Georgette thanked him by a glance. M. Pochemolle drew a sigh of satisfaction, having swallowed the explanation with entire faith. Mdme. Pochemolle, whether her woman's acuteness accepted it or not, pretended to do so; and thus the Prince was enabled to divert the conversation into a new channel. He had brought tickets for a new play which was making everybody weep at the Théâtre de la Gaieté. If there was one thing Mdme. Pochemolle liked more than another it was to have a good evening's cry over a melodrama, particularly when this satisfaction was afforded her in a stage box presented by some generous donor.

"And you will go, too, Mademoiselle, if you allow me to counsel you," said the Prince, speaking not very loud.

Though she had not yet recovered from the quiverings of her nervous excitement, she answered with more attention than she had ever lent him before: "What is the play about, Monsieur?"

"It treats of a young girl," said he slowly, and looking at her, "who has been faithlessly abandoned by a man she loved . . . ."

"Yes," continued she, interrupting him whilst her eye flashed, "abandoned for a woman who had gold to give. Go on, Monsieur, the story is an old one."

"Another man—of a different character—touched by her condition, pitying, admiring and loving her, offers her his heart . . . ."

"And she?"

"Accepts . . . ."

"I think not, Monsieur le Prince," returned she calmly. "The girl answered that she stood in no need of pity; that admiration is not always a tribute to be proud of; and that for a man to offer his heart to a girl who is not his equal is but another way of saying that he thinks her fallen lower than she is."

CHAPTER II.

Canvassing.

GEORGETTE'S outburst of wrath and abrupt revulsion of feeling as regards Horace were not mere caprice. They were due to her knowledge of what had passed between him and Angélique. In her dismay at the unforeseen climax brought about by her negotiations in favour of her friend, Angélique had at first known neither what to say nor what to do. She had taken four weeks meditating over the matter. Then the conviction had gathered within her that it would be honest to tell Georgette the whole truth: and she had done this, concealing no detail, but setting down everything as it had happened with the entire conscientiousness and want of tact which distinguishes those "who mean well." From this confession Georgette had had no difficulty in gleaning that if Angélique did not actually love Horace herself, yet his declaration had so far unsettled her that she would have no strength to resist him if he prosecuted his courtship with anything like insistance. The fact is, Angélique's first essay at diplomatizing had completely exhausted all her powers of initiative. She had laboriously collected all her weak forces for an attack, and had been not only repulsed, but placed suddenly in the position of assailed. She could do no more. If M. Gerold was in earnest in what he said, if he had really set his mind upon marrying her, if, above all, he had her father for an ally, as she

omehow suspected he would have, there would be no
se in her offering any opposition.

Georgette saw this, and her mild spirit was roused.
;he would have forgiven Horace for not loving her,
nd had he married any brilliant woman of his own
ink, rich or poor, from love or ambition, she would
ave excused him and borne her wound with resigna-
on. But that he should be aspiring to the hand of
.ngélique Macrobe revolted her. This match was too
ordid. Angélique could have nothing in her but her
ioney to attract such a man as he. She was devoid
f sense, her father's reputation was tarnished, their
ealth was sprung no one knew whence, and had been
iblicly denounced as corrupt by Horace himself less
ian a year before. She felt all her love shrink into
:orn for a man who could prostitute himself to such
debasing alliance: the more so as she was humiliated
at Angélique in her clumsy and unauthorized attempts
plead her cause, had probably degraded her in the
timation of this man whom she now blushed at
iving worshipped. It is to be remarked that the idea
nt Horace's affection might be owing to other causes
an inonetary ones, to Angélique's beauty, for instance,
is the only one that escaped Georgette. But this
a venial foible. Women are as much at a loss to
scover personal attractions in their rivals as men to
rceive talent in their adversaries.

The Prince of Arcola drove home in that state of
nd which inevitably follows a "scene" in the case
those who are unused to those incidents. He dined
his club—an English habit which he was helping to
:limatize by his example—and, being alone, had
sure to wonder how much truth and how much

comedy there was in Mdlle. Georgette's performance.
What puzzled him was the part Horace Gerold had
played in all this. He should have been glad to know
more of Gerold, who appeared to him a sort of social
enigma—a man credited with enormous wealth, and
living in the Rue Ste. Geneviève; a Republican whose
austere principles were cited, and who danced at fancy
dress-balls; a strictly virtuous youth who ravaged the
hearts of draper's daughters. Then whom did Georgette
mean by the woman to whom Gerold had sold himself
for gold? He thought there would be no harm in
trying to elucidate some of these points next time he
met Horace. He could ask him frankly whether there
had really ever been anything between him and Georgette,
and how far matters had gone.

In the evening, at a party in the Faubourg St.
Germain, he stopped Jean Kerjou, the journalist, who
was passing in all the glory of swallow-tails and crush-
hat.

"It's a while since I have seen you, M. Kerjou.
Can you give me any news of Gerold? He is, of
course, very busy?"

"You know, mon prince, he is on our paper now
—on the *Gazette des Boulevards*. Yes, he is up to his
neck in election work, and we are toiling by his side.
He will have the Orleanist votes, and the Legitimists
are not disinclined to support him. Indeed, it is
rather for the object of canvassing that I am here this
evening."

"Then his worst enemies are the Reds. What can
they mean by mauling him so pitilessly?"

"Heigh, it is their nature; but what makes the
thing rather hard to stand is that amongst them are

ome men Gerold knows and used to be friends with.
'he Radical candidate who opposes him is that fellow
Albi, and one of the writers of that rascally *Tocsin* is
o other than Max Delormay whom Gerold defended
i the libel action. He is not a bad character, but
as a soft head—in fact, he is a fool—and I expect
Albi corrupted him in prison. Then the *Sentinelle* has
ot behaved over well. Gerold counted that it would
ght for him, but Nestor Roche has answered some-
hat drily that his principles oblige him to remain
eutral: which, under present circumstances, is as
ood as being hostile."

"Then what do you think?"

"We shall win, I hope; but it will be a tough
ruggle."

Yes, it bade fair to be that, and an exciting
ruggle as well. For the first time since the *coup-
tlat* a Parisian constituency was to have the op-
ortunity of expressing its opinion with regard to the
versely-appreciated regime Frenchmen were under-
ing since 1851. Bonapartists argued that now was
e time to prove one's gratitude for the Crimean War,
e victories of Alma and Inkermann, the International
:hibition of 1855, the cessation of street riots, the
iolesale demolition of old houses, and the unexampled
osperity of trade. The Opposition retorted that here
s the moment for asking where France's liberties
re gone, what was done with the millions of in-
:ased taxes imposed upon the country every year;
d, finally, what was the equivalent in dignity, peace,
d happiness which the country was deriving from
e suppression of its Republic? Paris was the only
ality in the whole empire where the elections could

be conducted with any independence; and the tactics
recommended by the more acute amongst the leaders
of the Opposition were formidable. If adopted, the
Government could stand no chance against them.
They consisted in this:—To bring forward as many
candidates of various shades of opposition as was
possible on the first day of polling, and to bind them
by this common agreement:—That the one who obtained most votes on that *first* day should be left to
stand alone against the official candidate on the
second, all his brother opposition candidates retiring in
his favour—*i.e.* requesting their electors to vote for him.*

As soon as it had been published that the seat of
the Tenth Circumscription was vacant, a fair array of
Oppositionists had entered the lists: a Legitimist count,
who had not the ghost of a prospect; an ex-deputy of
Louis Philippe's time, who had sat behind M. Thiers,
and might be supposed to rally the bourgeois votes; a
second ex-deputy, former supporter of M. Guizot; and
finally Horace, who, at the cautious solicitation of
M. Macrobe, announced himself simply as "Liberal," and
whose candidature excited that interest which generally
attends youth, courage, and a promptly-won reputation.

* To illustrate this system of tactics, which led to the total defeat of the
Government in the Paris elections of 1863, we will take this example:—A constituency contains 35,000 electors. There are 5 candidates in the field, 1 Official and 4 Opposition, the latter comprising 1 Legitimist, 1 Orleanist, 1 Moderate Republican, and 1 Radical On the first day of polling the 35,000 votes
are distributed as follows: Official Candidate, 15,000; Moderate Republican,
8,000; Orleanist, 6,000; Legitimist, 4,000; Radical, 2,000. No one having
secured the absolute majority,—*i.e.*, the half of the votes *plus* one (17,501)—a
second day's poll becomes necessary; but this time, in accordance with their
previous agreement, three out of the four Oppositionists retire in favour of the
foremost amongst them; and the result is that the Official Candidate, who, on
the first day, headed the poll by 7,000 votes, finds himself completely swamped
on the second, the numbers being, Republican C., 20,000; Official C., 15,000.
The Imperial Government so much dreaded this strategy that the project of
abolishing the system of *ballotage* (second day's poll) was more than once
seriously mooted.

Everything was progressing favourably. That nu-
ierous section of Liberals who did not care who was
ected provided it were an opponent of the Govern-
ent, were looking sanguine, and the candidates had
ready entered into negotiations with a view to form-
.g the desired coalition, when the sudden entry of
ie Radical candidate on the scene, and his loudly-
:pressed intention of co-operating with nobody not
idorsing his own creed, had completely changed the
.ce of matters. M. Albi, or the Citizen Albi as he
illed himself, was too popular with the working-class
ement for the coalition to offer any probability of
.ccess without him. The policy to be followed now
as not to scatter the Opposition votes amongst the
'e or six candidates, but to put forward one man
hose popularity might outbalance both that of Albi
mself and the influence brought to bear in favour of
e official nominee. Horace's original competitors
:re modest enough to perceive that their own popu-
rities were not equal to this double emergency.
hey admitted that their only chance of entering the
ouse was through the reciprocal system, and there-
re they had retired at once, leaving the honour of .
hting the unequal battle to Horace.
Everything that could be accomplished by a power-
l committee disposing of considerable funds was now
ine to effect the return of young Gerold, who, bitterly
ing by the animosity of his former allies, had plunged
:o the struggle with a determination to spare nothing
win. He was the man on whom, for the moment,
: eyes of all Paris—nay, of all France—were fixed.
ople were hoping in him by hundreds of thousands
perhaps by millions. Journalists he had never known,

whom he was never likely to know, were advocating
his cause day after day in terms which made the blood
thrill in his veins, and sometimes brought tears to his
eyes. He had all the independent journals, both of
capital and provinces, behind him. Certes, it was a
fine position for a young man who had done nothing.
But this very unanimity only made it the more ex-
asperating that the paper he would have most liked to
possess on his side—the honest and esteemed *Sentinelle*
—had refused to speak a word for him.

"I should not be acting comformably to what I
deem my duty as a Republican, were I to recommend
you as deputy," had said Nestor Roche, coldly in answer to Horace's request. "The most I can do is to
remain neutral."

"May I know what is your ideal of a Republican candidate?" Horace replied, speaking with suppressed wrath.

"I doubt whether you would be able to realize
such an ideal, even in thought," responded Roche,
grimly. "It is not that you dislike Republicanism, but
you love other things more."

And Horace had been unable to elicit anything besides this.

As for Albi and Max Delormay, he had made no
efforts to ascertain the motives of their enmity. Albi
he had never liked, and Max Delormay was a personage who, ever since his imprisonment, had been
haunted but by one thought—how to turn his political
martyrdom to a good account. Now that he was out
of prison, his joining a paper where he was twice as
well paid as he had been on the *Sentinelle*, was a perfectly natural incident; nor was there anything very
astonishing in his battering suddenly, for wages' sake,

an old friend: journalists are used to these brotherly
emonstrations. What did surprise Horace, though,
id many others with him, was that Albi, Delormay,
id the rest of the set should have found the funds
eedful to start a paper; and still more, that the
overnment, which stringently prohibited new journals
˙ moderate liberalism, should have licensed such a
d-dyed, spit-fire organ as the *Tocsin*. This last cir-
imstance, taken in conjunction with the relentless,
rious war which the Radicals were waging against
m, forced him to the conclusion that Government
oked upon these men as its surest auxiliaries, and
s detestation of their ignoble scurrility became tem-
red with something very like contempt for, what he
is generous enough to consider, their blindness.

Police regulations allowed of no public meetings
which a candidate might address his electors, neither
is a personal canvass in a constituency numbering
her more than fifty thousand voters a very practicable
pedient. Official candidates got over these diffi-
lties by convoking meetings within covered buildings,
ch as a theatre or concert-room, stuffing those who
me with cake and wine, and then blandly declaring
it this was nothing more than a private party; but
e success of this stratagem would have been doubt-
in the case of liberals. Their only means of mak-
g themselves known was to scatter circulars profusely,
go the full length which the Press laws allowed in
e matter of newspaper-puffing, and to visit the
rkshops where a good many hands were employed
d there make brief speeches, if so be that the fore-
n allowed it.

Horace's committee, of which M. Macrobe appeared

to be the life and soul, though he only figured on it
anonymously, had undertaken the distribution of the
circulars; it disseminated them by cartloads, and not
in the Tenth Circumscription alone, but throughout all
Paris.   It had, moreover, set an army of agents afoot,
and a legion of bill-stickers, and a squadron of trusty
pedlars who went about the Boulevards hawking cigar-
ette-papers, lucifer-matches, and stationery, in boxes
labelled GEROLD, and were often dragged off into
custody for their pains. The newspapers launched leader
upon leader, paragraph upon paragraph, and printed
in flaming capitals on the top of their first columns:

"VOTE FOR GEROLD—CANDIDATE OF THE LIBERAL
AND DEMOCRATIC OPPOSITION."

Some published letters from eminent politicians
proscribed by the Empire, letters dated from exile and
wishing god-speed to their young successor.   Amongst
these was one from Manuel Gerold.   In a private
letter to Horace he had pointed out with emotion and
pride how great and unprecedented was the honour
which the liberal party of Paris were conferring upon
a man so young; in his public letter he recommended
his son to the suffrages of the electors in the name of
those past services for which he himself was suffering
banishment, and vouched for Horace's Republicanism
and fidelity as for his own.   The visits to the workshops were performed by Horace of an afternoon and
evening—he gave all his leisure time to them.

Emile accompanied him in these expeditions, and
generally Jean Kerjou or some brother writer.   The
electioneering stirred all Emile's energies into activity.
Nothing short of such an event as this could have
drawn him away from his books and his briefs, but to

further his brother's candidature, he abandoned both book and brief, gave himself up with all his steady power of application to the object before him, and was worth any dozen agents put together. Workmen are always delicate electors to handle. French workmen especially require to be managed with peculiar art, and Emile possessed that art; which, after all, was nothing but sterling sincerity. Where Horace failed to touch the sympathies of his hearers from speaking too much like a fine gentleman, and in language evidently coined for the occasion, Emile arrested their attention at once, and in a few pregnant sentences went to their hearts. They recognized in him a man who felt what they felt; his look, his voice, his gesture, all told it them. More than one sullen brow relaxed under the homely magic of his words, more than one stubborn foe was shaken, and there were days when murmurs of assent broke out, worth twenty salvoes of applause. Still, the canvassing in the popular workshops was woefully up-hill work. The candidature of Albi, and the denunciations of the *Tocsin*, made havoc of Horace's cause amongst the more excitable spirits; and the neutrality of the *Sentinelle*, favourite organ of the artisan quarters, damaged him sorely with the intelligent workmen.

In this manner, five or six weeks flew by, until the day when the writ was issued. This formality precedes the election by three weeks, and in the interval the zeal of both sides redoubles—it is like the final period of training before the day of the race. Bets were being offered on this election, and the odds were in favour of Horace; for people, as usual, judged by the superior noise which his candidature was making.

Emile received congratulations, and predictions of success; but he shook his head rather apprehensively: "I wish peace could be made with the Albians," he said; "we have a common foe, and when the enemy is so strong, disunion bodes little good."

This idea preyed upon him, and he had already turned over to small purpose an assortment of plans likely to operate a reconciliation, when one evening, not a week before polling-day, Horace decided upon canvassing a large workshop where some hundred men were employed in cabinet-maker's work. That day, as it happened, the *Tocsin* had been more than usually vituperative, and honest Jean Kerjou was indignant.

"By Heaven," he exclaimed, as he walked between the two brothers, "I don't know what withholds you from strangling these curs with your hands. It will be all I shall be able to do to keep my stick off Delormay when I meet him."

Horace said nothing.

"It is infamous, certainly," remarked Emile; "but we had better not strangle anybody. Disdain is as effective, if union be completely out of the question."

"You say 'if,'" cried Jean Kerjou. "Your brother has the patience of Saint Onesiphorus, who received a box on the ear, and begged the donor's pardon for standing in the way. Horace, you don't mean to say you could hold any terms with these vermin? I'd coalesce with the Government against them, and if any of those who voted for them on the first day offered to vote for me on the second, I'd throw their dirty suffrages back into their faces and ask them what the devil they take me for."

They reached the workshop. It stood in a not

'ery savoury alley, and was preceded by a dingy court-
'ard, usually resounding with echoes of wood-planing,
grinding of saws, and clanging of hammers. This time
t seemed as though the workmen must be absent, for
he place was silent, but as they advanced they caught
he sounds of an impassioned voice raised as if ad-
lressing an assembly; and as all three climbed a dingy
staircase, with a greasy wall on the one side and a
shaky baluster on the other, a tremendous shock of
applause burst like a thunderclap over their heads and
a hundred pair of boots pounded the floor with a din
hat made the building tremble.

"What's this I wonder," exclaimed Jean Kerjou—
hey were pausing outside the door. "'Pon my word
believe we've actually stumbled on the badgers."

Horace pushed the door and they entered. Jean
Kerjou's guess was right.

On a joiner's table, encumbered with tools, and
hoved hurriedly next the wall at the end of the room
n guise of platform, stood Albi, his hair dishevelled,
his quick, wild eyes glancing fire, and his parched
body drawn up in the attitude of one who is taking a
moment's breath after a telling oratorical hit. Max
Delormay, who had allowed his beard to grow, and
was trying, without much success, to look as if he
burned with hatred for tyrants, sat below him, glower-
ng under a wide-awake; and the body of the hall was
filled up with workmen in paper-caps and shirt-sleeves,
eaning against or sitting upon unfinished articles of
urniture, chests of drawers, cupboards and bedsteads.
The floor was littered with wood-shavings and glue-
pots; broad planks of oak, maple, and rosewood met

the gaze; a clean smell of saw-dust and French polish pervaded the atmosphere.

All eyes were fixed upon the new comers, and a dead silence supervened. Who were they? Albi and Delormay alone winced and changed colour slightly. Horace lifted his hat and introduced himself in a few words, amidst a long murmur of curiosity. He concluded by saying: "As you are being addressed by one of my competitors, gentlemen, I will wait and claim the favour of speaking to you in my turn when he has finished."

"But this did not suit Albi, who, feeling no desire to have Horace and Jean Kerjou at arms'-length of him whilst he proceeded with the rest of his oration, yelled out at the moment they were moving towards the platform: "This is no place for aristocrats and sycophants."

There was a sensation.

"No," roared he, following up his advantage. "Keep out those men, citizens, who come with smooth words to ensnare your confidence. The poor have suffered enough, I should think, from having put faith in men who betrayed them. If France is bowed down in chains and tears at this minute it is from having trusted in adventurers. Back! Tell them to go back to their masked balls, their operas—anywhere they please out of the sight of honest workmen whom they and their compeers have reduced to slavery. See! they have nothing to offer you but lying promises, and they quail miserably before your looks. Citizens! what the Workman wants is his lost liberties, his independence, the sovereignty that was ravished from him four years ago when he was off his guard—these men will bring you flatteries; your liberties and your sovereignty they would not give you if they could . . . ."

An ominous murmur rose. It is doubtful whether many there present cared much for their sovereignty, or were even conscious that they had lost it; but Albi spoke with a communicative fervour, his hand was stretched out menacingly, and the three strangers, instead of cowering under his harangue, seemed, on the contrary, both contemptuous and arrogant. Emile, it is true, sought to utter some words of quiet protest; but the Legitimist Jean Kerjou thwarted this endeavour by shouting with fury, "You rascally hound, if all your party were of the same mud as yourself, the ravishing of your liberties was the wisest thing that was ever done, for slavery and dog-whips are the only things you are fit for."

At this there was an immense clamour. "Knock him down!" cried a young workman, with solid arms. "Chuck them out!" chorussed twenty voices more. "Stand back!" roared Horace to an individual who was flourishing a rule over his head, and as the individual only answered with a grin, a crashing blow, levelled straight between the eyes, sent him backwards into the wood-shavings. The rest of the scene was enacted amidst clouds of dust, scuffling, blasphemies, heavy *thuds* of bodies rolled over on to the floor, and finally the opening wide of a door, and the precipitate descent of three persons down the staircase, with a tempest of valedictory howls from behind.

The candidate and his two companions found themselves in the yard, bruised, dusty, torn, but not bloodstained, and minus their hats.

Jean Kerjou felt in his pockets, and discovered that his watch and purse were intact.

"It must have been an oversight of theirs," he remarked quietly.

CHAPTER III.

Vox Populi.

At last the day of election dawned—a glorious day
of lustrous sunshine—the weather for great events or
popular solemnities. Horace awoke with confidence,
though pale and full of resentment, for the treatment
he had endured in the workshop was rankling in his
memory, causing him profound humiliation, mingled .
with a now burning desire to crush his rivals. The
Radicals had attempted to make political capital out of
the event, and the Tocsin had published a fantastic
account of how the "pseudo-liberal" candidate had
been expelled with ignominy "by the outraged artisans
whom he had sought to cajole." This had led to the
instant despatching of two seconds with a demand for
a formal retractation, which had been accorded; Max
Delormay opportunely remembering the fate of Paul de
Cosaque. But neither the fantastic account nor the
retractation had done Horace much good. His friends
opined that he would have done well to let the attack
pass unnoticed, and the Tocsin uttered piercing shrieks
at what it called this violation of the liberty of the press
by one who termed himself a Republican.

"This weather augurs favourably," said Emile, looking out of the window as the neighbouring belfry of
Ste. Geneviève chimed nine o'clock.

"Yes, the shopkeepers will not stay at home as
they do when it rains," added Jean Kerjou, who had
come early. "I have seen more than one French elec-

tion marred by showers which kept the rain-fearing classes within doors and allowed the tag-rag and bob-tail to have it all their own way."

A knock, and M. Pochemolle entered in his Sunday coat and hat, clean-shaved and most respectable. After much mental tribulation and long doubts as to the course he ought to pursue, he had arrived at the con-clusion that as the two votes of himself and his son could not possibly affect the general result in a con-stituency of fifty thousand, he would generously give them to M. Gerold. So he was now come to say that he and M. Alcibiade,—who, by the way, exercised his civic privilege for the first time—had risen betimes in order to record their suffrages as soon as ever the doors of the Mairie were opened. "And we were certainly the first who voted, Monsieur," added he, with effusion. "Ay, we were alone in the room with the Mayor and the gendarmes," chimed in M. Alcibiade, whose hair was profusely oiled for the occasion. "What they call the 'urn' is a long box with a slit in it, and when I saw that, I thought I might manage to slip in several voting tickets together—I'd got my pocket full of them—but the mayor didn't allow us to put them in ourselves. It's he who does it."

Another knock, and in sailed M. Filoselle with a new waistcoat of more striking tartan pattern than any before witnessed, and lavender gloves to match. He bowed with ease. He too had been voting, having come up to Paris for the special purpose the night be-fore. "Yesterday morning I was at Marseilles, M. le Marquis, and deep in a negotiation for sending a cargo of cracked bugles to China, where they could pass for new, the Chinese not being musical; but I said, 'Duty before profit,' and here I am. When that sun sets may you be deputy for Paris, then I shall return to Marseilles as pleased as if all the cracked bugles in Christendom had been shipped to Pekin, and I had received seven per cent. on the commission."

This cheerful commencement to the day removed the cloud from Horace's brow. He dressed himself with care and sallied out with the intention of paying a visit to the Hôtel Macrobe, professedly to see its owner, really in the hope of meeting Angélique. His interviews with the financier's daughter had not been many since the scene at the fancy fête. Whether it was that she avoided him, or that he was unlucky in his hours for calling, she never seemed to be alone when he was in her company. There was always the Marquis of This or the Count of That, and sometimes bevies of ladies engaged in solving grave problems affecting the shape of a bonnet or the length of a skirt. If he could have outstayed these nobles and these ladies—but then M. Macrobe remained or Aunt Dorothée, which was proper and correct but embarrassing, insomuch as when she was not actually obliged to take part in the conversation, Angélique sat, resplendent and divine, but silent.

On the election morning, however, M. Macrobe pretended having a letter to write before going out with Horace to the committee-room. He withdrew; Aunt Dorothée was upstairs, and Horace found himself for a moment alone with Angélique. It was in the boudoir which the financier had fitted up with such luxury and taste for his daughter. Rare objects of art gleamed on tables and consoles, choice flowers reared their scented heads out of exquisitely-tinted vases.

Angélique's beauty shone with greater radiance amidst these surroundings, like a peerless jewel out of a costly setting. She was dressed in white and wore a single rose in her hair. A glancing sunbeam fell upon a curl that rested on her shoulder and made it glisten like spun gold.

As the door closed behind her father she blushed and rose, feigning to examine a scarlet jardenia. Horace approached her with emotion.

"Will you let me offer you a flower?" she said, as if to ward off words which she expected yet shrank from, and she broke off the finest sprig. But, as soon, she clasped her hands, blushed deeper, and said, "But no, I am forgetting that this is the day of your election and I am offering you the colours of your adversaries—those bad men who, they tell me, say such cruel things."

"And does it pain you that bad men should say such cruel things? But give me the flower, it has a price now that you have culled it."

He took it from her hand and fixed it in his button-hole. She continued to gaze at the jardenias but found nothing more to say; so he gently drew her hand in his and murmured: "Do you know why this day is so anxious a one in my life? It is because it may prove the starting-point to a career of honour which I shall lay as my only fortune at the feet of her adore—at your feet."

She turned to him with blushing and almost piteous entreaty.

"Oh, why do you say that to me, M. Gerold, when Georgette is so much better and worthier of you than —you, who are a famous man, who will become a

great one, require a partner who is clever and can aid
you. I could not do that—I know I could not—and
I should make you unhappy, however much I tried to
do otherwise."

"I do not want a partner who would aid me by
cleverness," answered Horace, softly. "There is a
help more potent than that to brace the nerve and
smooth the path of man, and that help you could give
if you tried to love me a little. Promise me that and
you will make me more than happy."

Her bosom heaved, and in her trouble she could
only falter:

"If it were really for your happiness, M. Gerold;
but it is not. Oh, I feel it is not! But, tell me, did
you never, never love Georgette?"

This question, which revealed the first timid germs
of feminine sentiment, transported him. He pressed
her hand to his lips: "Never," he said, decidedly;
"never."

Footsteps resounded outside. Instinctively they drew
apart.

"Now then, my dear young friend, I am at your
service," said M. Macrobe, returning. "My child,
make your best curtsey to M. Gerold, who, before
you see him again, will be the most enviable man in
France."

Elections in France under the Imperial system
were not the noisy and boisterous events they are in
certain other countries. Although this election was
regarded with mortal anxiety by a full million of
French Liberals, who watched in it for the first feeble
symptoms of independent revival, the streets showed

tle or no signs that anything unusual was taking
ace. It was a Sunday, as French polling days always
e, the church bells rang, citizens, with glossy hats
ı their heads and smart wives on their arms, were
ooping to the Bois de Boulogne or to the railway
ations to catch excursion trains; and there was the
istomary sprinkling of soldiers in dress uniforms,
me of whom, to be sure, stopped and stared a mo-
ent at the yellow, red, and white candidate's addresses
aring on the dead walls. But this was all. It was
ily in the quarters comprised in the 10th Circumscrip-
on that any electoral movements could be witnessed,
d even here the proceedings were of the simplest
aracter. The Circumscription was divided into twelve
ctions, and in each one of these was a polling place
ovided by the Municipality—that is, a room hired
the ground-floor of some eligible house decorated
· the occasion by a tricolour flag. Anybody was
e to enter these rooms on condition of standing
iet. They contained two gendarmes, a deal box
th a slit in the lid, a table, and behind the table a
lf-dozen gentlemen, delegates of the Mairie and of
different candidates, seated on chairs. The electors
ne up one by one, handed their voting tickets folded
the municipal officer, who dropped them at once
ough the slit, and then retired in silence. No shout-
;, no cheers, no party cries. Outside some touters
tributed voting papers to new-comers, and knots of
) or three electors loitered in the roadway discussing
: prospects of the candidate they favoured. But
se groups were never allowed to congregate into
wds. A couple of *sergents-de-ville* paced watchfully

up and down, saying, "Circulez, messieurs, s'il vous plait, circulez."

Horace's committee-room was in a street not very far from the Rue Ste. Geneviève. When he drove up to the door with the financier he found the nearest approach to a throng that he had yet seen that day, and a good many hats were lifted as he alighted—one or two hands even pressed forward to shake his. Inside, the room was crowded with Horace's friends and with newspaper reporters come to pick up the latest news. The *Gazette des Boulevards* mustered in great force, so did Mr. Drydust, who had brought a youthful British peer with him, the Viscount Margate, and was describing to his lordship the mechanism of universal suffrage both amongst that and other peoples. A shout arose as Horace darkened the doorway, and fifty voices were raised to announce to him the results of the first four hours' polling, as gathered approximately from the ticket-distributors at the different sections:

Gerold	2,300
Bourbatruelle	1,200
Albi	450

There might not be much in these figures, for a large number of electors came with their voting tickets in their pockets and did not accept those proffered at the doors; still, they sent a flush to the face of the triumphing candidate. Mr. Drydust declared aloud that they must be taken as conclusive, the numerous elections he had seen having invariably been decided by the results of the first four hours' polling.

M. Bourbatruelle was the official candidate. It was not very easy to elect a personage suited to this de-

icate post in a city such as Paris, and under the cir-
umstances, M. Bourbatruelle was really not a bad
hoice. He was a manufacturer of clay pipes. Every
lay pipe in Paris issued from his stores bore the name
f *Bourbatruelle* printed in small letters next the
mouthpiece. On bringing him forward, the Government had suggested that it would do no harm to print
his name of BOURBATRUELLE a little bigger, to prefix
the words VOTE FOR, and to disseminate a hundred
thousand clay pipes, thus amended, gratis amongst
the population. M. Bourbatruelle had improved upon
the hint by causing screws of shag to be bestowed
along with the pipes—which was not bribery, although
it might have been deemed so had M. Bourbatruelle
been a Liberal, but simply a small token of affectionate
generosity. There was a general impression current
that M. Bourbatruelle was a fool—an erroneous idea,
for a man is not a fool who can make himself a millionaire by selling clay-pipes. If the Corps Législatif
were ever called upon to pass a law affecting the pipe-
industry, everything tended to show that M. Bourbatruelle would prove himself thoroughly competent to
defend his interests. Of course, as regards laws that
had no connection with pipes, M. Bourbatruelle was
different, and was expected to be so, for had it been
otherwise he would not have been chosen for official
candidate.

M. Bourbatruelle had behaved like a gentleman towards Horace, leaving a card upon him and bowing
to him with great civility once when they had met in
the street. Horace had followed suit in the matter of
the card, and returned the bow with respect. He had
no animosity for M. Bourbatruelle, and it gave him

keen pleasure to see that he was completely distancing
Albi.

"I see every hope of our obtaining the victory,
M. Gerold," said the grave and emphatic Baron
Margauld. "Madame de Margauld has charged me
to convey to you her good wishes. I think she has
been not unoccupied in canvassing for you among
some of her friends."

"I am most grateful," answered Horace, earnestly,
"and whatever be the result of the election, believe
me I shall never forget the kindness that has been so
freely lavished on me."

Jean Kerjou ran in breathless.

"I have just come from the section of the Rue de
Tournon. Emile came there to vote, and brought
ninety-two workmen with him—all rabid supporters of
Albi. He had talked them over. Ah, you should have
heard him! You've got a brother there who is not
made of ordinary stuff. If he had time to go the
round of all the workshops by himself to-day, you
would fly to the top of the poll like a flag to the mast-
head."

The voting begins at eight in the morning and
concludes at six, and it is from this latter hour that
the real excitement of a Parisian election commences.
But the centre of animation is not so much in the
voting quarters as on the Boulevards. On those three
hundred yards of holy ground between the Opéra
Comique and the Théâtre des Variétés every man
flocks who holds a pen or a pencil, who may wear a
gown or an epaulette, who is anybody or anything—
journalists, artists, barristers, officers, novelists, stock-
brokers, all jumbled together, smoking, chattering,

gesticulating, and waiting for the evening papers. At half-past six on the evening of the election you could not have dropped so much as a pea from the balcony of one of the houses of the Boulevard Montmartre without its alighting on the hat of somebody. The crowd surged rather than flowed. The cafés were crammed to suffocation — not a seat to be had in them.

The lamp-lighters, with their long ladders, found themselves unable to make any head against the current, and appealed distractedly to be allowed to pass. In the kiosks, the newspaper-women, worn out with counting money and folding broad-sheets, had hung out the announcement which is their signal of distress: "No change given." And amidst all the din, the clinking of glasses in the cafés, the rattling of dominoes on the marble tables, the cries of "*Oui, Monsieur; tout de suite*," from the waiters, snapped the exclamations, "Gerold wins!" "I'll lay on Albi: they say the Radicals polled in the afternoon." "I vote an address of condolence to Bourbatruelle."

Of a sudden, a tremendous rush. A string of news-boys were coming full tilt down the Rue Montmartre, metropolis of printers, with the second edition of the *Gazette des Boulevards*. They are mobbed. The kiosks are stormed. A deluge of copper coin ensues —those who have no sous give francs, and the papers are torn open:—

"LATEST NEWS.

"*At the moment of going to press with our second edition the results of the election are still uncertain; but the contest has been a very severe one. Until two o'clock the Liberal candidate maintained the head; but the majority of electors did not poll till late, and it is now supposed that the votes are so equally divided that a 'ballotage' will be necessary. The greatest order prevails."*

Ten minutes later the second edition of the *Sentinelle* appeared, and was cleared away in two minutes:—

"ELECTION OF THE 10TH CIRCUMSCRIPTION.

"The votes are being counted as fast as possible in the different sections, and it is now beyond doubt that the Government have sustained an overwhelming defeat, the aggregate of votes given to the two opposition candidates amounting to almost double the number polled by the official candidate. M. Horace Gerold's committee are sanguine; but at M. Albi's head-quarters it is confidently asserted that the immense majority of votes polled in the afternoon were for the radical interest. We have no means of ascertaining how far this rumour is correct."

Finally, at about eight, an impossible, indescribable scrimmage greeted the third edition of the *Tocsin*, brought damp from the press by men wild with excitement, and shrieking: *"Final Result!"*

This is what the *Tocsin* printed:—

"CLOSE OF THE POLL. ·
TRIUMPH OF THE RADICAL CANDIDATE.

10th Circumscription.

Number of Registered Electors . . 51,515
Number of Votes recorded. . . . 45,963
Absolute Majority required. . . . 22,982

Aldi 19,310
Bourbatruelle. . . 14,518
Gerold 12,125

None of the candidates having obtained the absolute majority, a 'ballotage' will take place this day fortnight."

This news was brought to Horace in his committee-room, and he managed to glide out unperceived amid the consternation and tumult which it occasioned. He had not eaten since the morning, excitement having left him no appetite, and he now felt faint; his steps were hurried and unsteady. People passed him with contented faces, returning home after their Sunday walk; and how he envied those people, who probably led uneventful lives and had no ambition! In a quiet street an Italian was grinding an organ and a ring of little children danced around him filling the evening air with their gay, crowing laughter. He rather wondered that these children did not read on his face how disappointed and unhappy he was, and pause in their merry-making; but he tried to smile to them kindly, and he thought the music the sweetest, most pathetic he had ever heard. When close to his lodgings, he stopped, remembering Emile. His brother would take this to heart more than he himself would. He must go in looking unconcerned, cheerful, if he could; he rehearsed one or two things which he could say to console Emile. And so he reached the Rue Ste. Geneviève.

But just as he was about to cross the road opposite M. Pochemolle's house, he was arrested by a loud and jubilant clamour proceeding from the end of the street and a joyous crowd ·debouched uttering shouts of

triumph and escorting a man perched high aloft on a
pair of stalwart shoulders. It was Albi's constituents
chairing him from his committee-room to his home.
The police had made some sort of effort to prevent it,
but they were too few, and the men too many—something like a couple of hundred; besides which, the
procession was only noisy, not obstreperous, so that it
was best to let it alone. On they came, cheering with
all the power of their lungs, and tossing their caps into
the air; and the inhabitants, attracted by this sight of
by-gone times, came out on to their doorsteps, to look
and nod, and clap their hands: success excites applause,
like sunshine the song of birds. Horace remained
standing where he was, motionless; but just as the
exulting troop approached, a window facing him was
opened, and Georgette appeared. She looked out and
saw him at once. He was standing in the full light of
a gas-lamp—she at an angle where her features were
plainly visible—and their eyes met. Rapid as lightning
she darted on him a look of contempt and derisive
triumph, and at the moment when the vanquishers
swept beneath her, leaned forward, caught up a nosegay
that was standing on the sill, and threw it to Albi.

CHAPTER IV.

Macrobe à la Rescousse !

To have been during three months the most prominent man in one's country, to have dreamed of becoming, at an age when others are subalterns, the
unique representative and leader of a party that numbered the best, wisest, and greatest men of France—
and to find oneself suddenly fallen again to the position
of writer on a second-rate newspaper, was bitter enough.
But what redoubled the chagrin and mortification of
Horace was the way in which his supporters of yesterday—the journals that had been his champions—
hastened to desert him and passed to the side of his
rival. So long as it had been a question of choosing
between two candidates—one an educated gentleman,
the son of an illustrious patriot, and a proved Liberal
like Horace; the other, a darksome and not over well-
known revolutionist like Albi—the moderate, enlightened
organs of public opinion had not hesitated. But now
that the ultimative lay between taking the official candidate or having Albi, the issue was changed. After
all, Albi was a Liberal, he would not vote as the other
two hundred and sixty members in that servile, voiceless chamber. He would raise his cry on behalf of
proscribed freedom; he would protest against the laws
of tyranny passed in the name of France. It was
absolutely necessary that the Opposition should have,
at least, one spokesman; and the liberal journals un-
animously called upon Horace Gerold to retire in Albi's

favour. To make matters worse, Emile, though he did
not verbally urge this course, implied by his manner
that he desired its adoption; and Manuel Gerold, writing from Brussels, spoke of it as imperative—as a thing
that did not even admit of discussion. "The life of a
public man," he wrote, "must be one of self-sacrifice.
Personal ambition, predilections, rancours, must all
sink before considerations of public good. This man
was your enemy yesterday, to-day you must be his
ally; else your electors would have the right to think
it is yourself you wished to serve, not them."

To resign in favour of Albi, to further the return
of a man who had pursued him with uncalled-for spite,
marred his own certain triumph, and who, had the
positions been reversed, would never have given way
to *him*—having vowed not to do so when he started—
this was an act of magnanimity which demanded super-
human courage. Horace blenched at it; it chilled his
heart to think of. Nor did his judgment incline to it
readily; for was not this man a malicious, serpent-
tongued slanderer—had he not shown himself both
tortuous-minded and unscrupulous, and was it to be
supposed that the Liberal party could be benefited by
having such a personage as that for its representative?
In his perplexity he sought the Hôtel Macrobe, as
much to cheer himself after his cruel deception by a
look at and a word from Angélique, as to ask counsel
of the financier whom he was beginning to look at as
his mentor. But, as though all creation were conspir-
ing against him, neither Angélique nor her father was
at home. So he walked back sorrowfully and betook
himself to the society of his friends of the *Gazette des
Boulevards*, the only paper which had remained faithful

to him, and whose advice, as conveyed energetically by Jean Kerjou, was "not to abet the entry of a black-guard into Parliament."

M. Macrobe was not at home, because closeted in private conversation with M. le Ministre Gribaud. This time the financier was subjected to no ante-room delay as at his last audience. On his arrival the venerable Bernard had saluted him to the ground, and ushered him at once into the Minister's presence, and M. Gribaud had motioned to him with his finger to take a seat.

"Well, M. Macrobe," began his Excellency, rather sourly. "It seems we've overdone it."

"I certainly thought the official candidate would get through, your Excellency. It never entered my thoughts that this man Albi could make such a hit."

"Nineteen thousand votes, and twelve thousand given to young Gerold: thirty-one thousand Opposi-tionists in one constituency! Ah! how right we are to keep the curb well strained: how quickly this devil-city would overturn us if we let it! But now what is to be done? Albi of course will not retire; but will Gerold do so in favour of our man, as you predicted?"

"Things have not turned out as I had planned," answered M. Macrobe, with his brows knit. "I had counted that the two rival candidatures would divide the Opposition votes and allow the Government nominee to get in easily; but then I had not foreseen that the Opposition was so strong. As for Albi, we have no hold on him. He came forward on the understanding that his expenses should be paid and that he should have the funds to start a paper. It was necessary to find a name which would rally a certain number of

Radicals; but I imagined that he would get ten
thousand votes at the most and that when he had
served our purpose we could simply let him drop and
suppress his journal. But, for the present, it would
not be safe to try this. He does not know that it is
the Government who have brought him forward; he
fancies it is a Radical Committee, and if this committee were to play him false at such a moment, just
as he was on the point of succeeding, he would suspect
something and denounce it aloud; for though he be a
vicious, venomous brute, he is no traitor. No, he must
never learn that the committee under whose orders
he has been acting is composed of men in the pay of
the Prefecture, and that all his contributors on the
Tocsin, with the exception of that simpleton Delormay,
draw their inspirations from Ministerial source. The
scandal would become public and injure the Government. What we must do is to defeat Albi on Sunday
week; then the committee can say that, his election
having failed, they see no use in continuing the paper,
and withdraw their caution money. But first we must
beat the man, and now there remains but one way to
do that; only one."

"Which? If young Gerold will retire in favour of
Bourbatruelle we might manage. There cannot be
much love lost between him and the *Tocsin* I should
think." And his Excellency chuckled a little.

"No, there is not. He hates Albi ten times more
than he ever hated the Government, and if left alone
would throw the Radicals overboard without much
parley. But he is influenced by his brother—a young
prig—and by his father, so that although I should not
actually despair of bringing him to coalesce with us,

yet the thing would require an effort and more diplomacy than it would be worth. I say more than it would be worth, because it is not so sure that even if Gerold did resign in Bourbatruelle's favour, all his electors would obey him. The unexpected lead taken by Albi has roused the hopes of the Opposition. All their papers are now backing Albi, and supposing that out of Gerold's twelve thousand electors, eight thousand were to vote for the official candidate, and four thousand only for the other man, Albi would still win. I suggest, your Excellency, that the man who should withdraw is M. Bourbatruelle. His supporters would naturally poll for Gerold whether they were asked to do it or not, and these fourteen thousand votes would beat the Radicals out of the field."

"And Gerold; how will he behave when he is in the House? You were not encouraging on this score last time we talked the matter over."

"True, your Excellency; but the conditions are altered. If Gerold had been elected as an Opposition candidate, he would have given us trouble, but if he gets in now, he will readily perceive that he owes it to the Conservatives. The affair, however, must be managed with tact. Let Monsieur Bourbatruelle withdraw without recommending his electors to vote for anybody. The majority of the Opposition press, deeming that Albi, with his nineteen thousand original votes, has the best chance, will probably continue to support him; the Government press, on the contrary, will take up Gerold's colours, and this will serve to widen the breach which the first day's poll has made between the Liberal candidate and the Radicals. Once in the House, the conviction that he is virtually representing

a constituency of Bonapartists and temperate Liberals
will keep Gerold within bounds. He is not likely to
forget the party that opposed him so ruthlessly, and
he will feel proportionate gratitude for the men who
secured his triumph. A little courtesy and tolerance
on the part of his colleagues will do the rest. But if
the worst comes to the worst—I mean, if Gerold
proves unmanageable — he need not remain in the
House more than a year. We are in 1856; in another
twelvemonth come the general elections."

His Excellency M. Gribaud rubbed his left ear
thoughtfully, then cracked the joints of his tough fingers.

"Well, we will try your plan," he said, slowly.
"It's rather like admitting a young wolf-cub into a
sheep-fold to put this Gerold into the Corps Législatif;
but perhaps the cub's teeth are a bit blunted. I will
send for Bourbatruelle at once. We shall have to give
him something. H'm, the Legion of Honour will do.
Then we shall have to pay his expenses. By-the-way,
Gerold has not got a *centime*, of course; and I suppose you've not found out what he and his father do
with their money? I learn from the sub-prefect at
Hautbourg that charitable donations are sent by them
every quarter-day; but the town complains that it is
ruined, root and branch."

"Better days will perhaps come for it," answered
M. Macrobe, laconically.

"Yes, if you succeed in your *rôle* of General
Monk."

"Who is General Monk, your Excellency?" asked
M. Macrobe, for, though an astute financier, his historical education had been neglected.

"General Monk was a shrewd fellow who restored

a penniless young king to his estates and then helped
him to govern them," said M. Gribaud, grinning
broadly.

A slight tinge of colour came to M. Macrobe's
parchment countenance, but he laughed.

"Well, I hope he was well repaid, your Excellency."

"Oh, yes, it was a good speculation, as you
gentlemen of the Bourse say." And, continuing to
grin, M. Gribaud took up his pen and indicted a line
to M. Bourbatruelle, the clay pipe manufacturer. "This
will do the business," he said; "but mind, Monsieur
Macrobe, I am acting now in deference to your judgment, and we shall regard you in some way as surety
for this young fellow's good behaviour."

The financier made an obeisance, and, the audience
being now terminated, withdrew.

But he did not go straight off to Horace to hold
out the plank of safety which he had just hewn out
for him. Events had marched fast, but the time had
come for accelerating them, if possible. Horace Gerold had entered the net, the meshes must now be
closed upon him rapidly; he must be brought to propose for Angélique, to break with his party, and to
place himself in M. Macrobe's dependence, all at one
swoop. This could be effected by leaving him to his
misery for these next few days. He must be left to
drink to the dregs the cup of his humiliation—to chafe
and writhe under his abandonment; and then, when
all the world seemed bitterness and deception to him,
his future father-in-law could step in like a *deus ex
machinâ*, smoothe away his troubles, and send him
careering once more on the high-road to glory. So

M. Macrobe merely wrote a line to request Horace not to take any step as to retiring until the following Sunday—seven days before the second ballot—when his committee would consider the subject, and by the same post he arranged that M. Bourbatruelle's retirement should also be held in suspense until the same date.   This done he sent Mdlle. Angélique into the country with her aunt for a day or two, and took an easy opportunity of having Horace informed by a third person that this young lady was being wooed by the Prince of Arcola, and would probably soon be asked in marriage by that nobleman.   "If he really loves her," argued M. Macrobe, "this will make him miserable and furious; if it be a mere inclination, jealousy will stimulate it, and, no doubt, fan it into something warmer."

Thus the week passed by.   The posters with Albi's name were renewed on the walls; the *Tocsin* gloated over its victory and reviled the conquered; the chorus of journals which besought the liberal candidate to do his "duty" swelled every day, and Horace himself was as thoroughly galled, distracted, and despondent, as can be imagined.

On the Sunday he paced his room in an agony of doubt, trying to form a resolution, yet not daring to take it.

"I don't see that there's anything to hesitate about," grumbled royalist Jean Kerjou, who was imbedded in an arm-chair and puffed solemnly at a cigar.   "The moral sense of this generation seems to be blunted. What!   Here is a cur whom you would not admit into your back kitchen, and half the newspapers of France are laying their heads together to plan how they may foist him upon an assembly of gentlemen! God bless the days when there were no parliamentary institutions to make such tricks look excusable in the name of party tactics. Heaven bless the times when there existed a free-masonry between gentlemen to send rogues to Coventry, and when fellows like Albi were shunned like the pest."

"It's not the man we should be helping into the Corps Législatif, but his principles," answered Horace feebly.

"Oh, his principles, my dear M. Gerold," exclaimed Arsène Gousset, laughing. He had come with a dainty-looking volume of somewhat improper poems—his composition—which were being much read in fashionable spheres, and which he desired the *Gazette des Boulevards* to handle tenderly. "What principles do you think those men have, except this immortal one, to turn out every man that holds a place and to put themselves in his stead? You will say he is a Republican, but so is every man who has not a *centime* and sees no chance of ever possessing one; and this is no more a title of honour than to say that his trousers are ragged, his washerwoman's bill unpaid, and that he dines off boiled beef, not being able to afford venison. The rich and educated who join this band are either perspicuous citizens who want to climb the political ladder quickly, and know that there is no better stepping-stone for their purpose than the heads of the unwashed; or amiable enthusiasts, like your father, who would govern wolves with kind words and jackals with forms of logic. As soon as these excellent theorists get into power, they begin by locking up the dog-whips, chains, and collars; they proclaim the liberty of howling; and a few weeks after they are howled out of office—as your father was. The fact is, the doctrine of Republicanism starts from the assumption that, however ignorant and brute-like an individual member of the lower orders may be—and that he *is* both ignorant and brute-like is sufficiently proved by our interminable schemes for educating and refining him—yet, that a few millions of such individuals, putting their ignorance and brutishness in common, become a class full of sense and virtue, both worthy and competent to rule; which seems to me like contending that, although one of the jackals above-mentioned, lean and ravenous, might be a danger to the poultry-yard, yet that a good big troop of such jackals turned loose together among the hen-coops would show the world what abstemiousness was, and extend a brotherly protection to the fowls. I should like to get a Republican candidly to acknowledge— but they never will do so—that Republicanism, as we understand it nowadays, has never existed anywhere, and when tried has eternally broken down. Greece and Rome were aristocratical oligarchies, in which all the lower orders were slaves. It was much the same thing at Venice, Genoa, and in Holland: republican in name, virtually close vestries, in which no man was admitted to power who had not a square cash-box to recommend him. In South America, democratic Republicanism—considerably diluted, however, by the slavery of the negroes, who do all the servile work— has been on its trial nearly half a century, and has resulted in a revolution every twelvemonth. There have been in Chili since the independence something like twenty *coups-d'état*, in Peru rather more; in Mexico the people change their executive as they do their shirts.

As for the United States—where again we find the negroes, who represent the proletarian classes of Europe, kept under heel—Republicanism had hobbled along hitherto there because, the country not being half peopled, there is land, like air and water, for all comers; and the subversive gentlemen, who in Europe swarm in our large cities and overturn our governments for us, go out into the West and found states of their own, where liberty, equality, and fraternity flourish under the shade of the bowie-knife, the revolver, and the bludgeon. But in a hundred years hence, when the descendants of these squatters begin to wash their hands and fence in their properties, when there is not a rag more land to distribute to immigrants, and when it becomes a question of providing for several million paupers, I doubt whether apostles of the Albi school will be more appreciated in American upper circles than they are with us. State prisons and gibbet-trees will be erected on their behalf, as they have been in this land; persecutions, revolutions, and reactions will succeed one another like a rotation of crops, and the States will pass through their cycle of monarchies even as the rest of the world has done. You see, there are certain orders of things you will never be able to reconcile, and amongst these is the Empty Stomach and the Full One. To the end of time, the man who has not dined will be the foe of the man who has, and the history of revolutions is but that of the alternate triumphs of these two over one another. To-day it is Gribaud and Company who dine, to-morrow it may be Albi and Brothers. Only, to think that Albi Brothers have any object but to get this dinner, or that, if they once had the keys of the state larder, anybody save

themselves would be the better for it, is one of those
bright fallacies that denote a cheerful contempt for the
lessons of history. Revolutions never abolish abuses—
they only change them. We have gone through three
bloody revolutions, and four changes of dynasty, to set
over us M. Gribaud, who presses as heavily on mankind as ever did the Duc de Choiseul or the Marquis
de Maurepas; a fourth revolution would give us M. Albi.
Upon my word, I consider things are very well as they
are; the change would be insignificant in so far as results went, and it would cost money, to say nothing of
comfort."

The Court Novelist emitted all this in his most
lively tone of bantering persiflage, blowing wreathing
clouds of smoke towards heaven, and stroking his carefully trimmed yellow beard with a hand on which
glittered an enormous diamond, the gift of an empress.
But his paradoxes did not offer any solution to Horace,
and when, at length, he smilingly withdrew along with
obdurate Jean Kerjou, whose parting words were to
"fight till grim death, as my Breton countrymen do,"
Horace began striding up and down as before, but
more harassed, vacillating, and moody than ever.

"Duty!" he exclaimed, bitterly, "what do men
ever gain by performing it?" and he thought of Georgette and her unfeeling insult on the evening of his
defeat. It was an insult the more cruel as he was unable to divine the motive of it. He had been wrong
in flirting with Georgette; he had felt this, and retreated
before it was too late both for himself and for her.
But was this the way to be revenged on him? When
he met her by chance, she glared upon him with the
eyes of a little tigress, or, what was worse, treated him

with undisguised, aggressive scorn, as if he were some abject criminal. She was not even content to trust to fortuitous occasions for making him feel her spite. One evening, returning home, he had found the work-box which he had given her lying on the table, and not a word of explanation with it, not a line to mark what she was offended at, or what he might do to soothe her resentment away. She was behaving without any sense or reserve. Had she been a misguided girl quarrelling with her paramour, she could not have acted otherwise; for, after all, he had given her no direct cause for offence. His sins, if sins they were, had been of a negative kind. He had left off seeing her because he wished to conduct himself as an honest man; and when, after a long interval, he had ventured upon entering the shop again, he had found the Prince of Arcola there. And this had recurred several times: more than once when he had passed the shop latterly, he had seen either the Prince himself or his well-known phaeton waiting at the corner of the street.

At this recollection of the Prince of Arcola his brow grew black.

M. Macrobe had not misreckoned on the emotion which the report of Angélique's marriage would cause him. The news had gone into Horace's heart like a knife. Coming at such a moment, when the cup of his mortification was already brimming, it was a savage sort of blow. It put him roughly back in his place, showing him what a poor devil he definitely was, and how extravagant was the pretension for one such as he to espouse a millionaire's daughter. Till that moment he had never reflected on Isidore Macrobe's wealth in connection with Angélique; but he did so now, and

measured at a glance the distance that separated him
—him, a struggling journalist and barrister—from the
brilliant Prince of Arcola. So this Prince was destined
to thwart him in his love, as that man Albi was doing
in his ambition! At the outset of his career, he was
to be stopped dead short by a dandified sportsman
and a ranting demagogue; nay, more, he was asked in
the name of duty to connive in this result! Angry and
pale, he swore this should never be. He had torn himself away from Georgette, that she might be respect-
ably married and never know trouble; and what was
the consequence? She despised him for his pains, and
coquetted with a Prince whose intentions towards her
were clearly what those of most other men of easy
morals would be in such a contingency. Now, people
were soliciting him to make a new sacrifice, in order,
no doubt, that Albi might laugh at him in his turn and
take him for a credulous simpleton. No, no; as Jean
Kerjou said, this was a case for fighting till the end.
He would tell the Prince that a libertine, titled though
he were, was no fit husband for Angélique; and if the
Prince resisted, why there were means of settling these
questions, in France, without much loss of time or
words. As for Albi, committees or newspapers, friends
or foes, might say what they pleased—if he could
prevent that fellow from succeeding, he would do so;
and if he could not, it should, at least, not be said,
that it had been for want of the trying.

Whether by accident or design M. Gousset had
wrapped his pretty volume of improper poems in a
number of the *Tocsin*, and there they lay both on the
table together, the improper fashionable book, and the
improper democratic gazette. Horace suddenly caught

sight of the journal, and, full of his new resolution,
snatched it up and ran his eye over the leading article;
as usual, an attack on himself, written by Albi, not
without talent, but in a style of violence positively
reeking with hatred and injustice. It was one of those
infamous articles which are intended to stab deep, and
which do stab, however steeled we may be against
them by usage. Horace flushed all over as he read it.
He crushed the sheet in his hand, and darting to his
desk, penned a letter to the chief of the independent
journals who were calling on him to retire.

He was so intent upon his work, his pen flew so
rapidly over his paper, that he remained unconscious
of the presence of M. Macrobe, who having knocked
without eliciting an answer, had opened the door and
glided in. When he had dashed off his signature, he
looked up, gleaming.

The financier's eye was mutely interrogative. Horace
handed him the letter without speaking.

M. Macrobe perused it with a nod.

"So far so good," he said, "this will do as a beginning; but men like you must do more than talk,
they must conquer. You would not be sorry to crush
this Albi?"

Horace's eyes glistened, and he waved his hand—
an eloquent gesture—it meant, "Give me the chance."

"Then the day is yours," said M. Macrobe. "I
have come to tell you that M. Bourbatruelle retires;
you will remain face to face with Albi; but as you will
have the votes of all the honest people who, thank
heaven! are a majority, your return is assured."

Horace rose to his feet; it seemed to him in that
moment that the room swam.

"Yes," pursued the financier calmly; "I saw M. Gribaud, and he said, "The Government prefer being criticized by a man of honour like M. Gerold, rather than by a low-bred person like M. Albi. Besides, all the votes given to M. Bourbatruelle belong of right to M. Gerold, for the electors of the Tenth Circumscription are liberal to a man, and if some of them vote for the official candidate, it is only out of dread for theories which are neither liberalism nor republicanism, nor anything else but blasphemy and blunder. If these electors had not suspected M. Gerold of making common cause with the revolutionists they would have elected him the other day." This is what M. Gribaud said. "He is much maligned, I assure you, is M. Gribaud. He spoke of you in the highest terms, and affirmed that the Government were particularly touched by the strikingly honourable way in which you had carried on the contest."

A tumult of emotions welled up in Horace's breast, and broke upon his face in changes of colour rapid as a succession of waves.

"M. Macrobe," he faltered, springing forward, "I am sure it is to you I owe this—it is you who have been working to secure me this triumph."

"Pooh, pooh! my dear young friend, I have done my duty, that is all. You owe nothing to anybody save yourself."

"No, no. You say that because you are too generous to accept thanks. You are continually befriend-
.ing me, who have done nothing to deserve it; and how I can ever repay these acts of kindness and devotion is more than I know or can imagine."

"Why talk of that? Believe me, I am more than

repaid already by the pleasure of serving you," said the financier, smiling. "I have but one wish, M. Gerold, and that is to see you prosper."

"Then add one more to your benefits, and complete my happiness," cried Horace, impulsively. "M. Macrobe, let me speak on a subject that is nearest my heart, but which I might not perhaps have dared to mention, had it not been for this new proof of the interest you bear me. I have had the presumption to hope that we might some day be connected by a closer tie than that of mere friendship. Yes, though I have nothing to offer but an honest name, and can compete with none who have great rent-rolls to give, I love your daughter. Yesterday I heard a report that Mdlle. Angélique was already betrothed to the Prince of Arcola, and the news caused me inexpressible sadness. If you could only tell me that this was not true, and cheer me with the assurance that I shall not hope in vain—that when I have created myself a position, you will allow me to pay my addresses to your daughter—you would be fulfilling my fondest desire, and I should look back upon this day as the most fortunate in my life."

M. Macrobe's features very cleverly expressed the greatest surprise, and he became grave.

"I had never suspected this, M. Gerold," he said; "but I should be dissembling were I to conceal how much your communication flatters me. I am unaware that the Prince of Arcola has paid his addresses to my daughter. I think the report must be a false one; but, in any case, rent-roll is the last qualification I should consider in any one who aspired to become my child's husband. I was a poor man myself, and have not found that wealth adds much to one's happiness. Honesty, courage, and ability are the only riches I set store by. In a word, my dear young friend, there is no man I would sooner own as my son-in-law than yourself."

In England, a man would have grasped the speaker's hand; in France they manage these things differently. Horace flung his arms round M. Macrobe's neck, and kissed him on both cheeks.

If he could have known the pleasure which this embrace gave the worthy gentleman!

*　　*　　*　　*　　*

On the following Sunday, Horace Gerold was elected Deputy of the City of Paris; though it was a close shave, as cognoscenti remarked. The Radicals, encouraged by their first success, came up to the poll multiplied, united, and strong. The Bonapartists rallied round the "Liberal" candidate, and the result was:—

Number of votes recorded, 46,347.

GEROLD	23,258
ALBI	23,089

That is, a majority of ONE HUNDRED AND TWENTY-SEVEN VOTES!

A few weeks later, the *Gazette des Boulevards* announced to the world that a marriage had been arranged "between the newly-elected member for Paris, our ex-contributor, M. Horace Gerold (the Marquis of Clairefontaine), and Mdlle. Angélique Macrobe, daughter of the eminent chairman of the Crédit Parisien."

CHAPTER V.

Epistolary.

So M. Macrobe had won the first game of his rubber. Won it promptly, cleverly, and completely. The second now began, and from the outset it looked as if he would win that too. Ten months after the Paris election the following three letters found their way through the post:—

From Emile Gerold, Paris, to Manuel Gerold, Brussels.

"Rue Ste. Geneviève, January 7. 1857.

"MY DEAR FATHER,—

"I HAVE just come in from pleading a rather dry case before a not very intelligent judge, and I find your good, welcome letter awaiting me. This weekly correspondence with you, that is the reading of your missives and the pleasure of replying to them, constitutes the gleam of sunshine in my somewhat lustreless life. Not, mind you, that I complain of this monotony, for I have failed to perceive that those whose existences are more variegated seem much the happier for it. But it is nevertheless a relief to turn now and then from my habitual studies—the poor devices by which men may best outwit one another—to the perusal of language so vivifying in tone, so humanely loving, so full of generous truth as yours. It is like escaping for a moment into a purer world.

"Yet, on the present occasion, are there not traces of unusual depression in certain passages of your

letter; I mean those in which you speak of Horace?
I have no wish to allude unnecessarily to the events
of the last few months, which I can guess have pained
you and which I will not conceal have to some extent
disappointed me. But be assured that, in so far as
the heart goes, my brother is unchanged. He is,
perhaps, a little sore at your not having come to Paris
for his marriage, and it may be that this feeling reveals
itself, as you say, by a slight tone of pique in his
letters; but I do not think we should be altogether
surprised at this, for it only argues the great value he
attaches to your approbation and his extreme sensitive-
ness lest any of his acts should be susceptible, in your
eyes, of misinterpretation. On this last score, it is
true, I might reassure him; for that his marriage was
one of pure affection, unalloyed by any mercenary
thought, neither you nor I certainly ever doubted.
But it is not enough to tell him this. In his present
temper of mind, he requires us to approve without
reserve *all* his recent undertakings. Binding up, as it
were, his marriage, his friendship with M. Macrobe,
and his political course together, he resents any stricture upon one incident as a blame upon all three; and
it wounds him to the quick to suspect that you or I
can even remotely concur in any of the harsh criticisms
which these different occurrences have evoked from
his enemies.

"No doubt this morbidly nervous mood will give
way in time to feelings more in consonance with
Horace's naturally genial disposition; but until it does,
I for one—half of whose contentment in life would be
gone were I estranged from my brother—I submit to
the necessity of the case and tacitly acquiesce in

everything. I wish our party had behaved with a
little more fairness and tact to him. That they should
have called upon him to retire after that unlucky first
ballot was natural enough, but I do think it was wanting both in justice and generosity to support Albi
against Horace once the other man had retired, and
to reproach Horace when elected with being an official
candidate. From a mere party point of view it seems
to me that it would have been more politic of the
Liberals to claim my brother's return as a victory.
He would have served their cause then and faithfully;
but their almost disdainful repudiation of him, con-
trasting as it does with the singular courtesy and kindness shown him by the other side, are producing the
only fruits that could be expected under the circumstances. Horace complains that he has been ill-treated,
and never refers to the subject without indignant bitterness. Nevertheless, from what I can gather of the
debates in the Corps Législatif—scraps of which, you
know, reach the public ear through drawing-room
echoes—his is the only voice in that gloomy building
ever raised in defence of liberty. He opposes Government bills, advocates reforms which in times like these
might be called subversive; and, were he stimulated
by contradiction, I suspect he would go greater lengths
in liberalism than many of those who essayed to brand
him as a Bonapartist would dare do. But nobody
contradicts him; I hear on the contrary that he is
applauded. The plan of his adversaries appears to be
to enthral him by civility, and there could in truth be
no surer way of touching one who is as open to
kindly influences as he is quick to feel injustice. However, there is a boundary line dividing Horace's now

wavering attitude from total secession, and when he
has reached this line and sees the pit beyond he may
recoil. Such is my hope, I might add—my prayer.

"Meanwhile, domestically speaking, Horace is I
believe happy. He resides in his father-in-law's house,
and every time I visit him there I find him looking
bright and pleased with his lot. His wife is a gentle,
loveable young person, shy and rather silent, but I
think good. She submits to him in all things, and his
chief preoccupation seems to be to make her happy. M.
Macrobe, at whose table I have once or twice dined,
rather to satisfy Horace than myself, is also—I must
do him that justice—very zealous in catering for his
son-in-law's felicity. He bustles about, forms projects,
agrees with everything Horace suggests, and to me in
particular he is most attentive. The family circle has
lately been completed by the arrival of a Crimean hero
just returned at the Peace. His name is Captain
Clarimon; he was introduced to me as a kind of
nephew of M. Macrobe's, and is, so far as I could
judge, a pleasant fellow. Horace and he appear to
have already struck up a fast friendship.

"I perceive I had covered so much paper that I
will close here. I repeat, my dear father, how much
pleasure your letters always give me; but it continues
to be to me a source of daily increasing sorrow that
your voluntary exile should be thus perforce prolonged,
and that we should be compelled to exchange our
thoughts in writing instead of by word of mouth.

> Cui dextra jungere dextram
> Non datur, ac veras audire et reddere voces.

Why does not this Second Empire fall and open the

gates of France anew to all the great and good men
who are sharers in your proscription?

"With tenderest respect and sympathy,

"Your affectionate son,

"EMILE GEROLD."

"P.S.—I have forgotten to mention that I may
soon be obliged to date my letters from elsewhere
than here, owing to the retirement from business of
M. Pochemolle and the consequently possible sale of
this house. The news took me a little by surprise
when the good man brought it up to me in person
yesterday, enveloped in pompously deferential explanations that made the gist of the communication at first
a little obscure. He said that 'my esteemed connection by alliance, Monsieur Macrobe,' had been the instrument of his attaining more rapidly to fortune than
he ever would have done had he confined himself to
the beaten tracks of commerce. He had, by Monsieur
Macrobe's advice, invested money in the Crédit Parisien, buying shares at 500 which were now worth
1,500, and the result was that Madame Pochemolle
was recommending him to retire and purchase a villa
with a garden and a pond—Madame Pochemolle inclined, said he, for gold-fish in the pond—somewhere
in the suburbs of Paris. I could see that it cost the
excellent man a pang to relinquish the *Three Crowns*
to a stranger, and that so far as he was concerned,
the shop where his fathers traded and the modest gains
which they earned, seemed preferable to all the suburban villas in the world, with or without gold-fish. But,
neither Madame Pochemolle nor Monsieur Alcibiade
being of the same opinion, the draper is out-voted and

will be set to perform—will-he, nil-he—the comedy of
'*Le Rentier malgré lui.*' There was almost a touch of
pathos in the way he exclaimed, 'Our fathers made
their earnings slowly, and prospered long; I have gone
further in one year than they did in fifty; yet somehow it doesn't give me the pleasure I should have
thought. I keep fancying that money which comes so
quickly into the pockets of those who have done nothing to deserve it, must have come equally quick out
of the pockets of those who didn't deserve to lose it.'
I promised M. Pochemolle I would apprise you of his
change of condition. His words were, 'Pray, sir, inform my most respected preserver, with my humble
duty, that selling cloth or wearing it, I shall remain as
much his obliged servant as heretofore.'

"Ever affectionately,

"E. G."

*From M. Hector Filoselle, London, to Horace Gerold,
Paris.*

"Leissester Squarre, January 15, 1857.

"MONSIEUR LE MARQUIS,—

"I DATE this letter from the banks of the Thames
in the metropolis of the Queen Victoria, whither I have
journeyed upon business, and the occasion I seize is
that of the Sunday repose, which in this great country
reminds me of the repose of model convict prisons.
Great Heaven! figure to yourself a square as large as
the Place Vendôme, and not one soul visible in it but
a single policeman, who is melancholy; and around
and about this policeman closed shops and cafés her-
metically barricaded, as if they feared an invasion; for

the English law decrees that man shall not be thirsty
of a Sunday morning, and the publican who sells him
drink is fined by the tribunal of Queen's Bench two
sterlings. These laws astonish the stranger. Also, I
have noticed that it is interdicted to play music on
the Saturday, for yesterday I witnessed a milord chase
from his door, with indignation, a grinder on the
organ, who was presently pursued by a policeman, and,
as they told me, conducted to prison, where he will
be judged by the tribunal of Habeas Corpus. However, these are details with which I have not the heart
greatly to occupy myself; being sad, even to the point
that the business questions themselves lose their interest for me. Ah, Monsieur le Marquis, it was not
merely a superficial affection I nourished for Mademoiselle Georgette. I had long meditated the project
of making her happiness and mine, and on the day
when you interposed, speaking the good word for me,
I cried to myself, 'Ah, it will become a reality, that
dream I cherish!' But fortune and other causes,
amongst which I suspect the presence of a rival suitor,
have coalesced themselves to defeat my ardent hopes
and your benevolence. Already, at my last visit but
one to Paris five months ago, shortly after your own
marriage, Monsieur le Marquis, I noticed that the attitude of my future father-in-law, M. Pochemolle, had
undergone a change towards me, and that the demeanour of my future mother-in-law—whom I have
ever gratified with a moderate liking—was chilly, not
to say freezingly distant. On my next visit these impressions were more than confirmed, and now I am in
receipt of a letter from Monsieur Pochemolle, which
leaves no longer a place for doubt. He states that he

relinquishes the draper's trade to devote himself henceforth to a retired life, and he adds that, under these
altered circumstances, perhaps I shall see the propriety
of breaking off an engagement which has ceased to be
so suitable as it once looked. Alas, the good man! I
know very well that it is not he who would write in
this way; but husbands are the slaves of their wives,
notwithstanding the Code Napoleon, and Monsieur
Pochemolle does but express the sentiments that have
germed in the feminine but unelevated soul of Madame
Pochemolle. You will excuse me for making you thus
the confidant of my destroyed illusions, Monsieur le
Marquis, but I wished to assure you that even in this
moment of grief, when the faithlessness of woman is
once more exemplified at my expense, I retain a recollection full of gratitude for the manner in which
you deigned to befriend me. Life is a bale of mixed
goods out of which one draws at the hazard, to-day
stuffs of bright colour, to-morrow, mourning crape. I
this time have lit upon the crape. Well, well, it was
fated; but at least this consolation is given me, to feel
that Mademoiselle Georgette is, like myself, the victim
of destiny, not the willing accomplice of a plot for
ruining my well-loved castle in the air. Ah! the usages
of the world forbid my now seeking any communication with her who was my betrothed, and my own
pride will not permit me ever again to cross the
threshold of those who have closed to me their doors.
Yet should ever the opportunity present itself, I will
say to Mademoiselle Georgette—as I would respectfully pray you to say for me should the opportunity
come first to you—that I bear no malice, but wish my
rival well. This is for Mademoiselle Georgette's sake,

against whom I could not bring myself to feel anger even if I would. As for her mother—but no, I will take a noble vengeance on that woman. I will apply myself with aching spirit but with renewed ardour to the pursuits of commerce, in order that when I, too, have become rich, she may open her eyes to the mistake she has made, and murmur, 'I should have done better to give her to Filoselle.'

"Begging to enclose a prospectus of current prices of the house of Verjus and Tonnelier, wine-merchants, of Paris, whose goods I will guarantee sound; also the description of a new kind of bag-pipe, patented by Messrs. Doremi, for whose house I travel, and three of which I have recently sold to Milord Ardcheanochrochan, a Scotch peer of distinction, I have the honour to offer you, Monsieur le Marquis, the assurance of my deepest respect and gratitude,

"HECTOR FILOSELLE."

M. Prosper Macrobe to his Excellency M. Gribaud.

"Avenue des Champs Elysées, January 21, 1857.

"MONSIEUR LE MINISTRE,—

"I ACKOWLEDGE the receipt of the report from the sub-Prefect of Hautbourg, which your Excellency obligingly forwarded to me yesterday. I laid it, as arranged, on a table where it was sure to meet my son-in-law's eye, and he read it after asking me how it came that such a document should have fallen into my possession. I explained that the sub-Prefect was an acquaintance of mine who had sent me a duplicate of the copy he intended despatching to the Government in the hope that I would intercede with the

Clairefontaine family to do something for the perish-
ing town. 'Which,' added I, 'I should not have ventured to do had you not accidentally stumbled upon
that report which I had mislaid.' He made no answer; but, during the rest of the evening, he remained
pensive, and I could see that those passages of the
report in which the sub-Prefect contrasts the now
pitiable plight of Hautbourg with its flourishing condition when the Castle of Clairefontaine was tenanted,
had produced upon him all the effect which I expected. I need not add—for your Excellency has
doubtless been in a position to notice this fact yourself—how surely the great kindness and forbearance
of the Government are operating on my son-in-law. I
might adduce testimony of this in citing the very
words he used when your Excellency, in the name
of the Ministry, accepted the slight amendment he
moved to a recent Police Bill. He said that 'whatever might be his opinions as to the reigning dynasty,
Napoleon III. had a merit not common to his predeces-
sors, that of selecting able ministers.' I have the honour to remain, Monsieur le Ministre, your Excellency's
most humble and obedient servant,

"PROSPER MACROBE."

CHAPTER VI.

A Speech, a Vote, and a Surprise.

IT is two o'clock. Luncheon is just over, and a group of five persons are congregated in one of the most sunny morning rooms of the Hôtel Macrobe. The financier, with his brass-bound note-book in his hand, is jotting down the details of some pecuniary transaction in which he does not look as if he had been fleeced. Aunt Dorothée is counting, with an air of wobegone solitude, the patterns on the carpet, as if to divine what average sum in copper money each separate flower must have cost. Beside her on the blue satin sofa her niece unravels a skein of bright worsted which Captain Clarimon, the Crimean hero and her cousin, is holding with docility; and Horace, his back to the mantel-piece interrupts the silence to read aloud occasional paragraphs out of the newspaper he is skimming.

A footman enters powdered and majestuous, the incarnate image of "eight hundred francs a year and perquisites." "Monsieur le Marquis's horse is at the door," he announces. Horace no longer objects to be called M. le Marquis. Soon after their marriage Angélique—no doubt paternally instructed—remarked that she liked the title Madame la Marquise better than that of Madame Gerold. It was said in the same tone she would have adopted to state her preference for burnt almonds over candied cherries; but from that day Horace had suffered himself to be marquisized

without protest. He was not responsible, however, for
the sudden and violent eruption of coronets which,
after this little uxorial victory, burst upon every article
of furniture or piece of plate on which it was possible
to paint or engrave these symbols.   Even his linen he
now noticed had been secretly seized and branded.

At the announcement of the horse Angélique laid
down her worsted and ran obligingly to fetch her husband's hat and gloves. She was the same pretty, silent
Angélique as of yore.   A shade more of timidity in
her manner; a fainter shade of gravity on her beautiful
face, and that was all.

Captain Clarimon also rose, displaying, when on
his legs, a handsome giant six feet high, with bold,
military face, moustaches waxed at either end as sharp
as spear-points, and hands that must have held a firm
grip of the cavalry sabre when cutting down rebel
proletaries in the *coup-d'état* affrays or Russians on the
field of Inkermann. Crimean heroes being still the rage
at that period, Captain Clarimon had been made welcome at the Hôtel Macrobe, and, finding his quarters
good, evinced no disposition to desert them.

"So you are off to your legislative duties, Marquis,"
said he, with more veneration than might have been
expected from one who had learned by experience
what a poor show an assembly of legislators makes
against half a troop of horse.

"Yes," answered Horace, smiling to his wife,
and thanking her as he took his hat from her hands.
"Yes, Captain, but I don't know what we are going
to legislate upon to-day. I have not seen the notice-
paper."

"I think it is a colonial question," said M. Macrobe,

tting up his note-book with a well-satisfied snap;
ie political régime of Martinique and Guadeloupe."

"Dull countries," remarked the Captain, "and
sedly peppery—ahem, I beg pardon, ma belle cou-
e. I lived in garrison there."

"Amongst the poor negroes," observed Angélique.

"Ay, the poor negroes who used to be slaves," ex-
imed Aunt Dorothée dismally, as if the servitude
the black races had been the canker-worm of her
stence.

M. Macrobe on the sly launched a thunderbolt-
nce in the direction of Aunt Dorothée, and coughed
drown her misplaced sympathy.

"The negroes—yes, those poor fellows who used
be so happy a few years ago, and who now, by all
counts, are in a miserable state of destitution,"
culated he.

"That's exactly it," laughed the Captain. "The
ggars were happy enough until a number of Deputies,
f of whom had never seen a negro, and the other
f of whom had never talked to one, laid their heads
ether to set them free. Up to that time Martinique
1 Guadeloupe had been flourishing. The negroes
re well fed, well housed, and had no more work
n was good for them. But crack! down comes the
olition, and what's the result? Your nigger left to
nself won't work at any price. Planters are ruined,
de dries up by the roots, and our two colonies go
the dogs. That's what comes of making laws,"
ded he, sapiently.

"My father was amongst those who agitated for
olition," remarked Horace, rather drily.

"Of course, and quite right too," returned the

Captain, unabashed. "I am sure I should have voted for emancipating the poor devils; in fact, I'm for emancipating everybody, and letting them all do as they like. But if you'd been to Guadeloupe, I fancy you'd wish they had delayed the experiment until you were past visiting the place again. Why, I have ridden twenty miles along the coast and met not a living soul save three niggers, all stretched on their backs in the sun, and swearing it was too hot to work. Like oysters, 'pon my word."

"Well, as I know very little or nothing about the colonies, perhaps you wouldn't mind riding down to the House with me and enlightening me," said Horace, cheerful again. "One picks up useful waifs in conversation. I will order a second horse to be saddled."

The Captain good-naturedly acquiesced, and so did M. Macrobe, who seemed pleased with the arrangement. A second hack was soon brought round, and the Captain armed himself with a riding-whip.

"Au revoir, child," said Horace, kissing Angélique on the forehead. "What shall you do all the afternoon?"

"Long to see you return," she whispered, with a slight, sweet smile, which brought a ray of pleasure to his eyes, and to her features a little colour. "Then, I have my round of visits to make," added she, submitting to the second kiss with which he rewarded her pretty compliment.

The Captain also took his leave in cousinly style. Selecting by hazard, no doubt, a moment when Horace's back was turned, he said, "Au revoir, charmante cousine," and, bowing, lifted her hand to his lips.

As the gallant warrior was thus engaged, M. Macrobe's eye was fixed upon him with rather a curious expression.

The debate had already commenced when Horace settled into his seat in the House—if debate it can be called where every honourable gentleman was known to be of the same opinion, and would infallibly vote the same way when the hour of "division" arrived. The Corps Législatif, indeed, had not been created that it might make itself much heard or felt. Its function in the constitutional machinery was to spin as noiselessly as possible; to do its little piece of allotted work in the way prescribed, but just that and no more; above all to avoid clanking or in any way jarring upon the nerves of its imperial proprietor. The look of the session hall marked its altered destination from what the place had been in days passed by. Where was the tribune whence Royer-Collard had delivered his flashing orations; Manuel, Foy, and Benjamin Constant hurled their fire; and where Guizot had stood at bay, breasting the attacks of Berryer, Lamartine, and Thiers combined? Gone. Where were the strangers' galleries in which two generations of Frenchmen had trained themselves to love of parliamentary eloquence, to worship of freedom? Where the journalists' box, in which, turn by turn, had sat all the master penmen who had moulded the thoughts of young France—Courier, Carrel, Mignet, Vitel, Sacy, Girardin? Present, but closed. Where the benches on which at one time and in one array, had figured Victor Hugo and Beranger, Louis Blanc and Quinet, Montalembert and Lamennais, Arago and Cousin? Present again, but peopled by two hundred and sixty gentlemen of de-

bonnair aspect and facile manners, with not an idea
between them but plenty of small talk; gentlemen
culled pretty much to right and left as we gather mush-
rooms, from half-ruined estates, from the purlieus of
the Stock Exchange, from plethoric and, consequently,
loyal Chambers of Commerce, from the semi-official
press, from ministerial backstairs, last and least, from
court. All of which gentlemen had been shoved into
the Corps Législatif to do their duty, and did it—
voting as they were bid, and roaring very conscientiously, "Hear, hear," when a minister spoke, to the
tune of five hundred pounds a-year a-piece.

As a counterpoise to these two hundred and sixty
human and self-acting voting instruments, Horace's
seat, slightly isolated from the others, being a little to
the left of the President's chair, was the only one
which could, by any elasticity of expression short of
downright abuse of language, be termed independent.

As Horace entered, an obese legislator was sawing
the air with his right hand, proclaiming the reasons
which would induce him to vote in favour of the bill
—a gratuitous piece of good nature which seemed so
entirely superfluous to his colleagues that they serenely
busied themselves in different ways and didn't listen
to him. A large proportion of honourable members
were writing their private letters, a good number more
sprawling with legs outstretched, hands deep in pockets,
and countenances upverted with a beatific gaze at the
sky-light, were sleeping the sleep of the just. Four or
five, whom you had fancied poring with absorbed
interest over statistical blue-books, were palpitating
over the incidents of a steeplechase at Chantilly, described in the usual graphic language by a reporter of

Le Sport; and a pair who kept their backs turned to the rest of the world, and were pushing white bits of something composedly towards each other, looked suspiciously as if they were playing at dominoes.

Horace was soon surrounded in his seat—colleagues in squads came smirking up to kill time with a little quiet chat until the rising of the House. He was not unpopular, the Member for Paris. Deputies fat and lean, jovial and bilious, broke into smiles as he passed them. In the lobbies he reaped as many hat-salutes and shakes of the hand as he knew what to do with. The prevailing notion was that, although independent, which was certainly a point against him, he was not dangerous, and might be trusted.

A canine-visaged deputy, with a rasping voice and a nose like a fig, said pleasantly:

"Shall we have the satisfaction of hearing you to-day, Monsieur le Marquis? A debate in which I take some interest. Was a planter myself in the good times."

"In the time of slavery?"

"Precisely. I had five hundred slaves and devilish contented they were. Never cow-hided them except when they deserved it. Within three years of the abolition half of them were underground; floated themselves to the deuce on rivers of rum. Ah, the rascals."

"I do think it's so absurd to talk of niggers as human beings," giggled a young viscount with features livid from long vigils and hair in curl. "The Marquise de Vermeillon had a negro page she dressed in red, and an ape she put in blue—confoundedly *rococo* she was, the Marquise. And I used to say to her, 'Marquise, if those two exchange clothes I shall be giving sugar-plums to Snowball—this was the nigger—and my card to Adonis—this was the ape. Hee, hee, hee.'"

Everybody laughed. This was very funny.

"I lost a million francs by the abolition," resumed the fig-nosed planter, in a voice like that of a nutmeg on a grater, "but the colony lost more. Chaps that didn't understand anything about the niggers' interests, nor about anybody else's, those that suppressed slavery. Why, isn't there slavery in all countries more or less? Look at our peasants who are taken by the Conscription at twenty, made to serve seven years, and risk being shot into the bargain. The niggers risked nothing, there wasn't a cleaner, happier lot going; why, it was like a prime concert to see 'em squat in a row and whistle in the sun. Then we used to marry 'em——"

"Yes," grinned the young viscount; "and I've heard of a nigger who was henpecked like fun, until one lucky day his wife was sold to one master and he to another. That's an advantage that wouldn't have been open to him if he'd been a free Frenchman. Once spliced with us whites its always spliced."

More merriment, interrupted this time, however, by the sudden close of the obese member's speech. At this the House woke up for a moment and burst cordially, and without a moment's hesitation, into unanimous cheering. The members who were writing their letters, those who slept with their countenances heavenwards, those who were palpitating over the prose of the sporting writer, and the pair who played dominoes, all looked up and shouted defiantly, "Hear, hear!" as if there were an invisible opposition making itself obstreperous on the benches of the Left and requiring to be put down. Then the President, a dapper statesman, ornamented with a red ribbon and star, consulted a list on his table, and called out to another deputy to rise and say something. It was very much indeed like a schoolmaster crying, "Boy Duval, stand up and construe."

Unfortunately for the regularity of the proceedings, the honourable gentleman appealed to was absent, having been taken ill in the morning; so was the next member on the list, who had been summoned away by telegraph at early dawn to bury a relative; and the third deputy whose name the President called was not yet arrived—whence an unexpected hitch. These debates, to tell the truth, were all mapped out beforehand, like the programmes of a musical entertainment. In order that a sceptic public might have no handle for murmuring that honourable members did small work for their 500*l.* per annum, M. Gribaud, the Minister, and his Excellency the President, provided between them that no bill should be sent up to the Crown without a decent amount of preliminary speechifying to season it withal. They recruited talkative members—those preferred who had the great art of saying nothing, and putting it into a good many words. It would be arranged that Monsieur A. should get up and talk from two till a quarter past, that Monsieur B. should follow him from the quarter to the half-hour, and that when Messieurs C., D., and E. had each had their twenty minutes' or half-hour's turn, according as they felt in condition, Monsieur Gribaud himself should rise—towards five or thereabouts—reduce all their arguments to powder, prevail upon them to withdraw their suggestions or amendments, which they were not likely to

object to do, and get the bill voted by acclamation in
time for everybody to be home and dressing for dinner
at six. Now, when Messieurs C., D., and E., all failed
to come up to time together, it was tantamount to what
the unforeseen eclipse of the tenor, bass, and baritone
at one of Monsieur Hertz's morning performances would
have been. Some little consternation ensued. The
honourable gentlemen who were writing their private
letters nibbled the ends of their quills, the pair who
played dominoes looked guiltily apprehensive lest they
should be dragged out of their retirement and forced
to speak whether they liked it or not; Monsieur Gribaud,
who had been sitting with his arms folded and his head
drooping on his chest, in apparent slumber,—though
of all men in the room he was certainly the most wide-
awake, drew out his watch, but seeing it yet wanted
two hours to six, put it back again and frowned. What
was to be done? Propriety scarcely admitted of the
Minister making a general appeal for somebody to devote himself, and it would not have concorded with
the dignity of a legislative council for the President to
exclaim, "I vow nobody shall go out of here until I
get my three speeches." In this emergency all eyes
sought Horace. What is the use of an Opposition
member if he be not prepared to spout by the hour at
half-a-minute's notice?

So, drawn by that magnetic attraction which brings
orators to their legs, Horace, without well knowing
what he did, rose, and an instantaneous sigh of relief
went round. He had not in the least made up his
mind as to what he should say, neither had he caught
a dozen words of what the last speaker had uttered—
moreover, he was not quite clear as to what the bill's

scope was. These were disadvantages, but, being a Frenchman every inch, they did not appal him as they might have done the scion of a less glib-tongued race. Certes, there was a difference between the young man who had stammered the first phrases of his maiden speech before the judges of the Police Correctionnelle and the coolly confident deputy of the people. The confidence of twenty thousand voters must make a man self-trusting if anything will. Horace began by running his hands through his hair, which seems to be a physical necessity with most Parisian speakers, and then, without hesitation, started into retrospective survey of the history of the French colonial empire, which would be sure to be appropriate. He alluded to Duplex and Lally-Tollendal; compared Lapeyrousse with Cook, somewhat to the disparagement of the latter; grew lyrical over Montcalm and the fall of Quebec, and towered to patriotic heights when describing how "the fairest jewels of our colonial crown" had been reft away by the avidity of a nation now at peace with us. This brought him to the negroes and the question of compulsory and gratuitous instruction, which, like the Messrs. Somebody's pills, appears to be the panacea for all evils known and unknown. "The negroes were lazy and allowed our colonies to be ruined; why was that? Because they were not educated. If the negro were taught to read, and gratified with a free press to develop his liberal culture, not a doubt that he would take to work with an ardent zeal. Commerce would re-flourish under his efforts, and France would show herself in colonial prosperity, as in other things, to be the mistress of the world." This conclusion was hailed, as it deserved to be, with loud, long, and general ap-

plause, for the great merit of the speech was that,
although nobody had understood it, it had occupied
a good hour in delivery. All that now remained was
for M. Gribaud to reply, which he did with adroitness,
declaring he should not fail to remember the suggestion
of his honourable friend, and that the question of negro
instruction would for the future be foremost amongst
those involving his most attentive consideration. Whereupon there was more cheering, enthusiastic and long
continued; the question was put from the chair, and
carried *nem. con.;* the pens, newspapers, blotting-books
and dominoes were stowed away, and everybody went
home to dinner, France being the richer by a bill, and
the Corps Législatif the happier for three speeches.
Such is civilization.

In the lobby, going out, Horace was joined by the
Planter, who, raspingly and bluffly as ever, said, "Fine
wor-rds, Monsieur le Marquis, and a good deal of
body in 'em too, I don't doubt. Only, in practice,
reading and writing don't any more change the nigger's
nature than soap can whiten his skin. I've been to
Jamaica and there seen model schools built a good
many years ago by an Englishman named Guineaman——"

"Guineaman!" interrupted Horace, with a start,
for he recalled the name of his uncle's wife, the woman
whose slave-earned money had restored Clairefontaine,
and set a lasting stigma of indignity on it.

"Yes, a slave-trader," returned the fig-nosed
planter carelessly, "but, like all Englishmen, one who
kept the Bible in his tail-coat pocket and called it his
compass. When he walloped a nigger he took car-re
to quote the chapter and verse that gave him authority,

and I believe he wouldn't have exceeded forty stripes, save one, for any money."

"A hypocrite?"

"Wa'al, no, it's bred in the grain. Those English who are pr-ractical have discovered that they can do a good many more queer things by citing the Bible than we Fr-rench can do without it. But I didn't know this Monsieur Guineaman; he was dead and gone long befor-re my time. They used to talk about him at Jamaica, though, and show the schools he built when he'd made his fortune; for it was his theory that slavery being lawful—for the Government didn't for-rbid it then no more does the Bible now—he'd just as much right to tur-rn an honest penny that way as anybody else, provided, of course, he didn't bully his niggers, which I think good mor-rals. The-refor-re, as I say, he opened schools and preaching-houses to make the beggars lively, just as I at Martinique being Fr-rench, set up dancing booths to the same end. Only, my dancing booths tur-rned up tr-rumps and Monsieur Guineaman's schools didn't. The niggers danced jigs fast enough, but be hanged if they loved r-reading and writing any more than hoeing and digging. It's not in the nature of the varmin."

Which wise commentary brought the two legis-lators to the door of egress where both found their broughams. The fig-nosed planter wedged himself snugly into his and was whirled away to one of those banquets which kept his physiognomy in such per-petual glow; Horace was going to follow suit, and had already one foot on his brougham step, when a fami-liar equipage, drawn by two superb bays and driven with right British science, came like a hurricane down the Quai d'Orsay, ten yards off where he was standing, whirling up a spray of mud-drops and flint-sparks on its passage. The driver was the Prince of Arcola, who recognized him, and instantly reined in his steeds with consummate skill, clattering and champing on their haunches.

"This is a lucky meeting. I will give you a lift."

"With pleasure," said Horace, who was always glad to see the Prince; and he scrambled into the phaeton, which, as soon as released by the two cockaded grooms who had sprung to the horses' head, sped merrily on its course again.

"I have been on a call to some old friends of yours," said the Prince, as they debouched into the Champs Elysées with a speed that made the gaslights flit past them like flakes of fire thrown up by an engine in motion.

"I have almost as many friends as enemies now, Prince," was the smiling answer.

"I mean the Pochemolles."

"I have not seen them for an age," said Horace, with interest. "I heard last month they were going to retire, but when I went to congratulate M. Pochemolle on his rise in the ladder, he had already removed. They are all well, I hope, and the good draper is not yet counter-sick?"

"They are installed at Meudon," rejoined the Prince without smiling. "The villa is a pretty one, devoid of vulgarity, the dwelling of an honest man who retires on a loyally-earned competence. Both Monsieur and Madame Pochemolle are very well."

"And Georgette?" inquired Horace, after a mo-

ment's silence, though looking with something of archness at his interlocutor.

As if he had been expecting the question, the
Prince quivered slightly. He did not immediately
reply, but lashed his horses nervously into a faster trot.
Then abruptly he turned his face full on Horace's and
said: "Gerold, I have been wanting for the last twelve
months to put you a question, but have never dared
—you will guess why, perhaps, some day. Tell me
now, on your word, between man and man, has there
ever been anything between you and Georgette?"

Horace, though he had long suspected the Prince
of paying a more or less avowable court to the draper's
daughter, was little prepared for the attack, and
changed colour.

"Nothing of any importance," said he, evasively,
and rather trying to laugh off the subject.

"Then there *has* been something," muttered the
Prince, and it seemed to Horace that he turned pale.

"I swear to you that, so far as I know and believe,
Georgette is a virtuous girl, if that is what you mean,"
he said.

The Prince seemed relieved; but musingly he
exclaimed: "Then what is the significance of her
flaming up as she does whenever your name is mentioned?"

Horace wondered. Why Georgette should thus
flame up was to him inexplicable except under the
hypothesis that she was an extremely forward person.
He had not forgotten the whimsical display of spleen
to which she had treated him a few months before,
when the report of his marriage was beginning to
gain ground: but this was a thing of the past now,

6*

which he was fain to dismiss from his mind as not
worth brooding over. Besides, a woman's fair fame is a
thing against which a man with the least spark of feeling is
so loth to breathe a careless word, even when he has
cause for suspicion and motives of personal rancour,
that Horace checked himself on the point of making
a rejoinder that would have reflected slightingly on
Georgette's conduct towards him, and answered
guardedly: "As her father's lodger, I frequently saw
Mdlle. Georgette, and it may be that by occasional
civilities, by those unmeaning compliments which we
men pay without attaching any weight to them, I
suffered my intentions to be misinterpreted. In this
case the blame would be mine, not Mdlle. Georgette's,
and she might feel some resentment at what may seem
to her to have been levity on my part. This is the
explanation I suggest."

"And that is all that passed between you—positively all?"

"That is all."

"Well, you have taken a load off me," murmured
the Prince, with an unaffected sigh. He flicked an
invisible speck of dust off his near horse's collar, and
looked as though he meant what he said.

"But tell me now, in your turn, why you catechize
me like this?" inquired Horace, not without raillery,
as his former not very charitable misgivings as to the
Prince's own designs upon Georgette recurred to him.

They were not above a hundred yards' distance
from the Hôtel Macrobe, and the phaeton was still
going like wildfire. The Prince said: "Repeat to me
once more what you affirmed about Georgette's blame-
lessness."

"I do; I affirm her entirely blameless, upon my word," said Horace earnestly.

"Well, then," answered the Prince with gravity, "if Mdlle. Georgette will do me the honour to accept me, I will make her my wife."

Horace looked quickly round, as if his first thought was that the Prince was joking. But M. d'Arcola was perfectly composed. He spoke as if he had just announced his coming marriage to a princess of his own rank.

CHAPTER VII.

A Recognition.

THE Prince's communication ought to have left Horace indifferent, but somehow it did not. Let those explain this who, having ever formed the manly resolution not to love a girl because she was poor, or low-born, or anything else uneligible, find these scruples accounted as nought by others richer, higher, and prouder than themselves. Horace was aware that there was not a living man who would have shrunk more sensitively from a mésalliance than the Prince of Arcola. But, apparently, *his* notions of a mésalliance were not those of the common world.

At dinner, without alluding to the circumstance, Horace asked his wife whether she had yet called on the Pochemolles at their new residence.

"Perhaps it would be civil," said he pensively, "as they sent us a letter, mentioning they were going to move."

"I will call, dear, if you wish it," answered Angélique in her tranquil voice; "but I could not do so before, for they gave no address."

"M. d'Arcola tells me they are at Meudon," said Horace.

"Very wise of them to choose the country," remarked M. Macrobe: "pure air, broad fields, life healthy and cheap."

"And shooting for those who can shoot," chimed in the Crimean hero.

"And shooting, as you say, Captain," assented his uncle.

For some time past it had become a sort of mania with M. Macrobe to depict rural bliss. Virgil never took greater pains to vaunt the charms of a rustic life, the sweet breath of kine, the scent of new-mown hay, and the unadulterated purity of country milk and butter than did the financier. Especially was it good to hear him hold forth on the pride and pomp of a manorial estate, the waving acres, the waggons groaning under loads of storied sheaves, the rows of peasants bowing with glad homage before their lord, and the turreted castle gleaming majestuously in the summer sun over river, field, and wood. Angélique, as if repeating a music lesson, would take up this pastoral in a minor key, saying that she adored the country, and would "so like to have a small castle where they might spend the autumn." Captain Clarimon, not less bucolic, opined that a great noble should slaughter winged fowl on a grandiose scale, organize battues that would muster a whole country side, and run down a stag now and then with accompaniment of horn-tooting to stir up the minds of the clod-hoppers.

That was a true saying of the ancients: *Gutta cavat lapidem, non vi, sed sæpe cadendo.* Under the frequency of these Georgic aspersions Horace was imperceptibly beginning to feel that the man who had no landed property, nor horned cattle, nor preserves, had missed the preordained purpose of existence. To be sure, he might have purchased all these things on the very morrow with his wife's dowry had it pleased him. But he did not look upon this money as his. At her marriage M. Macrobe had given his daughter two millions and a half of francs, but Horace had insisted they should stand in Angélique's own name on the books of the Crédit Parisien, and be tied down absolutely to her by contract: and there he meant to leave them, never claiming the privilege of touching a centime. Besides, his notions of an enviable demesne were not associated with a brand-new estate, cut out to order and bought with ready money. When he thought of the matter the towers of Clairefontaine rose vaguely before him— Clairefontaine which might have been his, had his relative Guineaman made his fortune by swindling his contemporaries under the rose, instead of selling them openly in the broad light of day.

"Everybody likes the country," he remarked mechanically, in answer to M. Macrobe's observation.

It was Italian Opera night, and, on leaving the dining-room, Angélique was cloaked in a flowing white *burnous* by the attentive Crimean hero, who was continually and jealously on the watch to render little services. The same warrior brought the opera-glass, and took Angélique's fan into his special custody. He also made himself useful in fastening those six-button gloves which ladies were then inaugurating, and which, had they existed in the time of Job, might have added one more to that sorely-vexed patriarch's trials of patience.

"You will take me to the opera, won't you, Horace?" asked Angélique, helplessly surrendering her small wrists to the gallant Captain.

"Yes, dear," answered Horace with the docility characteristic of husbands during the first year of their marriage; and he inquired what opera it was.

"I think it's *Don Giovanni.*"

"Oh dear!" sighed Aunt Dorothée, whose venerable head was crowned with an assortment of limp feathers that gave her the appearance of a demoralized bustard. "That's the play where the stage opens up and swallows a living being in the flames. You'll come away before that happens, won't you, dear? I'm always afraid to see that young man burn his clothes."

"You shall come away when you like, aunt dear," promised Angélique. "Are you ready, Horace?"

Horace was ready, and so was the Captain, who, as in duty bound, offered the Marquise his arm. But as they all sailed out together, with the exception of M. Macrobe, who participated in the belief of M. Alphonse Karr that music is but the most expensive of all noises, a servant announced "Monsieur Emile," and this upset the arrangements. Horace, not over sorry to be reprieved from four hours' stewing in a grand tier box, settled to join his wife later in the evening, the Crimean hero meanwhile undertaking to guard her under his valiant protection.

"The night is so fine that Emile and I will walk down," said Horace; "and I will be with you about the second act."

"And will you come too, Emile?" asked Angélique a little timidly; for she never brought herself without hesitation to call her grave young brother-in-law by his Christian name.

"I am scarcely in opera attire, sister," he answered kindly. "I only looked in on the chance of finding Horace disengaged, but I blame myself for monopolizing him in this way."

"Oh, you are quite right to come, brother, but you should let us see you oftener, and be here earlier, so as to dine with us."

She said this amiably, glancing up a little to her husband for approval, for she knew it was the surest way to please him to show civility to his brother. Then she held out her tiny hand to Emile, which he shook, thanking her.

"Well, old fellow, it's a long while since we two took an evening walk like this," began Horace, as he and Emile paced together arm-in-arm.

They were in the Champs Elysées, under the crystal dome of a clear sky, blue with the darkblue of night, and irradiated by a moon of such silvery brightness that it made the gaslights look like dull red dots. Paris shows well on such nights when the trees throw long lace-pattern shadows on the pavements, rows of fair white mansions gleam like polished marble, and lovers stroll in pairs, whispering that *Je t'aime* which is of daily use in none but the "Latin" tongues.

"Do you remember those pleasant walks," continued Horace, "when we first came to Paris, three years ago? It seems like ten years off. We worked all day, often half the night, but now and then we gave ourselves a holiday, and took it out like this, wandering about the streets and guessing at the future. How gay they appeared to me then, the streets; and what smiles I used to see on the faces of the passers-by! Paris always struck me as a perpetual fair. Ah, those were the happy times!"

"But you are happy now, Horace?"

"Oh yes."

And there was a pause.

"But tell me about yourself," added Horace, breaking off from some internal reflection which had brought a flitting frown to his brow. "Let me look at you—you grow paler and paler. Why do you work so much, eh? Everybody talks of your indefatigableness. A judge told me the other night that if he had worked as you do at his age he would have been a Chief Justice of Appeal by this time."

"Then you see, work does lead to something," smiled Emile.

"Ah, but my judge added the proviso: 'Or I should have been in my coffin,' which didn't reassure me."

"I don't feel as if I were near my coffin, dear fellow. Pale men, like threatened men, live long."

"And you are happy in your way and satisfied?"

"Why should I not be?"

"But you have no ambition, restlessness, eagerness to outpass somebody or do something before the appointed time? I sometimes marvel at your calmness; we don't seem to be moulded out of the same clay."

"I suppose everybody has his small beacon of ambition beckoning him, Horace, but I fancy the surest way of attaining it is by plainly following the beaten track. It may be the longest road, but cuts across country often lead one into quagmires."

A short silence and then they reached the Rue de Rivoli, that noblest of modern streets, with its half-mile colonnade, forum of foreigners, *Via Sacra* of hotel-keepers. Broughams glanced along the broad highway, bearing muffled forms to theatre and routs.

Unbroken lines of flaming jets intensified by dazzling
reflectors flooded the arches with light.   Spaniards
Americans, Germans, Englishmen sauntered up and
down smoking their after-dinner cigars, and examining
the accumulated treasures of the shops.

"What wealth!" exclaimed Horace.   "Paris has
indeed under this reign become Cosmopolis.   But,
now, I wonder"—and he laughed—"I wonder if all
these people we see here, and all the people in the
shops there, were suddenly to sit down and say, 'We
will make restitution of every franc that we have ever
unduly earned, and of every franc that our fathers before us unduly earned and bequeathed to us in in-
heritance;' and supposing some power of another
sphere were to inspire them with the faculty of making
a faultless estimate of these sums—I wonder, I say,
when the balance had been struck, how many of these
persons we behold congregated from all the corners of
the globe would have money enough left to smoke
their cigars, or to keep those sumptuous shops going."

"What can have put such a thought as that into
your head?" asked Emile, astonished.   "This is disquieting philosophy."

"I was thinking about the nice discussions we
barristers could raise as to what was honest gold and
what was not.   Given two men with large fortunes
and relatives to inherit them.   The first has been, say,
a wine-merchant, and has conscientiously mixed his
wines with logwood and water for a stated series of
years.   The second has with integrity followed a
trade, which, during his lifetime, was lawful, but
which was prohibited later, though even then opinions
were divided respecting it.   Now which is the cleaner

money of the two: that of the wine-merchant who re-
galed the public with a purple decoction at fancy
prices or that of the other man, who, pursuing a
doubtful trade, yet conducted it according to his lights,
straightforwardly?"

"I should like to hear more about the doubtful
trade," answered Emile, quietly. "There are possibly
in this crowd some police-spies from the Prefecture,
sent out to worm themselves into the confidence of
unsuspecting men, trap them into anti-Bonapartist utterances, and get them transported to Cayenne. As
times go, the trade is a lawful one, but I should be
sorry to finger any of its profits."

"Naturally. You speak like the good fellow you
are. Still, I ask myself how many men would feel
bound to do what we have done, and renounce the
estate where their fathers lived because it had been
bought back after arbitrary confiscation, with the money
of a dealer who—well, who did what the custom of
those days perfectly sanctioned."

This was the first time since many a long month
that Horace so much as alluded to a subject which
Emile had dismissed from his own mind once and for
all as not admitting of discussion. Emile looked at
his brother with an expression in which sudden surprise and dismay were painfully blended, and it was
in quite an altered voice that he said: "You are surely
not regretting a sacrifice that was made of your own
free will, Horace?"

"Not in the least. No, there's no regret whatever," and Horace laughed again in an off-hand way,
though somewhat constrainedly. "To begin with, our
father made the sacrifice before us, and I know he

would take it so much to heart if either of us
abandoned our resolution, that I wouldn't assume the
responsibility even if I *had* changed my mind.   But I
haven't—no—so don't be alarmed.   I was only speaking on supposition—supposing there were two other
men placed in our predicament, and you and I were
commenting on what they ought to do, I think, then,
the case might afford scope for argument. That's all."

And argue it they did, walking slowly during two
hours through the streets, often retracing their steps,
occasionally stopping altogether; the one conversing
with animation but simulated unconcern, the other
too much troubled to say all he would have said had
he felt the debate to be as hypothetical a one as his
brother would have had it seem.   At eleven they stood
outside the Opera House, and the theme was not yet
exhausted, for, bidding each other good-night under
the portico of the theatre, Horace said, a little flushed
but cheerfully: "Mind, old fellow, all this is purely
speculative; talk to while away the time and nothing
else. It was our walk set me thinking of Clairefontaine. You recollect our visit there; that old woman
who shewed us over the place, our ovation when we
returned to the worthy town, and the stones with
which the good people pelted us in guise of *pax
vobiscum* to the railway-station. It was just such a
night as this. By-the-way, you hear oftener from Brussels than I do: our father was quite well, at the last
writing?"

"Quite well, thank God."

"I will write to him myself in a day or two.   But
his letters to me are sad; they give one the idea that
he is suffering.   Well, good-night, dear fellow, and

mind what I repeat, this evening's chat has been words, nothing more."

"Good-night, Horace."

They shook hands and parted; but had Horace followed his brother round the corner of the street he would have seen that, collected as Emile had been all the evening, tears started to his eyes as soon as his brother's back was turned, and that he walked home with the lagging step of one who had received a blow, whose faith in a loved being has been shaken.

Horace was conducted by a bustling attendant to the box of Mdme. la Marquise de Clairefontaine. A prima-donna was indulging in terrific screams under pretence of singing, and the audience hung spell-bound on the enchanting sounds. The fig-nosed planter, alone, whom Horace descried slumbering in a pit-tier lodge under the mutely reproachful eye of Mrs. Planter, appeared to protest by his attitude against this manner of spending an evening. Every part of the house was crowded, and the Italian Opera being the only theatre in which the play-going Frenchwoman will unveil her shoulders and the Frenchman submit to the tyranny of swallow-tails, the effect was not bad.

"Do you recognize any one you know?" asked Angélique prettily, making way for Horace on the chair beside her, which the Crimean hero had vacated on his entrance.

Angélique's large, limpid eyes were always so intently fixed when uttering the simplest questions that Horace detected nothing unusually attentive in their gaze on this occasion.

"Let me see, dear child," he said, taking her

glass. "On the tier above there's Mdme. de Margauld; is that who you mean? a pretty woman, and dresses sensibly; then there's Mdme. de Masseline, wife of my co-deputy. They say her pin-money comes from the Prefecture, where she carries all that she picks up in society. I refuse to believe it, though, for you ladies malign one another mercilessly, and it was a lady gave me that pretty piece of scandal. Then there's the Austrian ambassadress, and Mdlle. Cora, the dancer, costumed with infinitely more propriety than her Excellency, and Mdme. Gribaud—why, yes, dear child, I recognize everybody. But there's not a face"—restoring the glass and nodding with a smile, "more pretty, or a dress more tasteful than those of someone whose name you may guess."

"Look again," said Angélique, her mild eyes calmly, inquiringly, intent as before. "There, almost opposite us."

Horace looked again, and this time his researches were guided by several pairs of eyes in the stalls converging towards one point, a box where shone a truly imperial beauty. She was the most striking face in the house; but it took Horace some seconds to rally his fluttering impressions and to grasp who it was. Georgette!

"Their coming in caused quite a sensation during the first entr'acte," pursued Angélique quietly; but she never withdrew her eyes from her husband, who now did not put down the glass. "Everybody seems to admire her."

"Reminds me of those Georgian beauties whom I saw at Constantinople; lustrous faces, scarlet lips, and dark hair," struck in the Crimean hero; "but I prefer blonde features."

In spite of himself, Horace's gaze seemed rivetted. The box was occupied by Madame Pochemolle and the draper, but these excellent people, not knowing much of etiquette, had given the place of honour to their daughter. In the background the Prince of Arcola was dimly recognizable. Georgette was pensively rapt in the music, but at intervals she turned to answer some remark of the Prince's, or bent her head with modest grace in token that she was listening to him. Could this be the Georgette of the Rue Ste. Geneviève? Was it possible that a few yards of silk and a trinket or two had been able to convert the humble girl of the linen-shop into a beauty outvying all the most courted women of the chief city of cities? When Horace put down the glass it was with a slight tremor of the hand.

"Is she not beautiful?" said Angélique, in whose voice no unaccustomed inflection was noticeable, at least to her husband.

"Yes—that is, no—I find her altered a little, improved, perhaps," answered Horace, affecting an indifference which his reverie-struck mood belied.

"Good gracious!" dolefully exclaimed Aunt Dorothée, at this opportune juncture. "Here is that dreadful Statue come to take that young man down into the flames. My dear, I was quite unwell last time I saw this."

"Well, madame, we will leave then," said Horace, at once rising. "Angélique, child, shall we go?"

"Yes, dear," she murmured simply, and there was a putting on of cloaks and screwing down of opera-glasses, which called into play the Crimean hero's chivalry, and filled up a minute. During that minute, after assisting in the swathing of his aunt, Horace came to the front of the box and gazed again across the house. His glance may have been charged with something of electricity, for Georgette almost instantly looked up and saw him. But had he been a stranger seen for the first time, had he been one of those curly-pated dandies in the stalls, one of the box-openers in the lobbies, one of the chorus-singers on the stage, her expression could not have been more stony, more coldly unconscious. She turned her head away without vouchsafing a mark of recognition, either unfriendly or the reverse. Horace turned away too, and drew out his handkerchief to wipe away a drop of moisture from his brow. As he did so he observed the cypher on his handkerchief. It was one of those which Georgette had embroidered for him as a gift two years before.

CHAPTER VIII.

Prince Cophetua's Wooing.

THE Prince of Arcola's mansion was remarkable for other things besides the architectural perfections which made it one of the finest in a capital where, Revolution and Equality aiding, the only fine palaces extant are those belonging to Government, the rest of mankind lodging themselves in edifices showy enough when looked at by the hundred, but separately, cramped and partaking of the doll-house. The Hôtel d'Arcole had an essentially English aspect, which it owed to the Anglophilist tastes of its proprietor, and to the valuable counsels of the eminent Mr. Drydust, who had laid himself out to show the Prince, his friend, what the dwelling of a British noble ought to be, and had done so with success. An air of home greeted the invader. The floors both in corridors and rooms were covered with carpets; nobody was exposed to come down flat over superlatively polished boards as slippery as glazed frost. The doors all shut properly, which French-made doors do not, the Gallic workman being particular about the trim look of his panels and the smooth roundness of his handles, but careless as to his hinges and lintels.. Then you saw branching antlers and trophies of hunting-whips in the vestibules; bound books on the tables (not those disastrous *brochures* which tumble to pieces in one's hands); and the walls teemed with the works of British artists in oil and water-colour; for the Prince dearly

, 7*

loved English landscapes, and sporting cracks, and was a little severe upon the artists of his own country, saying that unless you gave them women to paint they were fit for nothing.

On the morrow, however, of the *Don Giovanni* night at the opera, the Prince might have been detected in the un-English act of putting himself into dress clothes at eleven o'clock in the morning. And he did this gravely, for the business he had before him is never a light one in any country, and in France is generally attended with a certain degree of ceremony —the asking a lady's hand of her parents.

Yes, he had taken the resolution to seal his fate that day; and as he adjusted his speckless white cravat in the looking-glass, said to himself, what so many have muttered before him, and so many since—that in another couple of hours he should be the most fortunate or the wretchedest of men. Not that he had any reason to foresee that he should be the wretchedest; this did not appear likely, but a little modesty never comes amiss. It ought, perhaps, to be mentioned that there is no binding necessity for a Frenchman about to call upon his prospective father-in-law to attire himself in black. Aristocratic fathers-in-law are content to regard many-hued trousers and buff-dogskins as sufficient evidences of the intention to render their daughters happy; but the bourgeoisie cling more fondly to venerable traditions. It was certain that M. Pochemolle must have plighted his troth to Madame Pochemolle in a dress coat, and the Prince was but evincing his natural tact in seeking to avoid in any way hurting the worthy man's sense of the becoming. In addition to the staidness of his apparel, the Prince had deter-

mined that his equipage would have a suitable degree
of solemnity. He had ordered round his family coach,
which habitually saw service only at the burial of his
kinsmen, and was an imposing vehicle with hammer-
cloth, four coronetted lamps, and room behind for
two vassals with cocked hats to overawe the populace
and staves to keep them at a distance.

The Prince was ministered to by a valet of such
unmistakeably British complexion, that one would have
sworn he had answered to some such advertisement
as this: "Wanted a man with red whiskers and a stiff
shirt-collar. Must have an impassive mien, drop his
H's with dignity, always look as if he had just been
brushing his hair, and say, 'Yes, my lord', in a tone
of well-bred composure. It is indispensable that this
individual should tacitly, but firmly decline having any
language but his own imposed upon him, and should
distinctly object to adopt either the diet, habits, or
sentiments of the foreigners amongst whom he may
reside." This loftily spruce gentleman stood behind
his master holding white gloves, crush-hat, and per-
fumed handkerchief; and the Prince conversed with
him, wielding his English with the intrepidity of a
nobleman who read his *Times* every morning and
really understood four-fifths of it.

"I am right, like this, Bateson?"

"Yes, my lord."

"And the cravat goes well?"

"Yes, my lord."

"I think, Bateson, I will wear my rosette; this occasion is exceptional."

Bateson extracted from the dressing-case a rosette
the size of a Napoleon and presenting a combination

of colours. The Prince had been decorated for an act of courage performed when almost a boy in saving somebody's life at the risk of his own; but he never sported this order for which half his countrymen would have given their ears; nor two others less striking, one conferred by the mighty monarch of Monaco, in whose principality he had won with éclat a gentleman-rider steeple-chase, and the other by the grand potentate of Baden, as a reward, perhaps, for once breaking the bank in that serenely gambling duchy.

"Now, Bateson, it is well," said the Prince, fastening the rosette to his button-hole. "For what hour have you commanded the coach?"

"For half-past eleven, my lord?"

"And it is now?—Mon Dieu, it is only eleven five! The time seems long when the heart beats."

At the moment when the Prince was emitting this aphorism, some similar reflection, though suggested by different causes, was possibly obtruding itself upon three at least out of the four members of the Pochemolle family. It is all very well to give up business and establish oneself at Meudon, but the difficulty is to devise the wherewith to make the hours pass, when one has been used all one's life to measure calico, and finds oneself suddenly deprived of that occupation. M. Pochemolle with newspaper under his arm, which he had read and re-read, advertisements and shipping intelligence included, was asking himself what on earth he should do to bridge over the interval between the *déjeûner à la fourchette*, just over, and the dinner yet five hours distant. An immense garden-hat that covered his honest head, gave him the appearance of a melancholy mushroom as he meditated this proposition. Madame Pochemolle with less reason to vex herself, seeing that she had her household cares to attend to, and the never-failing resource of slipper-working when those were deficient, nevertheless thought that there were days when the Rue Ste. Geneviève, with its ceaseless flow of customers, its lively gossip of all that was going on in Paris, and the hum of the great city, audible without, was not always such a very dull residence. Of course, she would have suffered herself to be tortured by the rack sooner than acknowledge, even internally, that she regretted that Rue Ste. Geneviève; only her opinion was that if M. Pochemolle had been "a little less in a hurry to remove into the country," if he had postponed his retirement for, say, another year or so, it would have done no harm. Note that the good draper had only been driven to retire after the most energetic and valiant resistance on his part. Domestic strife had raged long and ardently; and Madame Pochemolle had only carried her point by shedding tears, and exclaiming she saw M. Pochemolle was brutally bent on condemning her and her children to a life of drudgery. But ladies have short memories for these kinds of particulars.

As for M. Alcibiade Pochemolle, the exaltation of his sire to the *rentier* class had opened before him an endless vista of leisure hours which he had immediately inaugurated by a series of walks from one extremity of the capital to the other. After a fortnight, however, these excursions had become slightly monotonous, partly from being conducted in tight, new boots, partly because M. Alcibiade was forced to stride alone, his former friends, who had not risen to fortune simultaneously with himself, being busy behind their several

counters till long after the going down of the sun.
So M. Alcibiade now spent his days at Meudon, where
small occurrences assumed giant proportions in his
eyes.   The falling down of a chimney, the escape of
a neighbour's rabbit, the discovery of a mole-hill dug
furtively during the night under the shelter of a wall-
flower, gave him subjects for reflection and varied, if
not always entertaining, talk until it was bed-time.
And a true godsend was afforded him when three
workmen in fustian and with pickaxes, for all the world
like Paris workmen, came and took up the road in the
vicinity of the villa Pochemolle in order to lay down
a water-pipe.   M. Alcibiade, perched upon a garden
mound, followed their movements with absorbed interest like a Layard watching the excavations of Nine-
veh, and he was thus intent when suddenly his vision
was dazzled and his voice uprose, shrill and amazed.

"My eye! here's a swell turn-out coming down the
Paris road.   Coachman with a wig on, horses with
gold-plated harness;—what steppers, and what a dust!
It's one of the Court nobs going somewhere.   No.—
Eh, by jingo!   I say, father, mother, blessed if it
ain't stopping here!"

M. Alcibiade stood dumb-stricken on his mound.
Madame and M. Pochemolle looked up bewildered,
but instinctively began, the former to smoothe her
gown, the latter to rumple his necktie in a wild and
distracting effort to make it sit straight.   Who could
it be?   But they were not kept long in suspense, for
the maid-servant, arriving with the air of one who
heralds something startling and incomprehensible,
said: "Monsieur the Prince of Arcola."

Although the visits of the Prince were sufficiently

frequent to give him the character of an established friend of the house, yet his name was never announced without causing pleasurable emotions to the draper and his wife.   M. Pochemolle was relieved from all solicitude about the flight of time, which sped by fast enough when the amiable nobleman was there to chat and to listen, for, above all, the Prince was a capital listener, and Madame Pochemolle liked the finished manners and pleasant smile of M. d'Arcola.   Being, moreover, never quite able to forget that he was a prince, and a rich one, she enjoyed these advantages twice as much as if he had possessed finished manners and a pleasant smile, but been some one else, not a prince, and not rich—which is only natural.

On the present occasion, however, it was at once evident, both to M. and Madame Pochemolle, that the Prince of Arcola had not come to chat, or to make himself simply agreeable.   His mien was too serious, his deportment too ceremonious, and Madame Pochemolle's matronly heart went *thump, thump,* against her stays.   Was the mother's idle, impossible wish she had formed about to be realized?   It was an old dream, and had been more than once laid aside, then taken up again, like all other dreams good or bad.   For a while she had timidly dared to hope that Horace Gerold, who they said was a marquis, would ask for Georgette; but that had come to nothing.   Then the Prince had introduced himself into their small circle, and, with maternal quickness, she had begun hoping—very timidly and very silently, to be sure—again.   But it seemed as slender a chance as the first.   The Prince came, indeed, and was kindly, and there was a good deal in his ways and words that encouraged the supposition

that he was courting.   But it never went farther than
very friendly attentions, so that Madame Pochemolle
had often resolved that she had pitched her ambition
too high, and that she must be content with such a
son-in-law as her own draper's sphere could afford.
Still, she persevered in her fond fancy, and, womanlike, had, in view of possibilities, set herself to thwart
the Filoselle engagement—ultimately achieving success,
though it had cost her honest husband a pang, and
had made him feel uncomfortable and conscience-
stricken ever since.

Now, what was to be the issue of all this?

During the prefatory interchange of courtesies
Madame Pochemolle, in one glance, devoured every
article of dress the Prince had on, noticing also his
rosette—magic symbol, fascinating to the eye of Frenchwoman! The Prince had followed the servant-maid into
the garden, where Madame Pochemolle had been sitting
working under a tree, and M. Pochemolle staring at the
clouds.   Georgette happened to be indoors.

There was a moment's animated bustle on the part
of the maid and M. Pochemolle to get another garden-
chair, and then the Prince said, with quiet earnestness,
"I hope I am not intruding at this early hour, madame
and monsieur, but I have a communication of importance
—of great importance—to make, and I wished to be
certain of finding you at home."

Madame Pochemolle bent her head, and the heart
went *thump, thump,* at an accelerated pace. M. Pochemolle looked in the direction of M. Alcibiade, as
though to inquire whether that gentleman were one
too many.

The Prince saw and hastened to add: "I beg

Monsieur Alcibiade will remain. As a member of the family he has a right to hear what I am about to say." —He coughed.—"Monsieur Pochemolle, I do not think it necessary to search for circuitous phrases to prefer a request which, perhaps, you already divine. Besides, my emotion at this moment counsels me to be brief. I have the honour to ask your permission" (here he rose) "to offer my hand to your daughter."

A red blush suffused Madame Pochemolle's features. In that second the poor woman looked twenty years younger. For nothing she would have got up and kissed the Prince. As it was, her still buxom face broke into dimples and smiles, and her eyes sparkled as they had not done for many a long day.

The effect on M. Pochemolle was not so instantaneous. He sat as a man who would like to hear the thing over again; but presently, when the truth, with its flattering train of consequences, flashed upon him, the latent fire in his French nature burst out as a conflagration over eyes, ears, and countenance at once. He became purple. He let fall his straw hat, and, in trying to pick up that, let go his newspaper. There was he, Pochemolle, going to marry his daughter to a member of the highest nobility, and to become the cynosure and envy of the Syndicate of Drapers! The ground seemed to swell under his feet, and it is to be feared that M. Filoselle, that pearl of young men, was, for the nonce, relegated to a very obscure nook in the temple of memory.

With respect to M. Alcibiade, the idea that presented itself to this gentle youth's imagination, with the inexorable force of logic, was that he should henceforth be able to talk of "my brother, the Prince," and heap humiliation on the head of his best friend and schoolfellow, Jules Paquet, whose sister had married a doctor. He grinned, and, for the next quarter of an hour, fixed his gaze in enrapt contemplation on the Prince's white gloves. How they fitted him, those gloves, and what small hands those "nobs" had!

It would be superfluous to describe the rest of the interview; the inevitable vows proffered on one side, the assurances of feeling unspeakably honoured, touched, and so forth, on the other. Those who have witnessed one of these scenes have seen a dozen, and those who have never beheld one may satisfy themselves by dividing as much sunshine, smiles, pleasant awkwardness, and incoherent sentences among three people as may be managed without making all three ridiculous. The element which occasionally tempers these interviews with a little cold shade—the dowry question—was adroitly suppressed by the Prince's remarking at an early stage that it was his desire to take Mdlle. Georgette without a portion; and mentioning at the same time a settlement so overpoweringly and unprecedentedly handsome that a grand duke himself might have accepted it. Whereat Mdme. Pochemolle was very nearly entering into the melting mood; M. Pochemolle stammered and became purpler than ever; and M. Alcibiade, who was quite acute enough to appreciate the amelioration which was being thus introduced into his own share of the paternal heritage, giggled and formed an infinity of reflections favourable to the method in which "nobs" managed money-matters.

It was not until full twenty golden minutes had elapsed that it occurred to either of the delighted parents to call into council her whom the negotiations most concerned. But at a point where the conversation, emotional as it was, began insensibly to flag,

Mdme. Pochemolle rose, and, with a sweet smile, said: "Monsieur le Prince, I will call Georgette. She had a letter to write to one of her friends, but it must be finished by this time."

M. Pochemolle understood that this was a hint, and rose likewise to leave the coast clear. He would have retired with one of those bows which he used to reserve for customers who had bought a thousand francs' worth of goods at a sitting, but the Prince extended both hands together, and there was a cordial, sturdy grasp. Emboldened, and feeling that he had yet his part to play in the domestic event, M. Alcibiade thereupon came forward too, with the words "my brother" already itching on his lips. But he bottled them in with an effort, as, perhaps, premature, and vented his enthusiasm by working the Prince's arm energetically up and down like a pump-handle. Then he vanished.

It was not long before Georgette came out, sheltering her dark eyes under a light parasol, and glancing with some inquisitiveness to see who the "friend" could be whom her mother had announced with such mysterious archness as desiring to see her. She was so used to the Prince that she had not thought it could be he. Since that day, now distant, when he had offered her his homage in terms slightly ambiguous, and been indignantly rebuffed, he had behaved towards her rather as an affectionate elder brother. She had grown to feel at ease with him, and his visits were agreeable, but unexciting, events to her. When, however, she caught sight of the formal dress, the face lit up by a hopeful and expectant gaze, the ray of pleasure that greeted her appearance, she saw what was impending. Any other girl would have done so, for

there is an intuition in these things, and the language
of the eyes is plainer to comprehend than any. She
advanced, her parasol trembling a little, and a bright
blush mantling on her handsome cheek; and the next
minute she found herself confronting a proposal as
tender and respectful as lover had ever made, or as
maiden could ever wish to hear.

What passed within her heart at that minute she
herself, and the spirits who read the human heart,
alone knew. Considering the attentions which the
Prince had for so long a time bestowed on her, it
could scarcely be said that she felt surprised, yet the
quick heaving of her bosom, the sudden trouble of her
manner, argued that she had almost ceased to expect
the proposal, and that it had been a relief to her to
think it might never come. For a moment hesitation
painted itself on her features. A struggle followed that
no eye could detect, for the pangs of it only revealed
themselves by that quivering of the lips that resembles
the ripple on the surface of water when there is a
violent commotion very deep beneath. Then a forgotten passion seemed to rise amidst this strife, like a
combatant who has been left for dead upon a battle-
field and revives. She essayed to resist, she murmured
some uncertain words; but it was of no use. The old
passion mastered her; all the colour fled from her face;
and when she gave the answer—trembling all over, yet
endeavouring to show gratitude through the tears in
her eyes—it was a refusal.

The Prince was not prepared for this. Without
more infatuation than is the unavoidable lot of those
who have never found the other sex very hard of con-
quest,—rather the contrary—he had counted upon
success—an easy success. On hearing Georgette's

refusal he turned whiter than the cloud which at that moment darkened the sun, as if ironically to symbolize the eclipse of his hopes.

Georgette took pity upon his distress. She liked him too well not to be moved by the look of astonished pain that had settled on his features.

"Monsieur le Prince," she said, trying to keep in her tears and to speak calmly, "I will not conceal the truth from you. Generous and good as you are, you deserve to have a heart that would be wholly yours, and that I could not give you."

"Were my fears, then, founded?" he asked, sorrowfully. "Can it be that——?"

"You guessed many months ago that I had a secret grief," she continued, completing his thoughts, and leaning ·for support with her hand against a chair. "You guessed my grief, and respected it. I thank you for that very gratefully, and for all the kindness you have shown me since. I cannot tell you how gratefully I thank you. I thought I should surmount this—grief. By not thinking about it, by persuading myself that the person who had caused it was not worthy to inspire such a sentiment, I had brought myself to believe that I had done so. But it seems there are feelings which neither time, nor reason, nor contempt even, can extirpate. Perhaps—— But no; I was going to say that if it had been anybody I esteemed less than you I might have acted differently to what I am doing. There are men who would ask nothing more of me than to be a good wife, and would never have questioned my heart to know whether there was an image in it besides theirs. I could have accepted such a part, which would have required only obedience, and a show of cheerfulness. But I cannot bear to deceive *you*.   I might be your wife, but there would always be between me and you the thought of the man I once loved, whom I thought till just now I had forgotten, but whom I find I love still—for indignation, jealousy, resentment, are in these cases only other forms of love. You will forgive me," she added, looking at him with a timid, appealing smile, "for speaking so frankly."

Would he forgive her!   He would have cast himself at her feet in that minute and told her that he loved her more deeply and truly than he had ever done before, and this would have been true.   But if a habit of society does nothing else, it teaches a man when to pause, teaches him to know when pleading will be of no effect.   Georgette's sincerity, though mild and timorous, would prove as resisting as a wall of steel, and the Prince saw it.

"Georgette," he said, in a voice which he was quite unable to control so as to stifle the quaver, "I will not say that I shall go away from here resigned to my fate, for this would be promising beyond my strength. I shall leave you with a wound which Time, I know, will not heal; but let me assure you that if my respect and admiration had been capable of increase they would have been heightened by this interview.   And if I may beg a favour in this supreme meeting it is that you should remember, always remember, that there are circumstances in which the boundless devotion of a friend may be of help, and, should such circumstances ever arise, not to deprive me of the happiness of serving you."

Perhaps she was never so near loving him as after this simple and feeling renunciation.

————

CHAPTER IX.

Idle Regrets and Bad Resolution.

MEN make one great mistake with regard to women: they fancy they can deceive them, which they seldom can.   For all the good that dissimulation does a man, he might just as well write out his secret at full length and pin it to his breast—that is, of course, when his secret concerns a woman, and the person who wishes to discover it is another woman.   Horace was labouring under the convenient impression that Angélique had detected none of his agitation at the theatre; that his tremor, the last look he had cast at Georgette's box, and his subsequent paleness had all escaped her. Coming down the staircase of the opera, he had even had the naïveness to ask his wife why her hand shook slightly on his arm, and on her answering that it must be the cold, had accepted this reply with that undisturbed serenity which is one of the salient traits of husbandship.

The next day Horace rose pre-occupied.   He had no appetite for his ten o'clock breakfast; took up the *Moniteur* when the table was cleared away, and set himself to read it—but did not read it, and held it listlessly on his knee whilst his eyes wandered away to some point on the horizon, visible out of the window across an expanse of leafless garden.   And, again, he was intimately persuaded that no one observed his absent mood, that no eye followed his, that no change indeed was noticeable in his manner.   And what wonder?   Did he remark any change in Angélique?

Angélique was pretending to read too. Of late she had taken to reading, not because she found any greater interest in books than before, but because Horace had good-naturedly bantered her once or twice on not knowing who Bernardin de St. Pierre was, and on imagining that Jean-Jacques Rousseau was the inventor of the Post Office.* So she read as she would have done anything else to please him—taken poison, or put her hand in the fire. For her notions of wifely duty were simply summed up in this: passively to obey, and do all in her power to render happy the man who had married her in spite of her own timidly expressed forebodings that he would repent of his course later.

The book she held was *Paul et Virginie*, and, perhaps, at any other time the touching adventures of this loving pair would have arrested her attention; but now she turned the leaves of the old book with abstractedness, casting glances, which became each time more furtive and longer in the direction of her husband. This had been going on for some time when there was a knock, and a servant entered, bearing a number of letters and some more papers on a tray.

It was one of the little pleasures of Horace's married life to ask Angélique to read his letters aloud for him. She delighted in the practice so far as it was in her tranquil nature to delight in anything, so when the letters had been laid on the table, she put down her book and said: "Shall I read for you, Horace?"

"Yes, please, dear child," he answered, and as was his wont handed her a pencil with which she jotted down in the tiniest of handwritings the sub-

* The General Post Office of Paris is situated Rue J. J. Rousseau.

stance of the replies that were to be sent. The letters
were all collected afterwards and transferred to a
secretary, whose office, by the way, was no sinecure.

From all quarters of the empire came the letters
which matutinally worried the elect of the Tenth Circumscription. Constituents wrote in great force, begging
favours for themselves and for their sons, who were
ambitious of Government clerkships, or for aged and
afflicted relatives needing admission to privileged
lunatic asylums. The ballot system is a godsend to
those electors who regard political rights as blessed
instruments for the furtherance of private objects, for
when the suffrages are recorded openly one is exposed
to the unpleasant risk of not being able to ask favours
at all of one's representative, should he unfortunately
be a man whose candidature one has opposed. Then
there were letters from old barrister friends, or to
speak more correctly, young barrister friends, who,
having been rabid Republicans at twenty, aspired at
twenty-five to be appointed deputies to the Procureur
Impérial, and would feel eternally grateful if, &c.; and
petitions from inventors, and applications for charitable
subscriptions, and folio sheets from persons who had
been aggrieved and craved the favour of an interview
to relate their trouble; and heaps of invitations requesting the honour of M. le Marquis's and Mdme. la Marquise's company to various festive entertainments.
Finally there was a missive dated from Hautbourg on
the Loire.

"I wonder what possesses those people to write to
me with such importunity," broke in Horace, whose
attention had not been very well sustained up to that
point, but who shifted his place impatiently when

8*

Angélique read the heading of the letter. "There's
not a day passes," added he, "but I get a petition
from one of those Hautbourg burgesses. They seem
to fancy I am a free agent in this matter."

"This looks like a round-robin," said Angélique,
gently.

"Ay, that was inevitable. They have got to round-
robins now; we shall have deputations of them next."

Angélique continued to read. The memorial was
signed by influential citizens: Ballanchu, seed-merchant,
Market Place; Scarpin, boot-maker, Rue de Clairefontaine; Hochepain, tax-gatherer; Duval, hotel-keeper;
Toulmouche, Truchepoule, and Follavoine, farmers,
and many more of the same eminence. It set forth in
humble language that Hautbourg did not despair of
seeing its ancient lords return with splendour to fill
the home of their forefathers, but that whether the
ancient lords did so or not, "we, the undersigned,"
ventured to submit that there was a means open by .
which the Marquis of Clairefontaine might confer both
a great honour and a great joy upon the town. The
general elections of 1857 would take place within a
month or two, and it was, to be presumed that M. le
Marquis would stand again for the city of Paris. But
there was nothing to prevent his being put up in
nomination at the same time for Hautbourg, so that,
should the Parisian Constituency "fail to do its duty"
—which heaven forbid!—France might not be deprived
of M. le Marquis's valuable presence in the National
Assembly.

Whereat Horace fell a-thinking. What if the Parisian Constituency *should* fail to do its duty? The
thought of the general election had never presented

itself to him in that shape before; yet his colleagues, he knew, were already busying themselves about their own constituencies, and the papers told him every day what desperate efforts the Liberal Opposition intended making to secure the return of "uncompromising" candidates. It was not likely that *he* would be regarded as uncompromising—he whom the Liberals accounted as a black sheep. There would even be some incongruity in saying, "Here am I, a Republican, the Marquis of Clairefontaine, who live in a palace, exchange bows with M. Gribaud, and get on capitally with all the legislators who are keeping my country under the gag." The Press would laugh in his face, and the small boys in the streets hoot him. Then, what chance had he of winning his seat by the same sleight of hand sort of performance. as last time? Why, his majority was not two hundred votes, and at the next election, if the Opposition put forward some name less revolutionary than Albi's, more Liberal than his own—which would not be difficult—all the votes he should get would be those of his personal friends, and those of the Bonapartists—though how to accept these latter a second time without presenting himself frankly as an official candidate, and hopelessly damaging himself as a Liberal for ever after, was a point which now began to appear to him in the light of a problem. Insensibly he was led into reflecting on what his position might have been had he never known M. Macrobe, but followed the career he had first marked out for himself—that of a hard-working barrister. He might have been the rising hope of the Liberals by this time. Albi would not have dared—perhaps not have sought, to hinder his election, and, if elected once, he need have had no fears at future contests—for it is especially in electoral matters that possession is nine points of law.

The familiar acquaintance of M. Macrobe must have seemed a very insufficient compensation to him for what he had lost, since the picture he evoked drew from him something like a sigh; and his mind must have been very full of an image other than his wife's, since it did not even occur to him that, had his first projected destiny been accomplished, he should never have known Angélique!

He was plucked from his meditations by the question, submissively put, "What answer must be given to this, Horace?"

"What is your own opinion, child?" he asked, with a quick, searching look at her whom he was thus interrogating for the first time on a matter of importance.

There was anxiety in his glance. He was gauging the measure of his wife's intelligence.

"Why, dear," said she, a little troubled, and darting rather plaintive looks at the letter, "I see they are kind people, who wish you well. But—" She caught the words "Paris" and "re-election,"—"you will be re-elected at Paris, I suppose?"

"It is not sure."

"But why not?" And her blue eyes expressed grave astonishment.

"They say that I am not Liberal enough—that, because I choose the friends I like, and wear a name that is mine, and am not churlish as a bear to those who are civil to me, and do not flatter the people, I am no true man."

Her small hands clasped themselves in a sort of silent perplexity, and a little sigh broke from her.

"I wish, Horace, I understood these political questions; but when I try, it all seems darkness. I thought you were more Liberal—as you say—than all the other deputies together, and I am *sure* you must be, despite all that unkind people may think. Why," added she, looking up, "at the President of the Chamber's last party M. Gribaud told me you were an incorrigible Radical. He was laughing, I know; but he must have meant part of what he said."

"Yes; but this is an affair of optics. The grey silk dress you are wearing looks pink from this side, where it faces those purple curtains, and opal-tinted from the other, where it has the sun's rays on it. M. Gribaud and the Liberals consider me from opposite points of view."

She did not appear to understand, but continued, with some concern beginning slowly to depict itself on her features,—"But if you are not elected at Paris, Horace, you will be without a seat."

"Yes, I suppose so, and my political career will be broken, unless, indeed, I hack myself out as an official candidate to M. Gribaud. But that is a trade which brings a man a little too low. I would rather take to one of my old vocations—pleading, or scribbling, or even starving, which is sometimes synonymous."

This time she understood and changed colour. Besides the loss of position, there was another to which Horace had not alluded, the salary of twelve thousand five hundred francs which deputies received. Though Angélique's experience of money matters was absolutely null, she vaguely knew that her husband was morbidly scrupulous that every centime of the interest

derived from her dowry should be expended on herself; he himself confining his personal expenditure—
the keep of his brougham, pay of his valet and secretary—within the eight or nine hundred pounds, made
up of the above twelve thousand five hundred francs,
of three thousand francs a year, the allowance his
father gave him, and of three or four thousand francs
which he continued to earn by occasional anonymous
contributions to the *Gazette des Boulevards.* So the
first thing that struck her in connection with Horace's
possible failure was the diminution of comfort that
might accrue to him as a consequence. She saw him
discharging his brougham or disbanding his valet or
some such catastrophe; and therefore exclaimed in
distress, "Oh but, Horace, you will answer Yes to this
letter, won't you? They are good-hearted people at
Hautbourg, you see—they will elect you, and not cause
you the annoyance which these Parisians do. Besides"
—(for one of M. Macrobe's oft-repeated injunctions
was recurring to her)—"Besides, Hautbourg is your
own town, after all; that of your family I mean; and
it is quite right they should do something for you after
all that your family has done for them."

"Well, they complain that my family are starving
them now."

"Yes, but that is not your fault: you said so just
now."

"And what if they and I should not be of the same
political opinions?"

"But Hautbourg is in the country; there will be no
politics there," she rejoined seriously. "And they will
be of your opinion if you go down and talk to them;
and if you promise that you will return to live with

them some day, which I know you will do if you can;
for, indeed, dear"—and she glanced up at him art-
lessly—"I don't think it can so much matter about the
castle having been built by negroes."

Horace gave a puzzled stare, then laughed, and,
stooping, kissed her. But aside, he moaned and recalled the poor child's past words; that day when she
repeated to him so earnestly that Georgette was much
cleverer than she.   The fact is, all that Angélique
knew of the Clairefontaine business, was what her
father had told her; and he, not sanguine of ever being able to make her comprehend all the details of the
secret he had learned from Horace, had put the thing
into a nut-shell, by telling her that her husband's only
prejudice against Clairefontaine was its having been
reared by blacks—which she had believed calmly, as
she would have believed any other thing, possible or
impossible, that he might have told her.

"We will send the answer to Hautbourg another
day," said Horace, grave again; "it deserves to be
pondered over;" and he glanced through the memorial
himself, and thoughtfully examined its large, straggling
circle of signatures, something like a congregation of
clod-hoppers dancing in a ring.

There remained two letters to be read. Both were
from persons acknowledging and accepting invitations
to a dinner at Macrobe House—invitations issued by
Angélique, at M. Macrobe's desire, in her husband's
name and in her own. These disposed of without any
remark on Horace's part, Angélique sorted the letters
that required answers from those that did not, those
that were to be replied to in the affirmative from those
that were to be negatived, and so on, all for the con-

venience of the secretary.   The sun played upon her
pure features and cast a halo over her golden hair as
she noiselessly did this, and Horace, had he looked at
her, might have been reminded of some Madonna of
Raphael engaged in domestic work. But he had taken
up his *Moniteur* again, and was trying to decipher a
leader on some treaty question in which the words
"balance of power," and "M. Walewski," "supremacy
of France," and "Napoleon III." were blurred by, and
mixed up with, the names of "M. Macrobe" and
"Hautbourg," "Tenth Circumscription," and "Georgette," so as to render the whole not very intelligible.
Angélique, having arranged her letters, glided back to
her book, and beginning the same chapter over and
over twenty times, never succeeded in dissociating
Paul from the Italian Opera, and Virginie from a private box, whence she saw a rival in a box opposite and
her husband beside her fascinated and troubled by the
sight of that rival.

The silence was hardly interrupted until the discreet
clatter of silver and china which heralds the luncheon
has made itself heard in the adjoining breakfast-room.
Horace was not a luncheon man, holding by the old
French system of late breakfast and clear day till
dinner-time; but lunch was a transmarine institution
which served to bring all the members of the Macrobe
household together for the first time every day, and
led to varied conversation on the morning's events and
plans for the afternoon and evening.   Accordingly,
when the major-domo announced "Madame la Marquise est servie," Horace prepared to go through the
ceremony of shaking hands with his father-in-law,
making his bow to his aunt, and being greeted affec-

tionately by his cousin the Crimean hero, who was always demonstratively charmed to see him.

"Bonjour, belle cousine," exclaimed this distinguished officer, advancing with an enormous bouquet as Angélique entered with her husband. The nosegay was of white and dark violets, redolent with the perfume of budding spring.

"You have been to the flower-market, cousin," she said, thanking him, and inhaling the fragrant breath of the flowers.

"No, belle cousine, a country ride. A spurt straight away into the meadows, as if I were charging Cossacks; and, by the way, Marquis, I met a friend of ours as I was returning. It was on the Meudon road. A tremendously swell trap was cavalcading in the dust like the Pope's mule coach on a gala day, so I reined up, ready to salute if it should be king, emperor, or field-marshal. But it was the Prince of Arcola, draped in a swallow-tail, like a Roman in his toga, and looking whiter than the lawn cravat he was sporting. If his servants hadn't been so spruce and shiny, I'd have wagered he'd been to a funeral. But I daresay it was worse: he may have been to a christening."

"Meudon," said the financier, sitting down to table. "Perhaps the Prince was simply on his way from a call to the Pochemolles, Captain."

"A morning call in black and white, sir, with a powdered periwig on the box, and two pairs of pink silk calves holding on behind! That would be prince and magnate with a vengeance. Yet, I don't know——" (He unfolded his napkin.) "We saw monsieur in the same box as the Torche—Toche—what is it?—Porche—molles last night. Maybe he had been offering his

coronet to that handsome girl with the red lips, whom
the marchioness admired. If so, it looked for all the
world as if she had said to him what my colonel did
to me last time I asked for more furlough.—Ma cousine, I have a *mayonnaise* of lobster before me, will you
allow me to send you some?"

The captain's light words struck two at least out
of the four persons seated round the table much deeper
than he fancied. Angélique found the getting through
her *mayonnaise* a rather difficult operation; and Horace,
who had not been able to restrain an abrupt raising of
the head at the mention of the Prince's name, hurried
over his glass of hock and biscuit, and withdrew much
earlier than was his custom, to go down to the House.
On alighting, however, before the Palace of the Assembly,
he did not go in, but dismissed his coachman, and,
when the brougham was out of sight, walked up and
down on the pavement for a few minutes in evident
doubt. He was flustered and uncertain. He knew
that the Prince must have been proposing to Georgette;
but what answer had she given him? Could it be true
that she had refused him, and if so why? He was
surprised at the vehemence with which his heart beat
at the thought that Georgette was possibly still free.
He turned the thought over and over in his mind, and
the more he did so the more pleasure it gave him. At
last he said: "If I could only know for certain"—and
as this perplexing reflection occurred, his eye lit upon
a cab that was plying desultorily for hire along the
quay. He hailed it and jumped in. Once seated, he
appeared to hesitate, and pressed his hand to his eyes;
but on the driver asking him, for the second time,
"Where to, sir?" he answered rapidly,—"To Meudon."

CHAPTER X.

M. Macrobe's Aspirations.

A FEW hours after Horace had started for Meudon M. Macrobe might have been found in his study. The time of evening six o'clock, the curtains drawn, a warm fire shedding its glow on the hearth, and the low moaning of the February wind audible outside through the closely-barred windows. M. Macrobe, just returned from his office, sat poring over his desk and making what seemed to be abstruse calculations in pencil on a sheet of paper. Open before him lay a ponderous folio ledger, extracted from a strong cupboard with an iron door, and locks enough to defy all the burglars in Christendom. This ledger was marked on its chamois-leather back, "SOCIÉTÉ DU CRÉDIT PARISIEN."

Everybody in Paris, and in Europe, too, for that matter, talked about this "Crédit Parisien," and appeared knowing about it. Its shares were quoted at London and New York, Frankfort and Rotterdam; it was extolled in the money articles of the leading journals in these respectable cities; and in Paris— "sceptical" Paris—the confidence accorded to it was so entire that any person hinting his dissent would have been eyed askance, and found himself in a hopeless minority, and been held up to contumely. But the best of it was, that when you came to inquire into the titles of the Crédit Parisien to be regarded with esteem and proclaimed the pride and pinnacle of

financial enterprises, nobody could enlighten you.
Jules had bought his shares because advised to do so
by Alphonse; Alphonse had speculated in deference
to the loudly-expressed opinion of Antoine; and Antoine had expressed himself loudly because a certain
Auguste, who knew a certain Achille, had gathered
from the latter the unshakeable impression of a certain
Ulysse, himself a director in the concern, that the
Crédit Parisien was the safest investment going. So
that, reduced to its simplest terms, the fact amounted
to this—that the Crédit Parisien grew and flourished,
and absorbed the economies of high and low, of senator
and concierge, of washerwoman and ballet-girl, and
blazed at the top of the share-list, and occupied with
majesty the place of honour in money articles, because it enjoyed the unlimited confidence of its own
promoters.   -

It seems that there are, or have been, a considerable number of credit institutions based upon the same
sort of solid foundation as this; and under the circumstances, the only wonder is, not that a desultory joint-
stock promoter should now and then be signalled
landing at a foreign port with the funds of some eight
or nine hundred shareholders in his carpet-bag, but
that the whole universe should not blossom over with
migratory promoters like a fruitful tree with caterpillars.
In short, it is a marvel that humanity itself should not
be divided uniquely into two categories—the one jovial
and replete, having fattened itself with promoting, the
other reduced to a condition of hunger, collapse, and
manual labour, by a wilful, incomprehensible, and
utterly guileless course of shareholding.

On the earth's surface there was, probably, but one

man who really understood the Crédit Parisien, held
all the cues of the enterprise in his hands, and knew
to what extent the public were dancing on a volcano
in trusting to it, and this was the much-respected chairman and chief promoter, M. Macrobe. Of course his
co-promoters, the directors, were supposed to understand and hold cues, and all the rest of it, but they
didn't—which is not a rare occurrence with those who
are supposed to know things. M. Macrobe had originated
the idea of the Crédit Parisien at a fortunate moment.
On the morrow of the *coup-d'état* of 1851 there was a
large and most interesting class of persons, who, having
previously never possessed a centime, found themselves
suddenly raised to posts of honour and emolument.
These persons, whom a factious opposition styled adventurers, but whom History, more impartial, designates
simply as Bonapartists, with more loyalty than small
coin, were, not unnaturally, desirous to place their
private means as soon as possible on a level with their
public position. M. Macrobe had stepped in and
suggested the way. Being known to most of the new
dignitaries intimately—having, indeed, trodden the
shady paths of Bohemianism with some of them—he
was able to point out in the confidential language of
friendship, how superfluous a thing is capital when
one holds such an excellent substitute as place, and
the special information it gives access to. What else
he added—what alluring prospects he flashed before
yearning eyesights—are secrets locked in the bosom of
mystery; but the upshot was, that one morning the
Crédit Parisien rose like a star in the East, and that
forthwith it fared well with it. For the Company bought
land in Paris, and lo! by a strange coincidence, a new

boulevard would soon after be constructed thereon and quintuple the value of the land: it bought ships, and behold! the new line of packets were scarcely inaugurated, before it obtained Government contracts for carrying mails, transport of troops, laying down of submarine cables: it purchased houses, and straightway the Government found it necessary to expropriate these houses as sites for barracks, churches, theatres, for sums double or treble what they had cost. Perhaps it may be remarked that this mode of making money has a suspicious look of kinship with the time-honoured expedient of winning a game by means of loaded dice. But to such unsophisticated objections it will be enough to reply that hazard is often a strange thing; that men high in office are always maligned; and that if it certainly did happen that a few eminent functionaries, suspected of occult connection with the Crédit Parisien, became unaccountably prosperous in a surprisingly short space of time, there is nothing in this circumstance which may not have been purely fortuitous or a simple freak of Chance.

Anyhow, hazard or no hazard, M. Macrobe, as he dotted down his calculations, and threw occasional glances at his ledger, looked well pleased enough with the business in which he was embarked. The shares were at 1,550 francs; the evening paper showed a new rise of 5 francs that very day.

"There is no reason why this should ever stop," muttered he half aloud, "except that nothing here below is perpetual. So long as the Government holds its own, and keeps the Budget from being overhauled by a set of factious Radicals, we shall do. Our sources of information are inexhaustible for the moment."

He turned over the leaves of the ledger and came
to a series of pages entitled "*Names, Professions, &c.
of Original Shareholders.*" It was singular the array
of Duvals and Leroys, Joneses and Browns, Müllers
and Bauers, who were inscribed as holding the greatest
number of shares, and more singular still were the
vague addresses of these Duvals and Müllers, Joneses
and Leroys. But doubtless there was a key to this in
the asterisks prefixed to most of these apocryphal-look-
ing names, and in a small volume with a lock to it
which the financier drew from a secret drawer and
began to con musingly, comparing it with the larger
book.

"Some of them," he murmured, "have sold out
and bought in again several times, making good hauls
by each transaction, which is not difficult when one
can foresee the rises and falls on 'Change a day or
two before the rest of the public. Others have kept
firm hold of their shares, and will probably sell out
when we reach 2,000, which, considering they had
their shares for nothing, will also be no bad investment.
What a list of names they are, and what a pretty sensation it would cause if these columns were published
some morning in the papers! Um! it's my life-preserver,
this book. If ever things turned out badly I should
only have to threaten with it—the Second Empire could
better stand a revolution than the printing of such
pages. But things won't turn out badly in my time.
No;" (he closed the small book;) "when the smash
comes, if come it do, I must be clear out of the
concern. I don't see why the affair ever *should* smash,
but these giant enterprises that run such a whirlwind
pace to begin with, always do. Nature seems jealous

of greatness: great empires, great men, great companies, all break up before the time. I must hie me away to some secure position whilst the Crédit Parisien is still in its heyday, and there will be nothing suspicious in my retirement. I must get into power. Why shouldn't I? This is a reign under which a man of brains can hope for anything."

He laid down his pencil, threw himself back in his chair, and rested his chin in his hand.

"There are so many ways of getting into the Ministry or the Senate now-a-days, and such curious fish slip in there! But my plan was as good as any. With Horace Gerold in possession of Clairefontaine, we could both of us make our own terms with Government. The Clairefontaine influence would be enough to ensure our both being returned for the department, and then he, as a Duke of Hautbourg, might blossom out into an ambassador, by-and-by into a Minister for Foreign Affairs—dukes are the very men for those posts when Government can prevail on 'em to accept them. As for me I should not be long in the House as an independent member before Gribaud came over to me and offered me my own conditions. Gribaud doesn't like me—in fact he doesn't like anybody who has a longer head than his own; but he recognizes merit when he sees it, and if I struck for a seat in the cabinet—minister of finance, trade, public works, or something in that line—or for a barony and a senatorship, he's not the man to say me nay. But if he did, it wouldn't matter. Gerold and I could put ourselves at the head of a dynastic-opposition party, accepting the Emperor but attacking the Ministry; it might rally forty or fifty adherents after the next elections and lead Gribaud the very deuce of a life. I should get what I wanted then, in spite of Gribaud, perhaps by overturning him—who knows? Ministers are never thoroughly popular either with their masters or their followers. And all this might come to pass within a few months of this if Gerold had a little nerve in him! He's not much of a fellow, and it's uphill work leading him to where his own interest lies. Let us re-read what Louchard says.

M. Macrobe selected a letter from a portfolio in his pocket. The envelope was franked, not stamped, which indicated its administrative origin. It ran this wise:—

"Préfecture de Police, February, 1857.

"MONSIEUR,—

"ONE of my men has just returned from Hautbourg, where, under the guise of a commercial traveller, he has been sounding the opinions of the principal towns-folk with regard to M. le Marquis de Clairefontaine, your son-in-law, and pursuing your instructions as conveyed to me verbally last time I had the honour of an interview with you. He has suggested that the towns-people should separately and one after the other appeal to M. le Marquis, and collectively offer him the candidature at the elections, which has been, or is being, done. My agent reports, however, that public feeling in Hautbourg is the reverse of favourable to M. le Marquis and his family, and that his candidature would have little chance of succeeding if the Government were to oppose it. Supposing M. le Marquis were installed at Clairefontaine the case would be different; it seems the town and all the country around have been

9*

accustomed to take their cue from the Castle and would
be quite disposed to continue that course.   I enclose,
by your desire, the bill of expenses incurred by my
agent, and await, with respect, your further orders.
But I would beg again, as a favour, that you would
not let anybody into the secret that I have placed myself at your services for these negotiations, the Government objecting most strongly to the interference of the
police in private concerns.

"I have the honour to remain, Sir,

"Your most obedient servant,

"MOÏSE LOUCHARD."

"I am sure I don't know what further orders to
give," resumed M. Macrobe.   "Short of bringing the
whole borough of Hautbourg down by special trains to
memorialize him, we have tried almost everything without effect.   Angélique has no influence over him.   He
is fond of the child, I know, but treats her like a wax
doll.   By the by,—ahem!" (M. Macrobe frowned)—
"I must have that jolter-headed captain sent back to
his regiment.   He is getting on too fast with his 'Ma
belle cousines' and his nosegays; I don't understand
these modern husbands; they allow their wives to be
made love to under their very noses.   No, Angélique
has no influence over him, nor have I beyond a certain
point.   He feels as we do: he would like to go to
Clairefontaine, but daren't because of his father.   What
a man that father of his!   To have an estate of that
value and to pour the revenue every quarter day into
the poor-box.   There is some sublime lunacy amongst
those old Republicans!   Then he seems to be tough,
too, the old fellow; his health is all right.   Um, how

it would solve matters if he were to retire opportunely to a better world . . . ."

The jasper-faced clock on M. Macrobe's mantel-shelf tinkled the half-hour after six, prelude to the note of the dinner-gong, which sounded at seven. The financier restored his papers to their drawers and his ledger to its cupboard, locking and double-locking the latter with a key no bigger than his little finger, pigmy driver to such Brobdingnagian bolts. Then he went and leaned against the chimney-piece, and repeated thoughtfully: "How it would solve matters!"

It may be said that the words were yet on his lips when the house-door bell was rung with violence, startling the echoes of the silent vestibule and corridors. It was one of those unusual peals that bring a presentiment of something unforeseen. M. Macrobe started, and listened, motionless. A servant quickly crossed the hall, the door was opened, and, after a moment, footsteps were heard going in the direction of the reception-rooms. Then the servant appeared, and said: "Monsieur Emile Gerold is in the drawing-room, sir, and would be glad to see you for a minute, if you are disengaged."

Monsieur Macrobe, with his pulse at ninety, went to the drawing-room.

Emile had never thawed much in his reserve towards his brother's father-in-law. Their mutual relations were ceremonious. But this time there was nothing but unaffected grief and impulsiveness in the young man's manner as he advanced and said: "Do you know where my brother is, M. Macrobe? I have news which should be communicated to him at once."

Angélique, who was present, and looking with

alarm at Emile's discomposed features, answered: "But Horace must be at the House. He left to go there at two."

"No: I have been to the House," replied Emile. "They told me he has not gone there this afternoon; —at least, he went, but left immediately in a cab, and a linkman heard him tell the coachman to drive to Meudon. I thought he might have been back."

Absorbed and bewildered as he was, Emile was struck by the sudden pallor that overspread Angélique's face at the mention of Meudon, and by the way in which she pressed a hand to her side, as if to stop a sharp spasm.

"I hope there is nothing wrong?" began M. Macrobe with concern. "Horace will certainly be back for dinner. No bad news, I trust?"

"Our father has been taken ill," said Emile in a voice that he endeavoured to keep steady. "I trust the illness is not serious, but I have been apprised of it by telegraph, and must start for Brussels this very evening. There is a train at eight. I came to fetch Horace so that we might go together."

"He will undoubtedly go, and I will have some of his things packed for him," said Angélique, rising, with a look of sympathy surmounting the evidences of the shock she herself had just received. "But," added she, with unwilling bitterness, "if Horace is at Meudon, perhaps a messenger had better be sent for him: else it is not sure he will be back so soon."

"I am unfeignedly grieved to hear that your excellent father should be unwell," exclaimed M. Macrobe, dolorously, though inwardly that worthy man seemed to be reflecting how inscrutably providential are the ways of Fate.

"I don't think it is possible to send to Meudon and to return in time for eight," ejaculated Emile, glancing regretfully at his watch. "I must leave a note, and . . . ."

"There is a noise of carriage-wheels," interrupted Angélique, listening, and going to the window. "'This is, no doubt, Horace."

Emile sprung out and met his brother as he was descending from his cab. Horace wore the look of a man who has just passed through keen emotions, and is not prepared for more immediate trials, but, seeing Emile's face, he paused on the doorstep, and faltered: "You have bad news, Emile?"

Emile took his arm, and handed him the despatch.

"This is a visitation," exclaimed Horace, hoarsely.

———

CHAPTER XI.

One Good Man less.

THE Brussels of the Second Empire—a sentinel city perpetually on the watch: on the watch for all sorts of things;—for the whim of that Unfathomable Tenant of the Tuileries, which might bring an army of four hundred thousand Frenchmen within sight of its Brabantine streets; for a revolution in Paris, which might drive away the Unfathomable Tenant, Heaven knew whither, and empty the Brabantine streets of the Republican refugees, who clustered thick within their attics as mice in corn-lofts; for the British regiments, which some thought would come, and some were persuaded wouldn't, if the integrity of brave Belgium were ever menaced.

And meanwhile, that is, pending these contingencies, Brussels looked like a pocket-edition of Paris. Its streets were as clean, its boulevards as trim, its cafés as jingling and full of chatter, as those of the elder sister-city, and the Brussels theatres gave French pieces, and the Brussels publishers sold pirated editions of French novels, and the Brussels learned societies extended hospitality to proscribed French *savants;* and the Brussels people wore French hats, and grinned before the print-shops where, to the great disgust of the French Ambassador, figured comical cartoons, representing the Emperor Napoleon, and practised parliamentary government, and venerated the honest man and true gentleman who was their King, and eschewed revolution—for Belgians are Frenchmen, with the froth taken off.

In a secluded street of the Faubourg Ixelles, which is to the radiant quarter of the Place Royale, what the Quartier de Mont Parnasse is to the Parisian Champs Elysées, and decent Chelsea to proud Belgravia, stood the small house where Manuel Gerold was lying.

These houses were not built on the French system —of six stories, a large door, and a porter in a lodge to take care of the door. The architects of the Faubourg Ixelles have studied in England. Their structures are the three-floor lodging-houses we all know, and miles of which may be seen in all the London suburbs, where "*Lodgings to Let*" stares cheerlessly on stiff cards out of parlour-windows. There is always a woman with a hot face who answers the doors of these places, and a cat who comes purring behind, rubbing her sides along the walls of the narrow passage, and a smell of dinner steaming up from some underground recess; and, when you have examined the bleak parlour and chilly bedroom—limp white curtains to the bed, and blue pattern wash-hand basin—it is always the same reply: "The sitting-room and bedroom, sir, will be fifteen shillings a-week. Fire and lighting hextra."

Horace and Emile were driven up to a house of this model as day was dawning, rather after six. At the time they lived in Brussels with their father, their lodgings had been elsewhere, so that they did not know this house.

The hot-faced woman who opened the door for them was, in this instance, a girl, down at heel, with cheeks puffy, and eyes blinking from having been started out of sleep, and compelled to huddle on her clothes in a hurry. She guessed who the young men

were, and making a pretence of washing her face with
her sleeve, whimpered dismally: "He was took ill,
gentlemen, all of a heap like. The doctor's with him,
and have not left him since. It was him as sent the
despatch to Paris."

Receiving but a muttered answer, she closed the
door behind them, and, in hushed silence, the whole
party proceeded up a creaking staircase to the sick-
room, which was on the highest story, and looked out
on a grey back-yard. A night-light was flickering
feebly in a saucer, and vying in sadness with the
leaden hue of the morning sky. The ashes were cold
in the grate. The furniture, of the commonest, barest
kind, scarcely gave an inhabited look to the chamber,
and the poorness of the place was discernible in such
tokens as the cracked cup that had been used to pour
medicine in, and the battered tray, on which were the
remnants of the doctor's supper. It was not a room
to live in, much less one that should have been a
home during illness; but, when it was remembered
that the occupier of this poor apartment was a man
who had held the coffers of a nation in his keeping,
who had discarded a colossal fortune because he
thought that he could not honestly touch it, and who,
though he possessed a competence that would have
enabled him to live at ease, preferred pinching himself
in order to have more to give away amongst needy
fellow-refugees—there was something indescribably
great in all this misery. The poverty-stricken room
ceased, then, to be a garret—it became a sanctuary.
Nevertheless, when Horace saw this desolate scene a
great sob escaped him, and he threw himself weeping
on his knees by his father's bedside.

Emile, less demonstrative in his grief, grasped the hand of the doctor who had been sitting near the head of the bed, and in a sorrowful whisper asked him for particulars, and for a word of hope.

The doctor was a short, grey-haired man, with round eyes and rather lugubrious ways. In a tone of condolence he said what he knew. Manuel Gerold had been struck down suddenly by paralysis — that grim foe to men of mind; which lies in ambush for them treacherously and lays them prostrate as with a mace. Ever since the attack he had been in a state of coma. The usual remedies had been applied and he might revive; or, he might pass away unconsciously, like a man in sleep. He was a refugee, too, this doctor, and spoke of Manuel Gerold with something of the devotion of a soldier for a great, and revered chief.

"I have observed a decline in his health for the last twelvemonth," he murmured, shaking his head. "It came on slowly, but it was marked. He no longer smiled, and his gait had lost its elasticity."

Emile shivered and drew nearer to the bed. He wished to prevent his brother from hearing. But the doctor unable to divine and prone to diagnostic talk, like most of his cloth, pursued innocently.

"The symptoms of incipient paralysis were all there. It is the most insidious of diseases. I had seldom seen a man more vigorous in mind and body for his age than your father; but for this vigour to remain unimpaired to the end, there must be a complete absence of all shocks to the system. Men who undergo the natural infirmities of age will bear up better against certain chance accidents, than these exceptional and overwrought organizations will. I have

known feeble old men pass unscathed through physical
and moral trials that have proved fatal in cases where
the constitution of the patient was seemingly stronger;
whence I infer that strength of body or of the mental
faculties can only be prolonged beyond their accustomed time at the expense of the nerves.   Your father
was highly impressionable.   You are not cognizant of
his having experienced any great sorrow or disappoint-
ment during this last year?"

"No," said Emile, and taking one of his father's
unresisting hands in his, he gazed with hot tears in
his eyes at the saddest of all wrecks; that of a loved
being, of a great, good man.   Oppressed breathing,
as though there were some heavy weight on the chest,
and flushed features, told, indeed, that this was sleep
and not death in which Manuel Gerold was plunged.
But what a sleep this, whence the slumberer can only
awake to vacant-minded senility!   Is not death a
thousand times preferable?

The two sons sat watching beside their father all
the morning.   The doctor, who had gone through a
thirty hours' vigil and was knocked up, though he
refused to own it, went home, leaving directions as to
what was to be done in different contingencies, and
promised to return in the evening.   Then the hot-
faced servant girl reappeared dressed properly, but
grimy, from lighting the kitchen fire, and asked whether
the gentlemen would take anything; and soon after
came her mistress, a hot-faced, warm-hearted Walloon
lodging-house keeper, with a bowl of arrow-root which
could be of no possible use to any one, but which
she placed nevertheless on the table with an air of
profound conviction, as if it were instantly going to

set everything to rights. And then began the trivial, worrying, shabby round of incidents of which lodging-house life is made up; incidents all audible in the sick-room. The call for yet uncleaned boots by the first-floor lodger; the lamentations of second-pair back, who wanted to shave himself, but had not got his hot water, the ring-a-ding procession of tradesmen at the front door and their confabulations with the mistress about the last joint, which had proved to be three ounces short when weighed in the larder scales, and amidst all this the re-entry of the hot-faced girl with a slip of paper, saying that this was the day when M. Gerold was used to pay his washing-bills, and please, was she to tell the laundress to call another time? In which manner the forenoon glided by.

But at one, the Walloon landlady, with cheeks aglow, a tray laden with omelette-au-lard, and bottle of Macon on her arms, and a proclamation of beef-steaks to follow on her lips, swept into the adjoining sitting-room and, resolutely laying the cloth, declared that if the messieurs did not eat, there would soon be three patients in the house instead of one. So Emile and Horace had to take their respective turns of sitting down and attempting to swallow, whilst their entertainer discoursed with a well-meant kindness, which deprived them of every vestige of appetite they might have possessed, on what a good gentleman their father was.

"I never saw a gentleman that could talk so, nor look one so gently in the face," said she, warming up into emotion; "and you should have seen how his purse was open to everybody that had need, ay, and to them that hadn't. Why I've counted as many as

a dozen come here of a morning with begging letters,
stout, strong, good-for-noughts too, some of them who
ought to have been ashamed to take money which
they hadn't earned.   It was the same story with all.
They were Republicans who had been exiled from
France; and I'd have told Marie to republicanize them
with the broomstick if he had let me.   But he always
had a kind word to say for them: they were hungry,
or persecuted, or what not, and so he used to work
all day and the better half of the night, and deny
himself and starve himself to make money for the
vagabonds.   Ah, saving your presence, sir, you gentlemen are simpler than us women; it's not a woman that
would have allowed herself to be taken in in that way."

This was quite true, that Manuel Gerold had
worked indefatigably.   The heaps of books and manu-
scripts in the room bore enough evidence to the fact.
It was a plain sitting-room, but more habitable than
the bed-chamber, from the books just mentioned and
from portraits on the wall, prints before the letter
most of them, and representing well-known Republican
figures: Lamartine, Arago, Beranger, Dupont de l'Eure.
They were all signed, these portraits, with some such
dedication as *souvenir d'amitié* or *homage affectueux*.
Then there were a few keepsakes of a more curious
kind: a framed sheet of paper with a quill pen attached
to it, and underneath: " *Que mon ami Victor Hugo veuille
bien certifier que cette plume lui a servi à écrire quelques
pages de ses immortels 'Châtiments,'*" to which Victor
Hugo had subscribed a large " *Oui;*" a crucifix given
by Lamennais; an unedited ode to Liberty in Beranger's
own hand; a group of terra-cotta figures of the Pro-
visional Government of 1848 by the caricaturist Dantan,

humorously but good-naturedly conceived, Manuel Gerold being shown in the act of striking the fetters off a slave, who, to reward him, was picking his pocket. This group, by-the-way, was lettered: "*En matière de Gouvernement, faut de l'honnêteté; pas trop n'en faut.*" The numerous bookshelves revealed the only real luxuries of the apartment—rare editions of old works, and richly-bound volumes of modern authors, the latter gifts for the most part from the authors themselves; also, what Manuel Gerold must have considered his most precious treasure, from the prominent place he gave it, a unique copy of Montesquieu's *Esprit des Lois*, presented by the compositors of Paris after a speech delivered under the Restoration in defence of the liberty of the press. The compositors had printed this one copy of a unique quarto edition on vellum, and then broken up the type. It was more than a kingly gift, for kings never make such presents; it was a people's gift. On Manuel Gerold's desk lay the unfinished manuscript of a political essay he had been writing at the moment of his attack, with the pen lying slantwise on the blotting-book as it had fallen from his fingers, and a large blot beneath to show that when the pen had so dropped it was full.

When the landlady had at length retired, leaving Horace alone—for Horace had lunched after Emile, in order that both should not be away together from their father's bedside—he looked with dim eyes and yearning heart on all the objects in this modest room. But what moved him most was an album he found on the writing-table filled with newspaper cuttings relating to himself and Emile. There was his own maiden speech in the Affaire Macrobe, as reported in a Belgian paper, with a laudatory leader, and all the articles he had written in the *Sentinelle* and *Gazette des Boulevards;* but here the cuttings as regarded himself stopped. There was no account of his election, no report of any of his doings in the Chamber, no notice of his marriage; and these could not have been chance omissions, for the extracts relating to Emile's speeches at the Palais de Justice continued uninterrupted, the latest of them being but a few days old. Horace would have given a great deal at that moment could he have expunged the whole of his life during the last twelve months and brought himself back to the point denoted by the date of his last newspaper article. The silent censure implied by the exile of his name from this album during the past year cut him to the quick. "And yet," thought he, dejectedly, "what have I done? I accepted Bonapartist alliance to win a victory against a man who had goaded me to madness, but I have performed my duty in the Chamber as well as he would have done. He might have advocated liberty more rantingly than I do; he could not have pleaded for it more earnestly. Then I married, and that they seemed to think was another crime. But I imagined then, that I loved Angélique. In fact I do love her, but—but . . .;" and his mind strayed excitedly to a scene enacted not four-and-twenty hours before when he had called at Meudon, seen Georgette, and being alone with her, had pressed her for an explanation of her coldness towards him in such terms as to bring down an explosion of impatience and anger. Georgette, beside herself, had spoken all that was in her heart, not up braiding him indeed for his faithlessness to her —she was too proud to do that—but doing what women do, taking up a line that was no business of hers, and taunting him with uncontrolled bitterness and scorn for having married a woman whom he could never have loved, all on account of her money. Upon which, he, stung and infuriated by the unjust accusation, had retorted as a man never should retort upon a woman even when she is a hundred times in the wrong. He had made capital out of the unfortunate Filoselle, cast the jilting of that individual in her teeth, and left her speechless under the reproach that she too must have been actuated by a sordid motive, some scheming after a richer lover, in acting thus faithlessly. Altogether it had been a miserable scene of which it made him redden to think. And the more so, as he said to himself, that there was a time when no woman or man would have deemed him capable of the baseness Georgette had imputed to him; and when he himself would have suffered his tongue to be cut out sooner than to use it in insulting a defenceless girl as he had done. He experienced that undefinable feeling of having fallen in the estimation of men generally, and of being lowered in his own; yet without being exactly able to perceive why.

Emile's voice calling to him in a low tone from the bedroom aroused him. Manuel Gerold had shifted his head on the pillow, his breathing was less heavy, and the inflammatory hue of the complexion seemed to be subsiding. Horace hastened in, and the two brothers watched anxiously the signs of returning life. The patient's movements were those of a man trying to shake off in sleep fetters weighing down the whole of one side of the body. It was only the right side that could move, the other was inert. At one time it

seemed as though the attempt must be a vain one, and
exhaustion paralyze what little strength remained in
that once robust frame. But gradually—though this
was the work of hours, not of minutes—life resumed
a sluggish course; the blood slowly deserted the head
and flowed to the extremities, a feeble but restoring
stream, and, just as dusk darkened the small window
of the room, with its drab clouds, Manuel Gerold
opened his eyes.

At almost the same minute the doctor returned.

The brothers were leaning over their father in
watchful suspense, to see if he would recognize them.
Horace passed an arm under him, and propped him
up gently with pillows.

"Father," said Emile, "do you know us?"

Manuel Gerold turned his eyes vaguely from one
to the other, going through the efforts that follow the
awakening from a long and painful dream. There
was a hushed stillness whilst he laboured to join together the broken threads of memory. At last a ray
of consciousness stole over his features, and he strove
to speak; but the sounds that left his lips were in-
articulate, the tongue appearing to roll heavily, like a
once strong bark that has lost its rudder. The endeavour was renewed, once, twice, but without success, and then a look of distress painted itself over
the old Republican's face.

The doctor approached with a cheering word, and
felt the patient's pulse. The examination did not last
above a minute, but when the doctor turned there was
a verdict in his eye. He silently withdrew into the
next room to leave the sons alone with their father. His
science could be of no further help here, and he knew it.

"Father, do you feel pain," asked Emile, trembling in every limb.

Manuel Gerold made a sign that he did not.

Horace lowered his head, and, after a struggle with himself, faltered: "Father, if I have done anything that has displeased or grieved you; if I have—if I have acted otherwise than as you would have had me act, will you tell me that you forgive me . . . .?"

Manuel Gerold fastened on his eldest son a glance full of mournful affection; and the tear that glistened in his eye and then coursed furtively down his wan cheek showed that the forgiveness sought had been given and given over again long before it had been asked. But at this same moment the old patriot's countenance became illumined as it were with a brightness not of this earth; there was no mistaking the presage. Both sons sank on their knees.

Emile happened to be on the left side of the bed, so his father laid his sound hand—the right—on his head in a mute, parting blessing. Simultaneously he strove to do the like with Horace, but his left hand refused its office. There was something plaintive in the look of embarrassment and sorrow that flitted over the dying man's brow as he recognized his inability to do what he desired. He summoned up all his remnant of strength in a last effort: but it was to no purpose. The attempt only exhausted what little strength yet remained in him. His head dropped softly back into his pillow, and he passed away.

So Horace rose from his knees without feeling his father's dying hand pressed with a benediction upon him as Emile had done.

CHAPTER XII.

Requiescat.

WHEN all was over, when the body had been laid
out, and the landlady, subdued and crying, had placed
upon the table the usual sad ornaments of Catholic
death-rooms—the two lighted tapers, the crucifix, the
cup of holy water with sprig of blessed box-wood;—
when the priest had arrived who was to watch all
night by the body and pray for its departed soul,
Horace sat down at his father's desk to write a line
to Angélique, apprising her of his bereavement. He
had promised her to write, whatever happened, and it
was more in redemption of this promise than out of
any natural impulse that he took up his pen. This
was the first time that he had ever written to Angélique,
and the words "your affectionate husband" looked
strange to him on the paper. Angélique his wife, and
the daughter-in-law of him who had just gone to rest?
He could only dimly realize this twofold relationship.
The truth is, a woman is only half a wife who is not
recognized by her husband's family, for the union between man and wife can never be complete if they do
not love the same people, if a death that bows down
one of the two with grief leaves the other indifferent.
The terms of Horace's letter, which would have been
tender and confiding had he been addressing one sure
to feel as he felt, were necessarily cold and brief. As
he wrote, his pen was clogged by the thought: "What
can she care about this death, she who never saw my
father, and had no reason for liking him?"

The next day there were those customary steps to be taken which relieve the mind of some part of its load of grief by occupying it. The declaration of the decease had to be made at the Mairie, the orders for the funeral to be given, the funeral letters be issued to friends, and, also, there was the will to be read; for, abroad, this formality does not follow the burial, but precedes it.

It was a very short and simple will, which a Brussels notary brought and read out before the two sons, the doctor, and a clerk, who came as witness. The date was of about six months back:—

"I, MANUEL GEROLD, called by some Duke of Hautbourg and Clairefontaine, being of sound mind, declare that this is my last will and testament; and I hereby cancel all wills made by me prior to this date.

"I request that my body may be buried in the foreign land where I may die, and this without pomp of any kind. Let my hearse be such as is used for the poor, and let no monument be set over my grave, but only a plain stone with my name.

"Should France become a free land again during the life-time of my sons, they will be fulfilling my very dear wish if they disinter my remains and transport them to the cemetery of Père-la-Chaise in Paris, beside those of my beloved wife; but so long as my country is ruled by its present Government I desire to rest, as I have lived, in exile.

"I bequeath all my books, papers, portraits, and personal property generally to my two sons, Horace and Emile, to be divided between them as they mutually shall determine; and I desire that the income derived from the sale of my literary works shall, so long as the copyright of those works remains by law the property of my heirs, that is, for the term of twenty-five years after my decease, be divided annually into three equal parts: one part for my son Horace, another for my son Emile, and the third to be devoted to some liberal and charitable object: that is, either to the relief of men who have suffered for their political convictions, or to the assistance of enslaved nations who shall take up arms for their emancipation.   And I appoint, as trustees of this fund, my son Emile and my friend Nestor Roche, to whom I bequeath as a token of my esteem and affection the copy of Montesquieu's *Esprit des Lois* given me by the compositors of Paris.

"At my death my son Horace will inherit the title of Duke of Hautbourg.   I desire that he will consult only his own choice as to adopting this title, or suffering it to remain in abeyance, for in these matters the convictions of one man cannot and should not influence those of another.   Let my son only remember that when a man assumes a great historical name he enters into a tacit covenant with his ancestors to keep it pure from all stain.

"I beg that my friend Nestor Roche and Maître Devinck, notary at Brussels, will act as executors to this will; and I sign in the humble faith of God, and the belief in an immortal life,

"MANUEL GEROLD."

"*10th September,* 1856."

Horace listened in silence to the reading of this will, which Maître Devinck scanned with monotonous solemnity as if he were perusing a *capias*. He could not be insensible to the passages which revealed how much his father's confidence in him had been shaken, and his mortification was increased, if possible, by the embarrassment of Emile, whom the substitution of Nestor Roche's name for Horace's as co-trustee of the charitable bequest truly surprised and grieved. This will could only have been written in an hour of dejection, perhaps of physical suffering. In his usual mood of health and kindness Manuel Gerold would never have put this slight upon his son, nor offered him such a serious rebuke as that implied in the paragraph relative to the title. So reasoned Emile, but his tongue was tied, for before he could venture on any consolation Horace forestalled him, and said resignedly: "Our father judged me like the rest. Don't let us ever talk about this, Emile. I bear no rancour, for I loved my father with all my heart; but some of the men in this Republican party poisoned his mind against me. It was just like them. You saw he died without giving me his blessing——"

The funeral had been fixed at a week's interval from the decease—this by request of a large body of refugees, who said that numbers of Manuel Gerold's political friends would come from London, Geneva, and from France itself to give him a parting token of respect. Horace was not much disposed at first to listen to these men, who arrived by scores every day to leave their cards, asked to be allowed to view the body, and did not kneel before it, being mostly "freethinkers," and who treated him—Horace—with a cold and studied civility of which it was impossible not to divine the meaning. He remarked to Emile that as

their father had desired to be buried without pomp,
there would be some transgression of his wishes in
suffering the funeral to be made the pretext of a great
Republican demonstration. But Emile interpreted the
absence of pomp to mean merely simplicity in the
arrangements; no plumes, emblazoned catafalque, or
mourning coaches, nothing but the plain hearse which
the will mentioned. Horace asked if there would not
be something like the pride that apes humility in the
contrast of a pauper's hearse with the position which
Manuel Gerold once held, and with the immense
concourse of mourners who would follow him to his
grave. He submitted that if the burial had been strictly
private a poor man's hearse might have been suitable,
but that if a great public procession were to be or-
ganized it would look less ostentatious to have the
funeral conducted in the usual middle-class way, not
pompously but becomingly. Emile, however, was too
sincerely a Republican to endorse these sentiments.
He could not see that there was any vanity in using a
pauper's hearse when one was not a pauper. Every
party has its foibles and Republicans dearly love a little
Spartanism. Accordingly Horace gave in, and the
hearse that drove up to the door of the lodging-house
on the appointed morning to convey the great tribune
to his last home was a common one of black wood,
open to the four winds, devoid of trappings, and drawn
by a single horse.

The evening before the brothers had received the
visit of a Brussels commissary of police, who came
with the scared countenance which Belgian officials
always wore when their country was being made the
scene of any episode likely to displease the great Em-

peror of the French, to say that the projected demonstration seemed much more important than had been
contemplated—whereupon he mopped his brow with a
red cotton handkerchief. "Refugees were arriving by
all the trains, and from everywhere; an enormous
number of French Liberals had also come by the last
expresses from Paris, and the French Government, as
usual, had sent a good many spies to accompany these
Liberals, and to attend at the funeral, to hear what
they might say. It was too late to ask the Messieurs
Gerold to alter any of the arrangements, but the commissary hoped that they would kindly exert their influence to have as few speeches as possible pronounced
over the grave, and, above all, to have those speeches
moderate; — it was the Belgian Minister of Foreign
Affairs who requested this as a very great favour."

Horace would have promised readily enough if
Emile had not interrupted him by inquiring somewhat
excitedly of the commissary if Belgium were not a free
land.

"Alas, yes!" answered that official; "a free land
bounded on all sides by the French ambassador."

Which meek reply disarmed Emile, though, said
he, they could promise nothing, for it was not their
part to dictate to their father's friends what they should
or should not say.

At which the commissary bowed; but added, dolefully, that he hoped the Messieurs Gerold would not
view it as a mark of disrespect to their father if the
Belgian Government took precautions against order
being disturbed on the morrow. And these precautions consisted in six policemen, who came to the
door at the same time as the hearse, with black thread

gloves on, and appeared extremely anxious not to offend anybody or to stand in anybody's way.

The commissary's evaluations as to the number of people who would swell Manuel Gerold's funeral train were not exaggerated; only, the concourse, from its very vastness, was, contrary to his timorous expectations, an orderly one. At ten o'clock a score of the leading French Republicans—great names all of them—who had been deputed to act as pall-bearers, entered the house between two dense but silent rows of spectators bordering the street outside, and claimed the honour of carrying the coffin themselves to the hearse. It was a plain deal coffin painted black, but it was not unadorned, for the wives and daughters of the refugees in Brussels had sent that morning a velvet pall with a cross embroidered by their own hands, and a beautiful wreath of white camelias. As the coffin issued through the door every head in the street was bared; and when Horace and Emile took up their positions behind the hearse they noticed that in every hand was a crown of yellow *immortelles*, to be laid by-and-by on the grave.

The hearse began slowly to move; but it was not one thoroughfare alone that was lined with spectators. As street after street unwound itself before the gaze, rows upon rows of people appeared, standing in black, with heads uncovered, and these wreaths of amaranths in their hands. There were not a few women in the crowd, who were crying; and here and there a Belgian soldier, who respectfully made the military salute. As the hearse passed, the throngs of mourners in perfect order and with a mechanical sort of discipline left the pavement, and formed themselves in rows ten abreast in the rear of the procession. This was done at every step, at every foot of ground along the road, so that the cortége, gathering in depth and strength as it advanced like a river swollen by tributary torrents, numbered thousands by the time the church was reached. All the shopkeepers on the line of the procession had put up their shutters, and every house, without exception, had its blinds drawn. Emile's tears rained fast, warm tears of thankfulness and pride; Horace was ghastly pale. What were the splendours and triumphs he had been courting beside this unparalleled homage offered to the memory of a man who had simply remained true to his faith?

At the church there was a halt. The building was too small to contain a tenth part of the concourse; so only the pall-bearers and the first two or three hundred in the close-pressed ranks went in, the rest remaining stationary in the road with imperturbable patience. Contrary to what the brothers had any right to expect from the price of the funeral, all the clergy of the church were assembled in the chancel. This is usually a matter of money, there being more or less priests according to the sum paid by the undertaker; but there is nothing so much flatters foreign clergies as a great Republican dying religiously and being buried pursuant to the ritual of the Catholic church: wherefore the priests of St. X——, ever full of tact, as all their order are, had waived the pecuniary question in this case, and mustered together twenty strong to impart unusual solemnity to the obsequies of Manuel Gerold. Also, the choir were at their post, but strengthened, as the custom is on such occasions, by some

singers of the Brussels opera, who had volunteered
their services, and sung magnificently the *Dies Iræ:*—

> Dies iræ, dies illa
> Solvet sæclum in favillâ.
> *   *   *   *   *
> Tuba mirum spargens sonum
> Per sepulchra regionum,
> Coget omnes ante Thronum.

The grand verses of the old anthem pealing under the
sacred vault, stirred hidden echoes in the breasts of
many unbelieving there present.   When this was terminated, and the absolution had been given, and the
coffin was being borne out again, whilst the organist
filled the church with the divine sounds of Mozart's
Requiem, Horace turned with his brother to follow out
the pall-bearers.   As he did so he caught sight of a
figure standing with eyes, or rather spectacles, down-
cast, and an air of devout unction, amidst a group of
Parisian Liberals. He knew the face, but without being
instantly able to recollect where he had seen it.   In
another moment, however, it flashed upon him: the
spectacles and the false moustache did not much alter
the physiognomy.   It was the honest M. Louchard:
and on either side of that worthy stood the two acolytes
MM. Fouineux and Tournetrique, who had assisted him
in the domiciliary visit to Horace's rooms.

Once more the procession started on its course,
and again it was swelled by increasing troops of
mourners, until it gained the Cemetery of Laeken, outside Brussels.

The hearse passed the gates, and debouched into
the long avenue of white tombs, and then, for the first
time, the immense host broke up, spreading like a
black sea over the whole of one side of the cemetery

—everybody being anxious to secure a place near to the grave.

The hearse, with a few score followers, branched off the main highway, threaded some by-paths, and reached its last halting-place just as the crowd had settled down—a countless multitude choking up all the footways, covering the tombstones, standing on and clinging to monuments, and stretching in a compact, surging mass as far as the eye could see.

The coffin was lifted out, and the priest recited the final prayers, and a "*De Profundis.*" Then the coffin was lowered with a grating sound of ropes, the parting "*Requiescat*" was pronounced, and the priest withdrew. At that moment, when a deep hush fell upon the whole assemblage in expectation of what was to follow, the scene was an imposing one.

Above, the sky glistening with a pale gold sunshine, and those opal tints which clothe the heavens at that neutral season, when it is no longer winter, nor yet quite spring; below, this ocean of human faces, the majority of which belonged to men who had devoted their lives to an idea, who had been persecuted for that idea, but who were sustained by a profound unwavering faith in the future; in front of them an open pit, with the coffin, and on the coffin a handful of clay.

A man stepped out of the throng on to the brink of the grave, and began to speak amidst a silence so intense, that a pebble, which rolled from under his foot, and dropped on the coffin with a hollow sound, was heard distinctly by everybody.

The orator was a man of world-wide fame. He had swayed assemblies, and his words struck upon responsive chords, awaking long and but half-suppressed murmurs of assent, as he confessed the creed that bound them all there together, and uttered the praises of the honest, steadfast Republican they were met to mourn.   To him succeeded a second speaker, and then a third—each of whom paid feeling tributes to the patriot, who had been the glory of his own generation, and would be looked back to as an example by those to come.   And these speeches, which made the temples of Emile throb, and poured balm upon his wounds, fell like lashes upon Horace.   Every word rang as a reproach in his ear.   The speakers seemed to revile him, to point ironically to the contrast between him and his father.   He fancied that all eyes were fixed upon him with wondering contempt, and when he tried to look up he could not; his glance was anchored by shame to the ground.   Suddenly he started, and raised his eyes, flashing and astounded, upon the fourth speaker.

After the third oration there had been a pause, for it had been in some way settled that three speeches only should be delivered; but, just as that hum was commencing, which precedes the disbanding of a multitude, a small wild-haired man had elbowed his way to the front, and, by a gesture of his hand, rooted everybody to the spot.

It was Albi.

As well nigh all the spectators knew of the enmity between him and Horace Gerold, astonishment and curiosity, not unmingled with apprehension, broke upon every face, and the people pressed forward closer as if they were nudging one another.

Albi paid no heed, but, in quick, dry, fevered

accents, began a panegyric of Manuel Gerold more glowing, more heartfelt, more thorough, than any which had been pronounced before. But there was the exaltation of a fanatic in the burning phrases, and when the orator had emptied his heart of all the good in it the fanatic's mania for invective re-took possession of him. His voice became sardonic, like a trumpet that cracks, and undeterred by the sacredness of the spot—forgetting it, indeed, and all laws of humanity—consulting only his political passion, his spleen, his hatred, he turned his eyes to where Horace stood and regretted aloud that Manuel Gerold had left no son—or, at least, but one son—who could follow in his footsteps.

Horace watched Albi as a leopard may eye a panther. He had submitted to a great deal. To the coldness of his father's admirers, to their ill-concealed scorn of him, to their speeches, in which—without meaning it, possibly—they had trampled all his self-respect underfoot; but nobody could expect him to stand this.

At the first words of Albi's speech he had clenched his fists, and held in his breath, and now that the man was doing what he expected he would do from the first—slavering his venom over an unclosed tomb—he sprung forward, and shouted, "Silence!"

A thunderclap bursting abruptly overhead could not have produced a greater commotion.

"Silence!" repeated Horace, in a furious voice, "who are you that come to speak beside the grave of an honest man? Manuel Gerold had nothing in common with Republicans of your sort. You and your fellows belong to no party. You murdered the first Republic, you ruined the second, and if our country is

fettered now it is that Frenchmen prefer despotism to
the crimes and follies by which you have rendered
freedom hateful. Stand aside! Patriots should shun
you like a pestilence, for you and those who think like
you are the enemies of the human race." And as
Albi continued to stand where he was, Horace laid a
hand on his chest and pushed him roughly back.

A great clamour arose, and immediately there was
a dismayed rush to keep the two men apart. Numbers
of acquaintances whom Horace had not noticed in the
crowd, Nestor Roche, Jean Kerjou, Claude Febvre,
M. Pochemolle, Mr. Drydust, the black-clad commercial traveller Filoselle, held him back, Emile aiding;
and another throng, amongst whom Max Delormay was
active, did the same with Albi. But Albi, glaring and
mad, shook himself free, and, rushing to his anta-
gonist, hissed: "The men who belong to no party are
those who will sell themselves to any. They are the
harlots of politics. Prostitute!" and he spat in Horace's face.

Horace sprung from the hands of those who were
restraining him, like a lion through a thread net, and
clutched Albi by the throat. The two men closed and
wrestled; and, amidst the appalled cries of thousands
horrified by this frightful scene, both fell and rolled
headlong together into the open grave, on to the coffin
at the bottom, which crashed under them.

CHAPTER XIII.

Declarations of War.

M. GRIBAUD, the Minister, was out of sorts again. Not that the Corps Législatif had voted against a Government bill, or evinced any inclination ever to do such a thing; but an individual member of that Assembly, a square-headed Alsatian count, Protestant and gaiter-wearing, had taken him privately to task in a rich German brogue about certain abuses flourishing in his department, to wit, the appointment of Catholic school-masters in purely Protestant parishes. M. Gribaud had answered that if the noble count would examine well, he would, no doubt, find in other parts of France Catholic parishes blessed with Protestant school-masters; but the noble count had shown himself sceptic on this point, adding that even if it were so he saw nothing to admire in the arrangement. M. Gribaud was not much used to these replies, the less so as the count had given him to understand, in accents more and more Rhenish, that the support he vouchsafed to the Government was quite conditional, for that he was sure to be re-elected by his Lutheran constituency whether the "administration" liked it or not—and hereupon had stalked away. Scarcely had this unsatisfactory episode been enacted than another nobleman-deputy had supervened—this time a Gascon marquis, Catholic to the roots of his red hair and twanging his words gaily through his nose—to ask that his brother might be made a bishop. Now there was not the slightest

reason in the world why this marquis's brother should
be made a bishop, though there were numerous reasons
against such a course. But as the marquis himself had
been made a deputy for no cause whatever, it was
quite natural that he should suppose the same qualifica-
tions would do for his brother; so that on being rather
curtly denied what he wanted—for smooth-speaking
was not M. Gribaud's forte—he had turned on his
heel in a huff, mumbling meridional expletives sulkily.
"This comes of having land-holding aristocrats in the
Chamber," growled M. Gribaud, rolling homewards in
his brougham. "It's the hobby of the court, not mine.
If I had my way we should send the departments their
deputies as we do their prefects and their dancing-
dogs, all ready reared and trained in Paris. Manufacturers make the best deputies. All they ever ask
for is to be decorated or ennobled, which costs nothing. Or failing manufacturers, I'd have sportsmen;
they let one alone and have no religion."

M. Gribaud reflected in this strain during his dinner, and again after it. The evening was that of the
day of Manuel Gerold's funeral, and happened further
to be that which M. Gribaud devoted every week to
the reception of his political adherents, masculine and
feminine. The saloons were always crowded to suffocation on these auspicious nights. Mdme. Gribaud
was "at home." Diamonds twinkled by the myriad,
laced uniforms blazed in dense battalions, veteran functionaries trod on the distressed skirts of heated dowagers
hopelessly jammed in impassable doorways, and younger
functionaries, with the administrative bloom still fresh
on them, breasted their way through avalanches of
snowy shoulders, embellishing but obstructing the stair-

case. M. Gribaud, in a swallow-tail coat with much gold to it, a red ribbon and star, and his hair brushed, stood on a hearth-rug and smiled a welcome to the company as they defiled before him. But when M. Gribaud was not in a good humour these smiles much resembled those which a man, who has a whitlow on his hand gives, when that hand is warmly squeezed.

M. Gribaud had returned about a dozen hundred bows and stretched as many of these yellow smiles just alluded to when he became conscious of the presence of M. Macrobe, who was performing a worshipful though collected obeisance to him. M. Macrobe ought by rights to have been at Brussels attending the funeral, but having heard that there was to be a great Republican demonstration, and feeling small inclination to figure in the midst of such an assemblage where he was not likely to be regarded with deep sympathy, he had sent an excuse to his son-in-law pleading a convenient indisposition. At the same time, as he much desired to see M. Gribaud on behalf of his son-in-law's interests and his own, he had come in the hope of obtaining a few minutes' talk with his Excellency, and was not disappointed.

"How do you do, M. Macrobe?" growled the Minister, holding out his knotty hand, which now that it was covered with a white kid-glove, looked every moment as if it was going to burst; and he eyed the financier with an interrogative glance which seemed to say: "I wonder what this rogue is going to tell me this evening?" But suddenly, as if recollecting something, he added: "By-the-by what is that Brussels telegram in this evening's paper?"

"I am sure I don't know," answered M. Macrobe,

whose countenance wore an air of perplexity. "I have no further details than your Excellency has. The despatch is very summary and only says that there was a disturbance at the funeral between my son-in-law and M. Albi."

"And that there was a tremendous concourse at the burial," grumbled the Minister, and he led the way to a table in an embrasure where lay some evening journals. Some other guests in the room seeing the Pillar of Politics, and the Pillar of Finance, engaged in loving converse, withdrew discreetly out of earshot. "Yes, you see, there it is, a countless multitude, all Brussels afoot, democratic speeches and the rest of it. Manuel Gerold was a great fool, I used to know him well. He might have become a minister like me if he had liked."

"But he had the infatuation to prefer being an exile . . . ."

"And that's a form of vanity like any other, M. Macrobe. I'll wager the man thought he stood higher on his pedestal than any of us."

"There's no accounting for opinions, your Excellency. But I am glad that his eldest son shows but slight disposition to follow his example. I desired to speak to you about him this evening. Taking the newspaper account as it stands, I gather that my son-in-law has had some brutal affront put upon him and that the breach between him and the Opposition will be widened beyond mending."

"So much the better."

"As your Excellency says, so much the better. My son-in-law has become Duke of Hautbourg now, and under that new name I trust to see him begin a new

and more becoming life. At the approaching elections
I look to his standing for Hautbourg, and soon we
may count upon seeing him return to the Castle of
Clairefontaine and take his proper rank in the world.
Your Excellency will not, I hope, throw any impedi-
ment in the way of the Hautbourg election?"

M. Gribaud's face assumed a cold expression, but
without beating about the bush he replied.

"I am beginning to ask myself what Government
is likely to gain by furthering the Clairefontaine scheme,
and I fail to see our advantage in it." His voice grew
business-like. "When first you broached the subject,
the conditions were not what they are now. Young
Gerold was an adversary who was giving us trouble.
It was essential to suppress him, and we should have
done so, had you not proposed to win him over to our
side. But he is harmless now, thanks to the way we
managed that last election. The liberals have cast him
off, and if Government does not give him a lift the
next time, it is not difficult to see that he will be left
without a seat."

"Perhaps he might not be returned for the Tenth
Circumscription," said M. Macrobe, beginning to look
blue. "But he would be safe of winning the seat
at Hautbourg if the Government helped him."

"But why should we help him?" responded the
Minister, gruffly. "He has never joined our ranks as
you promised he would. All he has done is to tone
down his speeches a little, but what we want are not
deputies who tone down, but deputies who don't speak
at all, at least against us."

"Everybody cannot turn his coat in a day, your
Excellency," answered M. Macrobe, with half a sneer.

M. Gribaud was generally as thick-skinned as a
rhinoceros where epigrams were concerned, but this
time the barb penetrated a little too deep.

"A man cannot turn his coat too soon who has
begun by wearing it wrong side out," he rejoined,
with a scowl. "If young Gerold will accept an official
candidature on the usual terms, that is, issue an address
we shall dictate, and pledge his word to vote as he is
told, we shall not oppose him. But his support must
be unreserved. We certainly shall not help him to get
into the House as an independent member." And M.
Gribaud folded and refolded the newspaper he was
holding in a deliberate way that signified: "This is my
ultimatum."

"Then am I to understand that in the event of the
Duke refusing these conditions, which he naturally will,
the Government will contest the seat of Hautbourg?"
asked M. Macrobe, gazing uneasily into his opera-hat,
as if to ask counsel of it in this emergency. "I beg
to remind your Excellency," he resumed, "that the
death of M. Manuel Gerold has removed what I believe
to be the last obstacle in the way of my son-in-law's
assuming his estates and adopting the rank that belongs
to him; and that as Lord of Clairefontaine the Duke
of Hautbourg will be in a position amply to repay any
courtesies that may be shown him at present."

"I should be sorry to speculate on any gratitude
of that kind," muttered M. Gribaud drily. "I know
it was a seductive scheme that which you first unfolded,
of winning over young Gerold to us, getting him to
put his name and landed influence at our service, and
so on, but these projects never become facts. Landed
proprietors are the stubbornest cattle in existence; you

can't drive, but must for ever be coaxing them. Why, two of them bandied words with me this very afternoon."

And at the recollection of his Alsatian count and Gascon marquis M. Gribaud grew agitated, and stuttered indignantly:

"Two beggarly clod-crushers whom we had put into the Chamber out of charity, simply that they might have a decent salary to add to their trumpery rents, and this pair come lording it over me, threatening me with their displeasure, and all because they know that the peasant electors vote stubbornly at each election, as they did the time before, and that to turn a landed proprietor out of the seat you have once allowed him to occupy is about as pleasant a job as trying to root up a live oak with a pocket-knife. May the deuce take them! But if these two, with their five hundred acres apiece, feel independent enough to bully in this style, what can the Government expect of the owner of such a holding as Clairefontaine?"

"All the more reason for not offending him," suggested M. Macrobe shrewdly.

"There would be reason enough for not offending him if young Gerold were already in his castle; but he isn't. Hark you, M. Macrobe," broke off the Minister, recurring to his favourite method of going bluntly to the point: "if young Gerold returns to Clairefontaine he will have no need to come begging our support, for we should give it him as a matter of course, there being no use in doing otherwise; but you have your doubts about this return, and you apparently count upon the Hautbourg election to advance your aims. Well, I wish you good luck: only, you won't get anything else from us. For the moment

young Gerold has ceased to be a danger to us, and
that is all I wanted. As Duke of Hautbourg and Lord
of Clairefontaine he would certainly become trouble-
some again, so that to help him thither would be uncommonly like sowing stinging-nettles on my own path.
I've given you our terms—unconditional surrender on
Gerold's part, or else war."

"Then I think we shall have to accept war," said
M. Macrobe with a feigned laugh on his lips, but a
gleam in his ferret eyes. "Your Excellency will excuse us if, when our turn comes, we give no quarter."

M. Gribaud assumed the Olympian attitude—half
wonder and half grim contempt—of Jupiter hearing
himself defied by Mercury.

"Why do you say 'we,' M. Macrobe?" he inquired. "Do you intend opening hostilities on us,
too?"

"I am in the same camp as the Duke of Hautbourg, your Excellency," was M. Macrobe's curt rejoinder.

The scowl on the Minister's countenance deepened
abruptly into a glare. Some of the coarse aggressive-
ness of the old days when he was a blustering criminal-
court barrister rose to his tongue, and was only re-
pressed with an effort. He laid one of his huge white
gloves on the financier's arm, and, first looking round
to see that there was nobody at hand, said in a husky
voice: "Don't you think this is enough fooling, Macrobe? Do you fancy I don't know how the Crédit
Parisien is kept on its legs? Why, man, beware what
you are doing in taking up the cudgels against us, for
we could smash your company like a filbert, and you
with it, so I give you warning."

But he found more than his match in M. Prosper Macrobe, who shot back his answer like a dart from a bow.

"I dare you to do your worst, M. Gribaud. You can smash the Crédit Parisien if those of your colleagues who are interested in its welfare will let you; but you can't smash me, nor even injure me in reputation or in fortune. And let me tell you this—that if those whom you serve were ever driven to choose between offending me or dismissing you, it is not me whom they would deem it most prudent to sacrifice. So it is for you to beware and take warning."

And with a disdainful shrug he strode away, leaving his Excellency disconcerted.

So disconcerted that left alone M. Gribaud began walking straight ahead in a purposeless sort of way through the crowded rooms, his gilt sword-sheath beating on the thick calf of his leg, his cocked hat crushed under his arm, and his hands pinching each other and cracking each other's kid teguments behind his back. Before him, as he advanced, the subservient throng parted in two rows of bowing heads right and left. But many a sub-prefect, who had come up to town to urge a claim to promotion, many a fair dame who had decked herself in her gayest robes and softest looks to wring from the great man's generosity a post of emolument for her husband, brother, or peculiar friend, forbore their suits on marking his Excellency's eyes fixed with no inviting expression on the carpet. Mechanically M. Gribaud made a series of curt bows as he proceeded, throwing them at haphazard to any one who chose to take them, as one flings half-pence amongst rabble. Then, presently, he stopped, having caught sight of a brother statesman making himself agreeable to a bevy of ladies on an ottoman.

A glance from his chief brought this eminent politician to M. Gribaud's side. He was a lanky celebrity with not more than half-an-ounce of hair on his head, and that half-ounce dyed coal-black. His moustache and tuft were of the same jet. He had false teeth, wore a double eyeglass on the bridge of his nose, and evidently considered himself handsome. Rumour affirmed that he had been appointed minister because his aunt—— But this is beside the question. He simpered to M. Gribaud, who at once whispered to him: "I say, De Verny, you have shares in the Crédit Parisien, have you not?"

The coal-black dyed colleague changed colour a little, and exclaimed, "Yes; but how do you know?"

"Well, you see I do know; but there is nothing to be ashamed of in the matter. Only, if I were you, I'd sell out."

"Why, is there anything wrong?" and the dyed one's visage lengthened of a sudden visibly.

"No, not as yet. But of late these joint-stock companies have been running riot. Paris has become a gambling hell. In high quarters they don't like it; they say it gives a raffish colour to the Dynasty." Here M. Gribaud lowered his voice and muttered some words scarcely audible. "So you see," he resumed, "if it should ever be necessary, for form's sake, to make an example, we must be certain that the company we attack hasn't any of our own men on its books. I don't say the Crédit Parisien is in any danger, but you would be doing wisely to cut the connection. One never knows what may happen."

And two minutes later M. de Verny might have been seen scuttling downstairs to his carriage, with what little hair remained to him standing up on end, oblivious of the bevy of ladies on the ottoman, and bent only on gaining the Cercle Impérial to see if perchance he might find his stock-broker there, and instruct that worthy to sell out to-morrow morning—the first thing.

Further on, M. Gribaud observed a second brother statesman, who had just been treating himself to a glass of Malmsey, which was good at the Hôtel Gribaud, as are most wines purchased with the money of the tax-payer. This second statesman held his head high, as if there were a set of plumes on the top of it, which was the more imposing as he could hardly have measured five foot one, boots included. Almost the same dialogue ensued as before, with this difference in the results, that at the first mention of the Crédit Parisien the small grey head crested with invisible plumes sunk to below the owner's shoulders, causing him to look forthwith as if he had lost a cubit from his stature. M. Gribaud reassured him, but said: "Doesn't that long bit of land that skirts the fortifications in the Faubourg M—— belong to the Crédit Parisien, and wasn't there a talk of buying it for Government magazines?"

"I believe there was," replied the second statesman, rather sheepishly.

"But the bargain isn't struck yet?"

"No, the affair was to be concluded next week. A very good affair for every one concerned."

"Well, I think it had better stand over. There's

no great hurry for magazines, and I don't think the site a good one."

And five minutes afterwards the second statesman might have been seen hurrying through the hall of egress, and leaping into his brougham like the first, with brow knit and thoughts intent upon selling out there and then, if by chance a buyer could be found.

M. Gribaud continued his walk, glad within his soul at what he had just done. But he felt the need for a little rest and diverting talk, so he raised his eyes and cast about him for a likely guest, that is, one who would converse with him without asking him for anything.

A few of the ambitious sub-prefects, accepting this look as a hint that M. Gribaud's glumness had quite melted away, smirked forward precipitately. But his Excellency rebuffed them with a hasty "Good-night—good-night," uttered in the same tone as the "Down, Dash, down," with which we regale an affectionate dog who jumps upon us with muddy paws; and so passed on till he beheld that valuable member of the Corps Législatif, the fig-nosed Planter, who had escorted Mrs. Planter to the entertainment, and seemed to be enjoying himself thoroughly, being profoundly asleep in a corner; and not far distant from this legislator, the Prince of Arcola, a little languid, but sociable, and conversing with a lady. There was no hesitating between these two. If he awoke the fig-nosed Planter, that deputy would infallibly ask for promotion in the Legion of Honour; so M. Gribaud made for the Prince of Arcola.

The Prince was chatting with Madame de Masseline—the lady who rendered important services to the cause of order, as represented by M. Louchard, and the Prefecture de Police. She was a brilliant dame, with winning manners, eyes like sloes, and pretty confiding ways, that convinced every man she desired to pump that her one fond wish was to nestle under his strong arm, and unfold to him the whole tale of her chequered existence. Man being the silliest of bipeds, this stratagem never failed, so that, in half-an-hour, she had generally coaxed out of her interlocutor all she cared to know, and restored him to Society squeezed morally flat as a biffin. Nevertheless, though there was not an event occurred within Paris but that she was as familiar with all its details as though she had been on the spot and taken ocular notes, yet it was part of her delightful system to feign ignorance of everything; and she would go into little ecstasies of wonder to hear that it had rained in the morning; clasp her charming hands in amazement at learning that So-and-So—whose wedding she had attended—had just been married; and exclaim, in her silvery tones, "Dear, dear! that's news, indeed!" on being apprised that her own husband—every one of whose steps in this life she had directed—had secured an honour or an appointment, which she herself had obtained for him. Women saw through her, called her an odious, mischievous, affected thing, and detested her. She returned the compliment, and, in the prettiest way possible, without seeming to be aware of what she was doing, would pick the most virtuous woman's reputation to bits in five minutes—leaving not so much of it as would suffice for the needs of a courtesan. For all of which things men adored her, stoutly took her part when she was attacked by her own sex, and gave her credit for all the innocence, good-nature, and candour to which she chose to lay claim.

The Prince of Arcola was one of her admirers; or, rather, she was one of the thousand women to whom the Prince had, at different times, paid a languid court, without ever being able to make up his mind to love one of them. Indeed, the principal secret of the Prince's attachment for Georgette was that women in society seemed to him so similar—that is, so uniformly pretty, frivolous, insignificant, and wax-doll-like, that it was impossible to choose between them. It had required a woman who was not of his class—who contrasted totally with all the women he had ever seen— to fire the latent spark in his amative, but rather *blasé*, heart; and his rejection had been such a blow to him, that the first remark Madame de Masseline made when, obedient to her beck, he had subsided into a seat beside her, was, "Mon prince, you are becoming Byronian. You wear a tired, disenchanted look, as if you were joining the horrible army of misogynists."

He smiled rather wearily, but answered gallantly, —"If ever I take to hating women it will be when you have left P. P. C. cards on us all, which will be never—at least, in my time."

Madame de Masseline being of that elastic age called thirty-five—that is, by her own computation, seven or eight years the Prince's senior—viewed this as a compliment, and replied mincingly, with much fluttering of her fan, and sparkling of her dark eyes, —"Well, that's pretty, and more like yourself. But I am sure, my poor prince, you have some *peine de cœur*. Ah! what a tyrant the heart is. How it does make one suffer. I have often thought we should be better without hearts—I know I should. For instance, *She* must have no heart—I mean that cruel creature, who is making you look so—so—interesting."

"Oh, yes, she has plenty of heart," rejoined the Prince, naïvely, "but not for me."

"Then she has none for anybody else, you may depend upon it, unless she be blind, or deaf, or both. Perhaps she is." And she laughed, beating her skirts down, and moving her chair a little, so as to make more room, and said, sympathizingly,—"Draw nearer, mon pauvre prince, and tell me all about it. You and I are old friends, and can confide our sorrows to each other with platonic affection."

Men are never quite insensible to the interest which pretty women pretend to take in their affairs. It is an old, but not the less true, saying, that the surest way to flatter them is to talk to them about themselves. Moreover, it relieves a sorrow to confide it to a commiserating listener.

So the Prince acknowledged, with tolerable frankness, that he had been wooing, and failed. He omitted, of course, all mention of names or particulars that could put his hearer upon the right clue; but this happened to be quite a superfluous precaution, for Madame de Masseline was acquainted with the whole story from first to last. The Pochemolles had been far too much dazed by the offer of the Prince's hand to their daughter to be able to hold their peace as to the fact. Even when the refusal of Georgette had plunged them abruptly from the seventh heaven to the seventh region of Hades, they had found no rest until they had asked all their kinsfolk and acquaintances to condole with them in their sore trial. And thus the story was beginning to filter its way through Paris with the proverbial rapidity of all such kind of news, and Madame de Masseline, according to her wont, had been amongst the first to be informed of it.

She ignored, however, wherefore the Prince had been refused; so, on learning it from his own lips, exclaimed, with an astonished sigh, "Dear, dear, how shocking! Loved some one else, did she?—and that some one else a married man. That is always awkward, because a man of wit has but one revenge open to him in such a case."

, "And what is that?"

"Oh, you are pretending to be more innocent than I," said she, simulating an air of bashfulness, and giving a tinkling little laugh. "Why, what was it the Duke of Richelieu said? 'When a married man crosses my path, I make love to his wife—on principle.'"

"The Duke was evidently wittier than I am," sighed the Prince; "but I might fare no better with my rival's wife than I did in the other quarter."

"Impossible to be more modest. But don't you long for revenge of some sort? You talk with distressing placidity about your rival. I should not deem that flattery if I were the lady in the case."

"I have no great love for my rival if that is what you mean," answered the Prince, and he knit his brow. "I am certain he has not behaved well. He deceived the—the lady, and he deceived me; for I asked him before proposing, whether some suspicions which I had were founded, and he swore to me they were not. But the only revenge we witless men can resort to in such a contingency is not to believe the perjurer again, and to show him that we do not."

It was at this moment that the Minister Gribaud loomed in sight, steering straight for the nook where the two were seated.

"How provoking! Here is that wretched mummy of a Grand Vizier coming to break our *tête-à-tête*," muttered Mdme. de Masseline, pouting, and the same instant, with a charming smile,—"This is an unhoped-for pleasure, your Excellency. I was just saying to Monsieur le Prince what a delight it is to get a few minutes of your society; but it is so rarely one has that good fortune."

"Your humble servant, madame," grunted M. Gribaud. "Good evening, mon prince;" and he took a chair with the air of one who says, "I know this woman is humbugging me, but it does no harm."

"We were talking about the elections," resumed Mdme. de Masseline, with radiant fascination. "We were computing the majority Government would have, and M. le Prince agreed with me that the Opposition would scarcely win a seat."

"Then you take interest in politics, mon Prince?" remarked M. Gribaud, looking with interest at the nobleman. "Why don't you come forward? There would be no difficulty in getting you elected."

"What could I represent, your Excellency?" asked the Prince, laughing. "A deputy should have land, and I have none. My fortune consists of dogs, horses, and Crédit Parisien shares; it would hardly do to come forward as the representative of those interests."

"Oh, the land idea is a fallacy," returned M. Gribaud, bluntly; "it is just because you have no land

you would do so well. We could present you anywhere; start you as a candidate untrammelled by
landed or any other interests, and consequently offering every guarantee of independence."

"Yes, that is what my husband put in his last
address, and he got thirty thousand votes," observed
Mdme. de Masseline. "You have no idea, M. le
Prince, how good-natured the peasantry are—and be-
lieving!"

"We have a seat that would exactly do for you,"
pursued the Minister, as an idea appeared to strike
him; and his tone curiously reminded the Prince of
his horse-dealer saying, "A mare that will just carry
your weight, mon Prince." "A mixed constituency,
half borough, half country," continued M. Gribaud,
vaunting his merchandise: "the present holder of the
seat is old and used up: we have promised to put
him into the Senate. Anyhow, he will not come forward again. The place is Hautbourg, and, as a sport-
ingman, the contest will amuse you. Your competitor
will be young Gerold—you know the man; he calls
himself Duke of Hautbourg now."

The Prince gave a slight start, and a flush rose
to his face so rapidly that Mdme. de Masseline, ever
observant, fastened her two sapphire eyes upon him
like a pair of coruscating points of interrogation.

With a prompt determination that amazed but
amused the lady, and gave pleasure to the statesman,
the Prince answered,—"To tell your Excellency the
truth, I had never dreamed of embracing politics; but
the name of M. Gerold would almost induce me to
accept your proposal. I do not think that gentleman
worthy to sit in a National Assembly."

"No, he is not; and it pleases me to hear you say so," returned the Minister, with satisfaction. "He is a Radical, and makes speeches—we have tried everything to convert him, but it was of no use."

The Prince did not think it necessary to undeceive M. Gribaud as to the motives for his stricture on Horace Gerold. The Minister was therefore left to suppose that the remark proceeded from an exuberance of Bonapartist zeal highly natural in a Prince of Arcola.

"Then we may rely on you," said he, with something like a gracious snort, "and we may order the prefect to start your candidature—enter you for the running, as they say at Chantilly?" and his hard mouth bordered on a grin.

"Of course your Excellency offers me an independent candidature?" asked the Prince seriously.

"Undoubtedly, my dear Prince," rejoined the Minister, who knew that there was not much to be apprehended from one bearing the name of Arcola and a sportsman to boot. "You shall tell your electors what you please," and his contentment was such, that, rising to go, after a few minutes' more conversation, he said: "By-the-way, didn't you say something about the Crédit Parisien? If you have shares in that concern let me advise you to sell out. I don't understand much about those affairs, but a shrewd financier, whose opinions I value, told me to-night that there were symptoms of a break-up. I give you the warning for what it's worth, and in confidence."

M. Gribaud guessed that a thing communicated in confidence within the hearing of Mdme. de Masseline was likely to be repeated confidentially to a good many persons before the week was out.

Soon afterwards the Prince offered his arm to Mdme. de Masseline, to conduct her to her carriage. On the staircase she said to him, with gay malice,—"So it's the new Duke of Hautbourg who is your rival, mon Prince. Well, you can spare yourself the trouble of trying the revenge à la *Richelieu* on him, for I suspect somebody else has already done it for you."

"No, no, you mistake," answered the Prince, stopping her and looking rather shocked. "Horace Gerold's wife is the purest little thing in existence. Rather silly, I know, but nobody has ever breathed a word against her."

"Nor do I, my dear Prince," said she, drawing her cloak closer round her, with a pretty little shiver; "and, indeed, I was quite astounded when I heard it. Very much pained, too, I was, I assure you, for I love the little thing. I often go to see her, and she comes to see us. But why does she go about everywhere with a Captain of Carbineers? And why does that captain sit behind her in her box at the opera and whisper compliments in her ear when her husband is not there? Those were questions I heard asked this very day, and I stood up for the poor child, and said it wasn't true, and that I wouldn't have such things said about her."

"And you did quite right," rejoined the Prince, gravely, "for those facts you mention are the best proofs possible of her innocence. If she and the captain were guilty they would act more cautiously to avert suspicion."

"Well, I like to see men so chivalrous in defending

us poor women," said Mdme. de Masseline, smiling, and holding her little hand out of the brougham window for him to shake; "but we mustn't be so confident in everything, my dear Prince. Mind, for instance, you don't forget to sell out your shares in the Crédit Parisien. That old Grand Vizier's warning made me feel quite cold, for my husband has shares, too, and we must get rid of them at once."

"I can't see that at all," muttered the Prince, in perplexity, as this charming apostle of morality was whirled away. "If the company were all right we might sell out;—in fact, I personally *was* thinking of doing so. But now that I learn there's a screw loose, it would be as good as palming off a spavined horse on somebody, and letting him believe it was a sound one. That old Minister and this giddy woman can't have reflected on what they were saying."

And so this guileless nobleman sought his mansion, rather upset by M. Gribaud's warning. For the interpretation he chose to put upon it was, that he must not part with his shares on any account, lest by so doing he should pass them on to some unwary man and cause his ruin. Which for the year of grace one thousand eighteen fifty-seven was as out of date a piece of reasoning as well might be.

CHAPTER XIV.

Affairs of Interest and of Honour.

As for M. Macrobe, he went home from the Minister's reception in as fine a temper as he had ever experienced in his life. He did not attach much importance to M. Gribaud's threats concerning himself or the Crédit Parisien, but he was stung and exasperated by the opposition his projects respecting Horace had encountered. The hostility of the Government was going to plunge him into dilemmas. If Horace returned from Brussels re-puritanized by the week he had spent near his father's death-bed, and if he were still averse to installing himself at Clairefontaine, the realization of all his, M. Macrobe's, day-dreams would be indefinitely adjourned. Luckily for the financier's peace of mind and night's rest, his thoughts reverted to the newspaper telegram reporting the fracas between his son-in-law and Albi, and he blessed this Radical from the bottom of his heart.

The next morning M. Macrobe entered his daughter's boudoir early, for the purpose of instructing her as to what she should say to her husband, who was expected home during the day. Angélique was dressed in the deepest mourning. Mr. Girth had been called into requisition to furnish the most elegant and appropriate black costumes he could devise; and M. Macrobe had also put his entire household into sables, the footmen gliding about with black epaulets, and aiglets, and Aunt Dorothée as much covered with lawn and crape

as if she were inconsolable. M. Macrobe might, perhaps, have trusted his daughter to see to these not
very arduous details herself; but his distrust of her
capacities seemed to increase instead of diminish as
she grew older. His was the mind that bustled and
superintended everything; and he had not forgotten,
as soon as Manuel Gerold was dead, to have all the
Marquis's coronets on the carriages and hall chairs of
the Hôtel Macrobe replaced by ducal ones, and to
direct the servants to address the new duke on his return as "Monseigneur."

Angélique was alone. The evening before she had
let fall a few words in her cousin's hearing about the
difficulty of getting some worsted matched; and the
Crimean Hero had started off, immediately he was up,
to scour Paris with a ball of the rare wool in his pocket,
and the determination to find one like it at any hazard,
in his gallant soul. Aunt Dorothée was in the seclusion
of her own chamber darning pocket-handkerchiefs, or
some work of darkness. She hid and barred herself
in to perpetrate these crimes, for her brother allowed
her enough pin-money to keep ten families in comfort,
and having once discovered a basketful of stockings
she had carefully mended, had pitched them unhesitat-
ingly into the fire, and bought her six dozen pairs of
new ones—an act of wastefulness that had kept her
sleepless for a week.

"My child," began the financier, throwing himself
on the sofa beside his daughter, and speaking much
more brusquely than was his wont, "I hope you feel
the importance of inducing your husband to renounce
the Quixotism that is keeping him out of his estates.
That was all very well for a time, whilst your father-in-

law was alive; but the comedy would turn to a farce if
it were played much longer."

"I do not think Horace intends it for a comedy,"
observed Angélique meekly.

"No, but it is one nevertheless; and now is the
time for you, if you are a woman of sense, to insist
upon your husband doing what is proper and becoming. You should direct all your energies towards this
object. What were you reading there?" and he took
the book she was holding out of her hands. "*Vies des
Grands Hommes par Plutarque, Édition expurgée.* Fancy
reading such trash as that! Who cares now about
Epaminondas of Thebes, or Lycurgus of Lacedæmon?
Why don't you take to Balzac, who painted our own
times, and gives you a glimpse of the world we live
in: or to M. Gousset's novels? He brings us one
every six months, and I'm sure they're very good reading. Gousset is a witty fellow; he would enliven you,
teach you what a *grande dame* should be, and how she
should manage her husband."

"It was Horace who recommended me to read this
book," said Angélique.

"Then do; but read the others as well. You're
not a school-girl now, and your happiness is in your
own hands. What I tell you is for your good. If a
woman can't do what she likes with her husband her
life is a blank, and so is his. Men like being led, and
they only like the women who lead them."

Angélique sighed.

"I always knew I was not the wife for Horace,"
she said, with sadness.

"Stuff!" answered the financier, bluntly. "But the
way to secure a man's affection is not to be in perpe-

tual adoration before him, as before a shrine. A woman
must have spirit, and bring her husband to respect her.
Look at that young Georgette Pochemolle, whom you
took under your protection and wanted me to abet in
her husband-hunt. She has spirit enough for two. She
had set her cap at your husband and would have probably married him if you hadn't, and depend upon it
that, counter-girl as she is, she would have twirled him
round her little-finger, and been starring it as mistress
of Clairefontaine long before this time."

"I know she is cleverer than I am," answered
Angélique, wiping some tears, which had sprung to her
eyes. "She would have made him happier than I do,
and I believe he sees it now."

"You are a little goose," cried M. Macrobe, with
anger. "You are in hysterics because your husband
looks dull in your company, and because it turns out
he spent an afternoon at Meudon last week. But what
rivalry have you got to fear now? You are married;
your husband can't divorce you; and as for Georgette,
she is too shrewd a girl to become Horace's mistress.
So all the cards are in your hands, and if your husband finds your company dull, it is merely because
you sit and mope, reading *Plutarch's Lives* instead of
being up and stirring and remembering that you are
Duchess of Hautbourg, and clearing your husband's
mind of that mawkish, cheap-newspaper philanthropy
which has got there like a cobweb into a knight's
helmet. Lead him, push him to Clairefontaine, girl.
You will make my fortune, and his, and he will thank
you all his life for it."

This was the first time Angélique had seen her
father so peremptory. His counsels were more often

conveyed by hints than by direct injunctions; and the
hints, though broad, were always given in cheerful,
sanguine terms, with a kiss to seal them at the end.
But now M. Macrobe gave no kiss; his words were in-
cisive; the expression of his face was anxious; and
Angélique, as she looked at him through her tears, felt
frightened.

She had not the remotest hope of bringing Horace
to do anything by her own powers of persuasion, and
it was adding to her miseries to think that her father
had any direct interest dependent upon her efforts.
What could he mean by saying that she might make
his fortune—he who was so rich already?

She was pondering over this in helpless silence,
after making the faltering answer that she would do
her best, when M. Macrobe was summoned away by
a servant, who came to say that Monsieur Drydust and
Monsieur Gousset had called to ask for news of the
Duke of Hautbourg.

For news of the Duke! Why should they come
for news of him?

Angélique had not seen the telegrams relative to
the disturbance at Brussels, for, when Horace was not
there to tell her what was in the paper, it was generally
her cousin the Captain who read the chief items of interest to her, and as the Captain was this morning
absent, she had been deprived of this recreation. But
there was something in the word "news," as pronounced by the footman, with an air of bewilderment,
as if he only half understood what the two visitors
meant, which startled her.

"What news?" she asked, forgetting, in her sud-

den stupor, that she had been crying, and that her
eyes were red.

"The gentlemen said news from Brussels, Madame
la Duchesse," replied the servant, with hesitation.
"They spoke of an accident."

"Accident?"   And Angélique rose, her face abruptly bleached of all its colour.

"No, no," ejaculated M. Macrobe, motioning to
the man to withdraw.   But Angélique was too deeply
alarmed to be thus easily pacified, and though her
father attempted to dissuade her, she followed him into
the drawing-room.

Mr. Drydust and M. Gousset were both there,
dressed in that complimentary mourning implied by
grey gloves, and a hat-band, two inches broad.

They pressed forward with looks of condolence
befitting a visit to a house bereaved of an illustrious
member; but M. Gousset did not open his mouth, for
where Mr. Drydust was, a second spokesman was superfluous.   To do the eminent Englishman justice,
however, the sight of the young wife in her woeful
crape dress, and with her terrified countenance, for a
moment paralyzed even *his* eloquent tongue.   But per-
ceiving that there would, after all, be more cruelty in
remaining silent than in speaking, he launched forth,
and described, with picturesque vividness, just as he
had done it already for the behoof of the readers of
his penny paper, the scene at Brussels on the preceding day, the fineness of the weather, the speeches at
the cemetery, the appearance of Albi, his insult of
Horace, the retort, the tussle of the two men at the
graveside (at which Angélique turned icy cold), and
the final climax, where both had been dragged out of

the pit, bleeding, and half-stunned by the fall. Then had followed, it seems, an indescribable uproar—a tumult of shouts and excited recriminations. The great majority, who had not caught the sense of what Albi had said, looked upon Horace Gerold as the aggressor. They regarded his outbreak as a rancorous bit of spite that, considering the circumstances and the place, was ignoble and sacrilegious. He had been hissed as he left the burying-ground, and the event had thrown the whole French colony of Brussels into the wildest state of commotion. But Mr. Drydust knew no more than this, for his important duties did not allow of his absenting himself from Paris more than twenty-four hours, and he had left Brussels by the evening mail, just hearing, as he departed, that a meeting had been arranged between Horace Gerold and Albi for that night or the morrow morning.

Angélique sank on a sofa fainting, and some confusion followed with ringing of bells and racing about to fetch salts and glasses of water. Mr. Drydust, whilst experiencing an artist's pride in the effect his well-told narrative had produced, made himself useful in prescribing the way in which the salt-bottle should be held, the quantity of water that should be used to chafe the temples, and in recapitulating the symptoms of faintness he had observed after violent emotions in other people of his acquaintance. Then, when Angélique had been so far restored as to be able to say it was nothing, and that she should be well again immediately, he offered more valuable consolation by the remark that no news was good news, and that if no tidings had come it was certainly because no disaster had happened.

"You say the meeting was to take place last night or this morning?" said Angélique, trembling.

"I think last night, for it was moonlight, and they would want to get everything over before the Belgian police had time to interfere," answered Mr. Drydust; "but this is the more reassuring as we must have heard by this time had there been any accident."

"Duels between civilians, both ex-journalists, are not very serious," put in M. Gousset, soothingly, with a smile. "I have been in many of them. We penmen bark more than we bite," which was an observation he repented of a moment after, in recollecting the affair between Horace Gerold and the unlucky Government writer Paul de Cosaque.

M. Macrobe was more unsettled by the intelligence just brought than he cared to show; and asked in a low, quick voice, whether Mr. Drydust knew what weapons had been selected, and who were the seconds.

Mr. Drydust did not know about the weapons, but opined they must have been either foils or pistols. His Polish friend, Count Cutandslitski, had fought with a cavalry sabre, and he had been present at the duel of his other friend, El Conde y Colero, y Masticados, y Podagras, who had done battle with his grand-uncle's rapier; but such occurrences were exceptional. As for the seconds, Mr. Drydust had heard that all the Liberals, even one of Manuel Gerold's executors, Nestor Roche, had refused to act for Horace; but as Jean Kerjou was there, and had energetically taken part on Horace's side in the Cemetery riot, there was little doubt that he would be one of the seconds, and probably Emile Gerold would be the other. Mr. Drydust followed up with a story of his Bavarian friend,

Baron Kortpflaster, who had been attended on the ground, in an emergency, by his under-gardener and his head cook.

"At what time does the next train come in from Brussels?" inquired Angélique, resisting her father's advice that she should go and lie down a little whilst a telegram was sent to Brussels with a request for an immediate answer, if Horace had not already left.

"I believe a special train was to leave two hours after midnight, on purpose to bring back the Parisians who had been to the funeral; and it ought to be due about this time," replied M. Gousset.

"Then let us go to the railway-station," pleaded Angélique to her father; "anything is better than this suspense."

M. Macrobe offered no opposition, and the carriage was ordered. But it was not required for this journey, for Angélique had scarcely returned to the drawing-room from putting on her bonnet, and Mr. Drydust was still expatiating to the financier on the possibilities and probabilities connected with affairs of honour, when the unconscious cause of all this anxiety, Horace himself, entered unannounced. He had let himself in with his latch-key, and was accompanied by Emile. His right arm was in a sling. Angélique started, gave a cry of joy, and—for the first time in her life—ran forward to throw herself in his arms. He kissed her, but coldly; and the poor child thought he looked ten years older than when she had seen him last. The men clustered round to shake his hand, and question him about his wound, which he hastened to declare was a trifle.

"And Albi?" asked M. Macrobe, impatient to satisfy his curiosity.

Horace threw down his hat and answered in a way that made his hearers' flesh creep: "After my first duel I promised my father, I would never again take human life. But I have shattered this man's wrist; and if ever again he edits a libel about me, it will not have been penned with his own hand!"

CHAPTER XV.

Sub Rosa.

THIS second duel was the one thing wanted to give the definite stamp to Horace's reputation. The Liberals were unanimous in holding that Albi had been as good as butchered by a bravo; and as Liberals, being the loudest talkers, generally end by imposing their opinions on the rest of the community, so it came to be generally admitted amongst the public, that the eldest son of Manuel Gerold was becoming a dangerous character. At the Café de Madrid, opinions were unshakeable on this point; so unshakeable that Horace's friend Jean Kerjou exchanged warm words, that were nearly begetting warm blows, in trying to din into an obtuse head that Horace had been first insulted, and that anybody else with an ounce of pluck would have acted as he had done. Of course this convinced no one, nor could it be expected to do so, for the question as to who was right in the dispute and who wrong, was quite beside the issues of the case. Albi had obtained twenty thousand opposition votes at the last election, and Manuel Gerold's son

had suffered himself to be returned in the official interest—these were the true bases of the problem; and
the conclusions to be drawn from them self-evident.
In picking a quarrel with Albi and then maiming him,
Horace Gerold had been actuated by the basest motives of personal vengeance, and all talk about provocation received was so much wantonness, a slander
on the fair fame of an ill-used Liberal. By the end
of a week, there was a great majority prepared to
swear that Albi had never unsealed his lips by the
grave-side at all; nay, that Horace had first invited
him to speak and then clutched him by the throat as
he was going to begin.

As for the Government supporters on the Boulevards and in drawing-rooms, they waited before expressing an opinion to hear what the great M. Gribaud
would say, but that statesman having remarked humorously to somebody: "Bah! two Radicals fight and one
wings the other: *c'est toujours une patte de moins,*"
the fiat went forth that there was one Radical paw the
less, and that was all. Some even pretended for a
day or two not to remember which it was that had
damaged the other, a good joke that took very well in
ministerial ante-rooms, and Horace's only champions
were his fellow deputies, who from *esprit de corps* were
naturally pleased that a member of their House should
have bruised one of the outer world; and the women,
who, following the tender bent of their sex, thought
the whole incident sensational and shocking, but admired the hero of it, deeming there was something
mediæval and chivalrous in his readiness to go out and
smash a fellow-being's limbs for a yea or a nay.

The event, however, served to draw down public

attention on Horace in more ways than one. It was
known that the Member for Paris inherited a dukedom
by his father's death, and it was said that he also inherited a large fortune. During Manuel Gerold's life-
time the Clairefontaine mystery, as it was called, occupied few people, for. the reason that Society is not
prone to credit particular individuals with virtues that
it does not possess itself as a body. The construction
put upon Manuel Gerold's self-banishment from Clairefontaine was simply that he preferred spending the
revenues of that estate abroad; and when a few people
hinted that the Republican exile laid out the whole of
his income in charities, Society smiled at such cre-
dulity—many answering that it was a notorious fact
that Manuel Gerold owned a large mansion at Brussels,
that he might be seen driving there any day in a
barouche and four, that they had seen him there themselves—all of which things were religiously believed,
for if it takes a long time to make us swallow truth,
we gulp down slander without asking questions. Now,
however, that Manuel Gerold was dead, and that
people could give him his due without humiliating
themselves, some began to admit that he had really
died in a garret, and that it was a mistake about his
barouche and four. But this only made them the more
anxious to inquire what his son was going to do with
the ancestral property; and they kept their eyes upon
Horace, who, living amongst them, could not hide his
acts under a bushel as his father did.

"It is all on account of ghosts," said Mr. Drydust
confidentially to an admiring circle of listeners.
"Manuel Gerold was superstitious. I never knew a
Republican who wasn't—and he believed Clairefontaine

was haunted. A very curious story, footsteps heard
along the passages at night; a screech-owl making
himself unpleasant at sunset, and so on. The Marquis
of Stronachlachar, who has a castle in the Shetlands,
told me a story like it. His great-grandfather comes
and bays the moon seven days out of every month
under the form of a black sheep-dog.. The keepers
have orders to let him alone. I shouldn't wonder if
the screech-owl were a Gerold who had done something or other in days gone by. All the old families
have an ancestor or two in trouble." And satisfied
with having caused the hair of his gentle hearers to
uncurl itself with horror, Mr. Drydust went home to
write an extremely clever column of ghost legendry,
which was devoured in Islington, Camberwell, and
Upper Peckham; though the denizens of these Drydust-
worshipping localities were informed that "my friend
the new Duke of Hautbourg" was above being frightened
away from his domain by disagreeable peculiarities just
mentioned, and would probably hoist his pennon on
Clairefontaine towers before the year was out. In
fact," concluded Mr. Drydust, "I may inform you
positively that he will do so. It is already announced
that he will stand for the Hautbourg circumscription
at the next elections; and I am told that the famous
upholsterers, the Messrs. Palissandre, have been sent
to the Castle to refurnish it from roof to basement.
Perhaps some of my letters to you next autumn will
be dated thence, as I count on going there for a few
days' shooting."

It would have greatly relieved M. Macrobe to be
as positive about all this as the English correspondent,
for the financier was beginning to see that a great

deal more hinged upon his son-in-law's resolutions
than ever he had intended should be the case. The
Crédit Parisien had been struck a blow in the dark—
a vital blow that astounded M. Macrobe by its sudden-
ness and alarming effects—and the question was now
coming to this:—that unless Horace did what was
required of him, and did it quickly, so as to place
himself on a vantage-ground whence peace could be
made on beneficial terms with M. Gribaud, the Crédit
Parisien might crash down and involve its chairman
in its utter ruin. Bitterly did the latter now curse
himself for the unguarded display of temper by which
he had exposed himself to the animosity of the power-
ful Minister of an autocratic Sovereign. But even the
shrewdest of us commit blunders, and M. Macrobe in
that precipitate moment, when he defied M. Gribaud,
really fancied he was the stronger. He had not given
himself the time to reflect that all the influential men
who supported the Crédit Parisien were the abject
menials of their despotic chief, and that just as in
their own interest they had founded the Crédit
Parisien, so in their own interest they would desert it
at the first frown of the man who held their political
destinies in his hands. The financier saw this now
when it was too late. The credit of the Company
was not yet shaken amongst the bulk of the shareholders; there had been no public panic, but all the
principal holders of scrip were quietly withdrawing
their stake in the game. It was like the departure of
the rats before the crew of the sinking vessel have yet
perceived the leak. Then, there was the more serious
symptom of the breaking off of the bargain concerning
that land which was to have been sold to Government

for magazine building. The land had been bought
at a high price under the certainty that the tax-payer
would be made to purchase it for three times the sum
given; but if this arrangement were cancelled, the
Company must either re-sell the land—and there was
little chance of their obtaining for it the sum they had
paid—or build upon it at their own risks, that is, at
obvious loss, for the quarter was not a likely one for
building speculations. Anyhow, therefore, the operation would bear an ugly look in the next statement to
the shareholders—those statements which the chairman
was wont to make from an enthusiastic platform to an
audience wild with confidence and delight! Yes, there
was ruin lurking under those rocks ahead, towards
which the gale he had invoked was driving the financier; though by ruin must not be understood in this
case pecuniary destitution, for the chairman of the
Crédit Parisien had taken good care that whatever
befell the Company he himself should always remain
well provided for. But the collapse of the Crédit
Parisien would damage him morally, wreck all the ambitious schemes that were his passion; and under the
circumstances his position would perhaps be worse
than if he was beggared. For when a man of restless
mood has more money than he wants, cares nothing
for love, has no artistic tastes, and is so far shattered
in reputation as to find the road to all the honours he
covets hopelessly closed to him, what has he to live
for?

Horace would have pitied his father-in-law if he
could have divined the sickening anxiety that was
gnawing at his heart. But the financier cloaked his
feelings so that there was nothing of them visible in

his face. Only, he was more deferential with Horace than ever, agreed emphatically in all he said, and in the matter of the duel especially gave his approval without stint, in a hearty admiring way which was imitated in various keys by all the members of the household circle. Horace, however, abstained from all mention of the subject that was preoccupying so many heads both under the Macrobe roof and without it. He threw indeed a ray of hope across the financier's path by announcing *proprio motu*, on his return from Brussels, that he should accept the offer of the Hautbourg citizens; but allusions to Clairefontaine seemed tacitly adjourned until the day when the agent to the estate should pay the quarter's rents into the hands of Messrs. Lecoq, Roderheim and Macrobe, and when the latter would have to ask in his banking capacity what was to be done with the money. It was Manuel Gerold who had always disposed of the funds hitherto, for, notwithstanding the deed of gift, his sons had insisted upon charging him with this trust; but for the future Horace and Emile were the masters, and the payments would be made in their name. M. Macrobe looked forward to this day of rent much as a criminal does to his trial.

Meanwhile, he one evening received a call from M. Louchard. That functionary had not been sent for, but sneaked in at nightfall with a false beard on, and giving a card with a fictitious name on it to the servant. A few pencil hieroglyphics on the back of the card, however, revealed his identity to M. Macrobe, and he was at once admitted into the financier's study.

He never looked at peace with himself, did this

official, and on the present occasion he was more than usually agitated, as though he had been followed all the way from the Rue de Jerusalem by one of his own men, and expected to be apprehended by the neck. On the other hand, the troubled glance he cast at M. Macrobe, and the dishevelled appearance of his spurious black beard, might have given one to suppose that he had private orders to arrest the financier and did not like the job.

"M. Macrobe," he began, removing the spectacles that encumbered his eyesight, and staring in alarm at the financier, "you have been quarrelling with M. Gribaud?"

"Yes. How do you know it, and what are your instructions with regard to me?" answered M. Macrobe calmly.

"Not many instructions about you, sir," rejoined the Director of Police, making as if he would remove his beard also, but, on second thoughts, allowing it to remain, as not easy to re-fix. "Not many instructions about you, but we are to send down five men to Hautbourg to sap your son-in-law's candidature."

"That is, to tell lies about him?"

"Well, M. Macrobe, you know how we generally work in such cases. We must say as much good as possible about the official candidate, and spread all the rumours we can about his opponent."

"What kind of rumours, for instance?"

"It all depends on the locality, on the character of the candidate, and on that of the electors," said M. Louchard piteously. "What answers in one case will not always do in the other. This time we have to whisper that your son-in-law is stingy, that he is a

Radical who hoards up all his money, and will never go to live at Clairefontaine because of the expense it would entail. Also, that he doesn't pay his bills, and one of our agents is to pretend to be a small tradesman who has had a debt owing to him for years. This will disgust the men. Then, to put the women against him, we have got to report that—I beg your pardon, sir—that he drinks, and beats his young wife; that he seduced a girl in Paris, and deserted her with her child, refusing to give her a centime; and that he killed two poor men in duels, leaving their wives with children to bring up and no money to do it with. Then we should urge that if the official candidate were elected he would buy Clairefontaine of the new duke, and hold high state there, which, being a rich man, he can afford to do."

M. Macrobe quietly went to his bureau, unlocked a pigeon-hole, and fingered some bank-notes.

"What is the pay of the five men who are to do this work?"

"Bribery is not possible here," answered M. Louchard, with a shake of the head. "Besides, it would be of no use, for the mayors of all the *communes*, the priests, the justices of the peace, the schoolmasters, will every one of them be against Monsieur le Duc. An election in the country is not the same thing as one in Paris; if I were M. le Duc I would retire. The defeat will be certain."

"Here are ten thousand francs," remarked M. Macrobe, paying no heed to what the other was saying. "If I thought they would be of no use I shouldn't give them you. The five men must be bought, and, instead of running down the Duke of Hautbourg, they must

malign his adversary.   Now tell me about the prefect:
what sort of a man is he?"

"H'm, one of the usual sort," replied M. Louchard,
not resisting above a quarter of a minute to the temp-
tation of the notes.   "He has nothing but his pay,
thinks a good deal of himself, and is an ass.   He used
to be a journalist."

"I fancy I remember the man.   Used to be in the
Republican press, then became one of Guizot's semi-
officials; after '51 found himself a Bonapartist."

"Those men are expensive to bribe when they get
to be prefects," observed M. Louchard, despondingly.
"His salary is thirty thousand francs, and M. Gribaud's
rule is inflexible.   A prefect who lets a member of the
Opposition through loses his place."

"Well, listen, Louchard," said the financier, sinking
his tone and speaking quickly: "Gribaud trusts you,
and you have power.   I have put you in the way of a
fair number of good things since we first became acquainted, but all that is nothing to what you will reap
if you serve me in this.   I *must* win this election;—do
you understand; I *must?*   Now manage in your own
way.   Give the prefect his price, and tell him we'll see
he doesn't lose his place.   Buy the sub-prefect of the
arrondissement, and as many priests and schoolmasters
as you may deem it worth while.   I don't care much
about the mayors, for country mayors are dolts, and
obey either the vicar or the school-teacher, whichever
happens to have the most intriguing head-piece.   But
cajole the women.   Women are the hinges of the political door, it won't swing to order without their help.
As to money, I give you carte blanche;   and, if we
win, your own fee, mind, is five thousand napoleons."

M. Louchard was unnerved.

"If we fail it shall not be for want of efforts," stuttered he, drawing out the pocket-handkerchief, which was the signal he hoisted in cases of mastering emotion.

"Yes, but we mustn't fail. You must go to work as I've seen the Government do in past elections. There's no Opposition paper in Hautbourg, of course. You must supply the deficiency with lampoons against the other man. Circulate them widely, slily; have them pasted everywhere in the villages, scattered broadcast in the fields—good, unscrupulous, plain-spoken lampoons such as the peasants will understand and commit to memory. Those were capital lampoons your office circulated against that Orleanist count who contested the Charente last year."

"Ay, they were, and they almost drove the man mad," exclaimed M. Louchard, brightening at the recollection. "It's a very clever fellow who writes them. He is one of our *jays*."

"One of your——?"

"I beg your pardon;"—and M. Louchard grinned slightly—"*jay* is the name we give to the writers of the Opposition press who are in our pay, and whose business it is to sow dissensions in the other camp by accusing the foremost men in the party of being backsliders. The trade requires talent. One of the *jays* shall do us these lampoons. The work will be the easier here, as the Duke's opponent is a stranger to Hautbourg, and there will be no prejudices in his favour to overcome."

"Who is he?" asked M. Macrobe, without interest,

for official candidates were generally the personages
of least importance in the contests to which they lent
their names.

"Why, it's the Prince of Arcola.   Has it not appeared in the papers yet?"

The financier dropped a packet of letters he was
holding.

"The Prince of Arcola!" he echoed pensively.
"What can this mean? Why, he is one of the Duke's
intimate friends."

"He may have been, M. Macrobe; but the friendship has cooled now," answered the police director
glumly. "I heard from M. Gribaud's own lips that the
Prince owed a grudge to the Duke of Hautbourg and
would fight him hotly; and a lady who *notes* for our
office—I may as well give you the name: it's Mdme.
de Masseline—told me that the grudge is one with a
woman at the bottom of it.   Stay, I have it on
paper . . . ."   M. Louchard drew out a dingy pocket-
book and read: "'*When Deputy, Horace Gerold lived
Rue Ste. Geneviève, seduced daughter of his landlord,
draper Pochemolle. Name of girl Georgette, N.S.;*' this
means that there was no scandal, that the neighbours
didn't get wind of it. '*P. of A. took a fancy to Georg.
I. I.:*' that is, in all innocence. '*Proposed to her and
was refused. Bec. mist. 1st lov.:*' because she is still
the mistress of her first lover. '*K. Meudon, styl. dec. 2
par. 1 bro.=resp.:*' he keeps her at Meudon, in a
becoming style, and she has her parents and her brother living under the same roof with her for respec-
tability's sake."

M. Louchard closed his pocket-book and restored
it to its lair, without appearing to reflect that there was

anything in his communication of a nature to jar upon a father's ears. "This accounts for the Prince of Arcola's animosity," he added, sapiently. "He is a very proud nobleman and doesn't like to be crossed."

M. Macrobe had stood staring whilst M. Louchard read his memorandum. He was inclined to credit every word of it, but the circumstances unfolded rather astonished than shocked him—for he was too much of a Frenchman and too little of a moralist to be over-scandalized at his son-in-law's keeping a mistress. What he ruminated was how the intelligence could be made to serve his own particular ends, and this pre-occupation took shape in his next words.

"Do you know whether the Duke goes often to Meudon?"

"I do not, M. Macrobe," answered M. Louchard, "but we could easily find out."

"Yes, I wish you would. Set a man to watch when he visits there, and drop me a line. As for the election, all that I have said before holds good. Commence operations at once, and ply your money cleverly."

M. Macrobe had a second recourse to the pigeon-hole, and M. Louchard, for the second time, drew out his handkerchief.

"There's not a person in the world I would do this for but you," said he, evidently anxious to compound a little with his own conscience. "You act very generously, M. Macrobe, and the pay at the Rue de Jerusalem is not good; indeed, I should have retired ere this, but for expecting the cross of honour and a small pension at the end of my twenty years' service. I risk both those, and my liberty as well, by doing this."

"Nothing venture, nothing have, Louchard; but you will lose nothing if you bestir yourself at your best."

"I will forward you daily reports of the progress we make," said the police director; and with a new attempt at self-compounding, he added: "After all I shall be acting according to my own convictions in helping the Duke of Hautbourg. I am of his opinion in politics. I don't like M. Gribaud."

"You are a Liberal then, Louchard?"

"Yes, and have been from father to son," replied the other, innocently; "and I admire M. de Hautbourg for his spirits. I was at Brussels the other day in a professional capacity and saw the fight in the cemetery. It was like a bull-dog shaking a pole-cat. M. de Hautbourg was very near shaking *me* once in that way; but I have forgiven that little unpleasantness: we were both doing our duty on that occasion."

There was a few more minutes' business conversation, after which M. Louchard made his bow. But on the point of regaining the door he turned round abruptly and ejaculated, "By-the-by, I was very nearly forgetting another matter—the Crédit Parisien."

"What about the Crédit Parisien?" returned M. Macrobe, sharply.

"Well, nothing that concerns me, sir, for when you were obliging enough to let me have those shares, I sold out six months after, as you directed me, and made a good deal by your advice. But I rather fancy M. Gribaud has quarrelled with the Crédit Parisien as well as with you, and I thought you might like being warned."

"What makes you think this?"

"Oh, there are signs by which to detect it," and M. Louchard's false beard smiled. "At the central telegraph station the C. P. telegrams had precedence of all except those of the Government, now they are made to take their chance with the ruck. Then we have our secret inspector of the Bourse, who is a barometer in financial matters. Not so long ago he scowled at one of his subs for saying that the Crédit Parisien was like an overblown balloon, and would burst some morning; yesterday that same sub remarked that the Crédit Parisien was certainly the best thing in the money market, and the barometer scowled again."

"The Crédit Parisien is a granite rock," said M. Macrobe, dismissing his interlocutor, "and next time you have money to spare buy shares in it and keep them. Good evening, Louchard. Don't forget about setting one of your men to watch when my son-in-law goes to Meudon."

The door closed behind M. Louchard, and the financier was left to his reflections. "My son-in-law is a better comedian than I imagined," he muttered. "Fancy his being able to keep a mistress within a year of his marriage, and whilst living under my roof, without my suspecting it! Well, there's comfort to be drawn from the fact in one way. If he makes so light of altar vows, he's not likely to let himself be hampered long by his late father's crotchets."

But M. Macrobe wished to make certain that there was no mistake in this, so he went and found Horace, and said to him at once, without preliminaries: "I

have just been told the name of your opponent: it's
the Prince of Arcola. Have you quarrelled with him?
They say he is very bitter against you."

Horace coloured, and the reply he made was stammered. The fact is, he felt surprised; but M. Macrobe
not unnaturally set it down to guilt. "Louchard was
right," said the financier to himself, whilst a gleam of
genuine satisfaction lit up his face. "Well now, my
son-in-law, this is lucky, for we can oblige you to do
what we desire. A man who wants to seem pure in
public life must begin by being so in private. You
shall take us all to Clairefontaine before long, or else
you will have to reckon with me as your wife's father."

CHAPTER XVI.

Inter Pocula.

UNCONSCIOUS of his father-in-law's suspicions, unconscious of his wife's drift in recurring daily, with
timid persistence, to the subject of Clairefontaine, un-
mindful of that pensive melancholy which was becoming her habitual mood, and which would have excited
the anxiety of a more vigilant husband, Horace was
wrapt in a state of mind that was none of the brightest.
He was conscious of not being happy, of being on the
brink of decisive events, and he asked himself with un-
certainty in his heart what he should do next. A
problem which only the weak pore over, for the strong
solve it at once by instinctive action.

There were few places more propitious for strolling
reveries than the equestrian alleys of the Bois de Boulogne, at that period of the Second Empire when

artistic designs and irresponsible control of the municipal budget had made of that suburban wood the modern
garden of Eden. Horace often rode there of an early
morning, whilst the fauns and dryads that haunt the
sylvan scene in the later day—vulgo the demi-monde
and its worshippers—were yet a-sleeping. . It was
pleasant to amble up the shady avenue of the Triumphal
Arch whilst M. Haussmann's watermen were laying the
dust with their flexible tubes, whilst the milk-carts
rattled into Paris with their hosts of tin cans, whilst
the air was fresh and the singing of the birds as yet
undrowned by the voices of men. In the wood itself
the lilacs put forth their first tender shoots, the drooping laburnums gave early promise of golden blossoms,
the spreading chestnuts ahead of their brother trees
dotted the spongy sand of the rows with white flower-
lets like snow-flakes. Horace had all the alleys to
himself. Not a human being visible, save the wood-
keepers, who, however, are not human, belonging to
the *genus* functionary: or here and there a matutinal
British colonist galloping away his spleen, according to
French notions, or simply giving himself an appetite
for breakfast, if we accepted his own view of the case.

The environs of Paris on the outskirts of the Bois
de Boulogne are so picturesque and varied that Horace
might have struck out a ride of new interest for himself every morning; and, as a matter of fact, he did
spur forward now in one direction, now in another.
But no matter what the line might be that he took up
on starting, the end of his ride always brought him
back to the same point, and that point was Meudon.

He would ride past the house where Georgette
lived, or rein up his horse under a clump of trees, and

survey it from a distance. He loved Georgette; there
was no rooting up that passion from his heart; it had
sprung like a weed, and like a weed it grew; steadily
and irrepressibly. At least, irrepressibly in this sense,
that he made no attempt to check it. He let it quietly
intertwine itself with all his thoughts, and if perchance
remorseful promptings crept up as thorns beside the
weed and threatened to choke it, it was the thorns
and not the weed which he pulled up and cast aside.
It seems a dismal thing that bad passions should thrive
so luxuriantly when good ones are often so slow to
take germ; but so it is all the world over; and in loving
a woman of whom he had no business to think—between whom and him stood the most sacred barrier
that laws and custom could interpose—Horace was
only pointing the old but eternally true story of the
forbidden fruit.

It would have been fair to suppose that the contempt with which Georgette had treated him in that
short, violent scene, which formed the subject of his
bitter musings at Brussels, would have helped to ex-
tinguish his senseless passion. But when did vitriol
ever quench fire? Smarting under the lash of the girl's
reproaches, stung to fury by the falseness of her accusation, he had in a first paroxysm repaid anger with
anger, invective with invective: but once this outbreak
over, he had felt more drawn than ever towards the
woman who spurned him. Georgette seemed to rise
above him in her indignation, and to be only the more
fascinating. Horace was too morally weak himself to
admire weakness in woman. Nevertheless he prowled
about her abode without daring to go in. He would
have had a pretext for a visit, for the draper and his

son had made a special journey to Brussels to attend
Manuel Gerold's funeral, and courtesy required that he
should thank them. But he left cards. When the
servant opened the door and he was about to dis-
mount, he abruptly changed his mind, and gave himself. as an excuse that it was too early for a call, it
being ten o'clock. Perhaps what he trusted to most
was a chance encounter. He might meet her one day
going to visit a neighbour or to mass. Then he would
speak to her, apologize for his insults; exculpate himself from the charges she had brought against him;
say all that men do say who wish to persuade a woman
that they love her. And Horace had a presentiment
that if he could obtain a meeting he should be listened
to; at least in silence, for he knew this much of human
nature—that where indignation is very strong in woman,
love is not quite dead; there is a spark still smoulder-
ing, which can, with a little effort, be revived into
flame. So to increase the probabilities of his chance
rencontre, Horace insensibly lingered a little later every
morning about Meudon, and sometimes would find
himself there long after the hour at which he usually
breakfasted. This occurred a few mornings after he
had heard from M. Macrobe that the Prince of Arcola
had become his foe. Looking at the clock of the
Meudon mairie as he rode down the trim main street
of that toy village, he saw it was nearing eleven. Upon
which he did as was his wont when he had tarried too
long—put up at the chief restaurant of Meudon, to
which a small hotel and stabling were attached, committed his hack to an ostler and ordered breakfast for
himself.

It was a charmingly fresh restaurant, with its pink

and white awning outside, shading a row of white
marble tables, where easy Meudonites were sipping
coffee, bitters, and reading those spicy collections of
false news, mad leaders and improper anecdotes called
French papers. Within, more Meudonites were discussing *déjeûners à la fourchette* at three francs a head,
wine included, and chatting in a neighbourly way to
one another from their respective tables—for all seemed
to know each other in the little place, and it was a
running fire of familiar inquiries, such as "How are
your crocuses coming up this year, M. Marchagy?"
"Captain, I noticed your syringas over the hedge
coming along. How do you manage to make 'em bud
so early?" &c. &c. And presiding over this scene of
comfortable retired tradesmen and half-pay officers, a
smart *dame du comptoir* in flounces, jewelry, and a
slight suspicion of rouge, who favoured Horace with a
gracious bow as he entered, and nodded to a waiter
to hasten and dance attendance on him.

Horace liked this rural restaurant, because he was
not known there, which was more than he could have
said in any public place within Paris, where he could
scarcely have presented himself since his last duel
without being mobbed as a curiosity. He gave his
hat and riding-whip to the waiter, who, in a trice,
had set a table for him, planted a swimming butter-
boat and pink radishes on it, and thrust the *menu* into
his hands. A French waiter always does this with a
glib accompaniment of the names of dishes ready, or
likely to be so, within twenty minutes; and thus did
this waiter, rattling out his items with a jerky action
of the head and many interrogatory pauses. But Horace
was not fated to breakfast alone, for at this moment a

lanky figure emerged from a corner somewhere, stalked giggling across the room, and put out a moist hand to be squeezed.

It was M. Alcibiade Pochemolle.

Now, if there was a person in the world who evoked conflicting emotions in Horace's breast, it was this M. Alcibiade. When Horace thought of Georgette, it was to ask himself whether he would not have done better to marry her; but when his eyes fell upon M. Alcibiade, the reflection that arose was that, if he had married Georgette, this well-meaning but utterly insupportable youth would have been his brother. However, as the paw was there, no course lay open but to squeeze it, and the ceremony was performed with a tolerably successful pretence at cordiality. For this once—and, probably, by accident—M. Alcibiade looked almost a gentleman, being devoid of the scarlet and green scarves, and the excessive hair-oil which were his customary adornments. It transpired later that he had been taking a bath in the river, and considered himself only half-dressed.

"Been up to the house, M. Horace—a—Monsieur le Duc?" he giggled, spasmodically. "No? Then come to have a chop here? That's what I was just going to order myself."

This was apparently designed for a timid hint, and Horace, foreseeing that if not invited M. Alcibiade might possibly invite himself, suggested they could both take their chops together. At the same time, not desirous of being seen publicly banqueting with M. Alcibiade, he remarked on the advantages of a private room, and the waiter was bidden to show them to such a one.

"Yes, a private room's more stylish," approved

14*

M. Alcibiade, raising himself with some little awe on his boot-tips, as if suddenly mistrustful whether the number of his inches qualified him for lunching in private. "But stay, though; I mustn't forget I expect a friend here by-and-by. You won't mind his being sent up to our private room, Monsieur le Duc?"

And M. Alcibiade articulated the words, "Monsieur le Duc," in an audibly stammered tone, with the intention of impressing them upon the waiter, who pricked up his ears.

But the waiter and the rest of the company were much more impressed upon when M. Alcibiade pursued, with the nervous boldness of one who makes a successful maiden-speech in public, "I say, waiter, a gentleman will be asking for me here, presently. His name's M. *de* Filoselle. When he comes, you'll show him up to the private room where I and my friend the Duke of Hautbourg will be eating. Mind you don't make a mistake."

Had the Czar of all the Muscovies or the Schah of all the Persias been announced, their names could not have produced a more galvanic effect. Every fork stopped midway to every mouth; every bottle paused at half-cock in replenishing every glass; the smart lady at the counter made a sudden blot with the pen wherewith she was adding up a bill; and Horace passed through the public room, up to the staircase leading to the *Cabinets Particuliers*, between two rows of fixed eyeballs, like a cutter running the blockade of a double row of forts.

When he had vanished there was a buzz, as of many startled wasps.

"That's the member for Paris."

"Horace Gerold, the new Duke of Hautbourg, who winged the Revolutionist the other day."

"He doesn't look a very pleasant customer, with those black clothes of his, and that frowning face," remarked an ex-blanket vendor, rather scared.

"He is very handsome," put in the smart lady of the counter, scratching out her blot. "I guessed he must be somebody when he first came here."

"Don't say but he hasn't good looks; but what a proud face to him—just as if he was ready to stick one through for a nothing," commented another dealer, also rather scared, and late in the pickle way.

"I've seen him riding about here pretty often lately, —fine nag," observed a retired captain, cross of the Legion of Honour, hair clipped into bristles, purple physiognomy.

"So have I," assented he of the ex-pickles.

"Did you say he rode about here every day?" quickly inquired a sociable stranger, who had entered the restaurant very soon after Horace, and seemed smilingly anxious to strike up a conversation.

"I didn't *say* every day, but I might have done it," returned the captain, with a praiseworthy regard for exactness. "The fact is, the duke *has* been here every day this past fortnight or more, I do believe."

"Ah, dear me!" said the sociable stranger, and he began assaulting a *bifteck* with great vigour. Nobody knew the affable gentleman, but it was noticed by-and-by that he somehow persisted in lingering over his finished breakfast until the Duke of Hautbourg had gone. Then he jumped up, went out and looked very much as if he were following the young nobleman.

Meanwhile, M. Alcibiade, always giggling and moist, was doing the best honour in his power to the breakfast which Horace had ordered, and ingurgitating Rhine wine with the admirable confidence of those who are unused to that class of beverage. He drank it in tumblers: "For," said he practically, "those 'ere long-stemmed glasses do slip about so in your fingers:" which was true enough, for one of the long-stemmed glasses had slipped about so from his fingers on to the floor.

"So you expect Monsieur Filoselle?" remarked Horace, as M. Alcibiade poured down his fourth tumbler.

"Yes, M. Horace—I mean, M. le Duc. This 'ere fizzing hock's good stuff, I've never tasted any of it before," and he smacked his lips.

"Pray let me fill your glass."

"Don't mind if I do, M. Horace—I beg pardon. I wish I could get into the way of calling you M. le Duc."

"Call me M. Horace. I prefer it."

"Oh no, that would never do; a duke's a duke,— hang it!—and it's not every day I get the treat of breakfasting with one, or off such a feed as this. What did you say this here dish was,—salmis of pheasant? Devilish good! But, as you was asking, M. le Duc, I expect Filoselle. And I'll tell you,—I don't mind telling you, for you'll keep a secret—me and him is mounting a plot."

"A plot?"

"Ay" (down went tumbler number five); "you know Filoselle was spoony off my sister. I don't mind Filoselle; he's not of our rank, for we're *rentiers*, and he's

obliged to work for his bread; but he's a good fellar.
When we used to be at the shop, and I was in my
school-days, he used to tip me a *nap.* now and then
when I was hard up. I don't want any of 'em now;
I've got plenty of cash" (M. Alcibiade slapped the twin
pockets of his trowsers, and some loose silver and
copper therein lifted up their jingling voices in testimony). "But all the same, I remember what Filoselle
did for me, and one good turn deserves another. Well,
Filoselle thinks he's been treated shabbily because he
was cut out by the Prince of Arcola. You've heard
about the Prince proposing to Georgette. No? *Tiens,*
c'est drôle, I thought the Prince might have told you,
per'aps, being your friend. Well, he did; he proposed;
came down in the nobbiest trap you ever saw, in black
togs, with his decorations, and pink stockings to his
footmen's legs, quite the swell. And as I said to Filoselle, 'You couldn't expect, old chap, we should think
about you when we had a chance of making Georgette
a Princess. Bis'ness is bis'ness, hang it. However,
Georgette refused the Prince—slap-up she did—told
him she wouldn't have him."

M. Alcibiade heaved a chagrined sigh that de-
generated into a hiccough. Horace was paying the
keenest attention.

"Yes, refused him," continued M. Alcibiade,
lugubriously. "It was a shocking sell for us all.
Mother she became yaller as a quince; father took it
better—said something about it's serving us right; but
I didn't like it better than mother, for I'd already cut
off and told some chaps about it's being cock sure;
and when they see me now some of 'em says, ''Ow

about the Prince?' which, you know, isn't pleasant for a fellar."

M. Alcibiade made an abrupt effort to reach the hock bottle, but only succeeded in knocking over the salt-cellar.

"Allow me," said Horace, replenishing his guest's glass, though not without some apprehension, for the sparkling iced liquid was beginning to produce its effect on M. Alcibiade's manner, but especially on his countenance.

"How hot it is!" exclaimed the latter, when his sixth tumbler had gone at one gulp the way of the fifth; and he drew out his handkerchief to fan himself. As he did so a key fell out of his pocket on to the carpet.

Horace picked it up and restored it to him.

"This is yours, I think?"

"Oh, thank you, M. le Duc—(hiccough)—I mushn' lose that. Admits into our house and garden. It's my latch-key, that I let myself in with when I go to Paris on the spree, and don't return—(hiccough, grin and wink)—t—t—till morning."

The impressed waiter here entered after the cannonball manner of his kind, cleared away the salmi and broken salt-cellar, introduced *omelette soufflée*, Roquefort cheese and pulled bread, and vanished with an order for coffee, *chartreuse*, and cigars. Whilst he was in the room M. Alcibiade endeavoured to maintain a dignified attitude, which resulted in his almost rolling off his chair and having to be propped up. When the waiter was gone, he fell to on the omelette and remarked perplexedly on the giddying properties of fresh air, which had almost knocked him off his chair just now. He rallied at the coffee, perhaps under the influence of a giant glass of seltzer-water, which Horace counselled him to take; and having inserted a flat *panatella* screw-wise into the corner of his mouth, and begun to suck it as if it were a stick of liquorice, showed himself disposed for more talk.

"You were telling me about the interesting plot between yourself and M. Filoselle," said Horace, handing him a lighted match for his cigar.

"Ha, I've got to go on with that—let's see where I was—I was saying how that silly girl had refused the Prince—yes, that's it—and how the chaps was chaffing me, which wasn't pleasant," resumed M. Alcibiade, with intermingled hiccoughing and puffing. "Well, we was down in the mouth for a good ten days afterwards, asking ourselves what she should be so stoopid for, and hoping she would think better of it, and send back for the Prince, but she didn't, but only moped and cried by herself. And then came your father's funeral, M. le Duc, to which me and the guv'nor both went, because M. Gerold (hiccough) once saved the guv'nor's life, and gratitude, as the guv'nor says, ought to come as regular after a good deed, as profits after a good investment. We was at the cemetery, M. le Duc, me and the guv'nor (hiccough), and we was quite close when you grabbed hold of that radical cove by the throstle and tort him to behave himself by rolling him into the pit and yourself on to the top of him. And we waited in Brussels till next day to hear what would come of it, and me and the guv'nor was precious glad when we heard that you'd spoilt his fin for him so that he wouldn't jaw away out of his turn again." (Two consecutive hiccoughs. M. Alcibiade struck a match to re-light his *panatella*, which had gone out.)

"M. Filoselle was at the funeral too. Is that what you were going to say?" interrupted Horace, frowning slightly, and with some impatience.

"Ha, I was coming to that. Yes, M. le Duc, that's just it. We met Filoselle there, too, glum and genteel in his black clothes, but he made believe to be short-sighted and stared the other way when we passed (hiccough), and I don't believe he'd have spoken to us at all, if the guv'nor hadn't waited for him afterwards, and held out his hand and asked him to make it up; for the guv'nor always stuck by Filoselle. Filoselle hesitated a bit, but then gave in and asked how Georgette was, in a stiff-starched voice like. But when he heard how Georgette had turned the Prince off—for the guv'nor spouted it all out—(hiccough); he brightened up—my eye how he did brighten up, and you couldn't have seen him happier if he'd become emperor. 'Ah my adored Georgette!' shouted he, right out aloud; 'I knew you'd remain faithful to your 'Ector;' then he almost blubbed, and so did the guv'nor (hiccough), saying nothing ever came of turning off one man to try and get a better one; and as I knew it was no good hoping to make Georgette understand reason, now, I said the same thing, and we all went and dined together, Filoselle standing treat, for he said he'd been earning cash by the heaps lately. And when the sweets was on the table—*compote d'ananas* and such like—the guv'nor (hiccough) drank Filoselle's health, and said that all might come right yet, and then us three—me, the guv'nor and him—

mounted that plot of ours, which is to help Filoselle to get married, as if nothing had happened."

"How so?" Horace's eyes peered anxiously into the besotted physiognomy opposite him.

"Oh, it's like this, (puff-hiccough-puff), Georgette only told mother, but not father, why she had refused the Prince, but father knows it was because she loved somebody else; and that somebody else can only be Filoselle, as he says, and Filoselle is of the same opinion. But mother wouldn't hear talk of Filoselle yet, for she's too sore about the Prince, and maybe she hopes he'll still come back and get Georgette to accept him—which 'ud be stunning, but too good to be true. So I come here twice a week to meet Filoselle, and take letters from him to Georgette and bring back the answers. This here cigar of mine won't keep alight, (hiccough)—this is the second time I've come. I took a letter last time, and I bring back the answer to-day. That is, I don't bring one, for there wasn't any."

"There was no answer?"

"No," M. Alcibiade grinned, hiccoughed, and put on an arch leer. "Georgette seemed surprised when she got the letter, but that of course was all gammon, such as girls love to play. She won't give me an answer just yet, but by-and-by she will; and meantime I'll warrant she'll get talking mother round on the sly, as Filoselle advises her to do in the letter. My eye, Filoselle does love her, and if you want to see a chap spoony, look at him—he says that the girl who'll turn off a Prince to keep faithful to the man she likes, deserves to be fed on gold out of a diamond spoon, that's what Filoselle says."

Horace swallowed his glass of chartreuse in silence and then said, looking hard at M. Alcibiade: "Did Mademoiselle Georgette refuse the Prince beyond recall?"

"Oh yes (hiccough), cooked his goose completely. Manette, our maid, said a pin's head might have knocked him down when he went out. This here second cigar won't (p-p-puff) draw better than the first —M. le Duc, when a gal is spoony off one chap, it seems it ain't like with us men; she can't abide the sight of the others. I'm not like that—I love all the gals. Still, I bet if Filoselle had had a sister that had been making love to me, and the Prince of Arcola had had another sister that had been doing the same, I should have sent Filoselle's sister to the rightabout in very quick time and not been such a muff as Georgette."

Horace looked at his watch. There was some agitation in his manner.

"I see it is nearly one, M. Pochemolle. You will excuse my ringing for the waiter."

"I wonder at Filoselle not coming yet," hiccoughed M. Alcibiade, "but, by gad, now I think of it, per'aps he may be in the billiard-room all this while, and so missed the waiter." He staggered to his legs. "I say, though, M. le Duc" (this as the bill was being settled) "it's awfully kind of your stumpin' up for me in this way, hanged if it isn't. I owe you a feed, mind, and we'll have some more of that fizzing hock. I shan't forget it in a hurry, that I won't." He clutched at his hat on the peg, but losing his balance at that critical moment, and being obliged to hold on by his head-covering, was within an ace of tearing it in two. "Will you come down and shake hands with Filoselle, M. le Duc?" was his next remark. He was grasping the back of a chair to steady himself, and speaking with a meritoriously determined attempt at gravity.

"I am afraid I must forego that pleasure: I must be at the Corps Législatif at two. Pray remember me to him."

Horace was obliged to submit, not to the hand-shaking, but to the affectionate embrace of M. Alci-biade, whose sole regret was that this brotherly ceremony was not witnessed by the whole population of Meudon assembled. The embrace of a duke had, however, this satisfactory effect, that it for a moment sobered him and enabled him to totter downstairs, holding his head erect, without breaking his neck, thanks partly to the kindly assistance of the waiter, the collar of whose coat he clutched. Horace, having to wait till his horse was round, did not immediately follow him. He paced the small room with an excited step but a beaming eye.

"Then she loves me still as much as ever," were the words he would have doubtless uttered had he spoke his thoughts aloud. "She loves me above everything on earth since she can make such a sacrifice as this for me. And I who accused her of having jilted that wretched traveller so as to win the Prince! I who cast in her teeth that her refusal of the Prince was only a comedy she was playing to some scheming end or other! How see her now to ask her pardon, to make my peace with her and vow that nothing shall ever come between us again. I must see her alone, but how?"

His foot struck against something on the ground.
He looked down.   There was the key which M. Alcibiade ought to have put back into his pocket, but
which he had put on to the carpet instead, his faculties
being absorbed in hock.   The key, M. Alcibiade had
mentioned, admitted to the garden as well as to the
house.   Horace had only to go downstairs to restore
it to the owner.   He hesitated half a moment, and
then kept it.

CHAPTER XVII.

M. Gribaud makes a Speech.

ON leaving Meudon, he rode straight into Paris.
Like most ambitious men, whose range of mind is not
extensive, Horace Gerold could devote himself but to
one thing at a time; but to that thing, whatever it
was, he gave himself up wholly.   When he was pursuing love affairs the entire world might have been
dead for all the thoughts he bestowed upon it; all his
own interests even, except the particular one in hand,
were for the time being banished from his reflections.
On the other hand, when he was engaged in politics,
politics were the only aims he had present before him.
They engrossed him as if he loved them, which he
did not; or as if he understood them, which he did
still less.   Thus it was that twenty minutes after leaving Meudon, where he had resolved that before long
he would see Georgette, and see her alone, he was
riding down the Champs Elysées in a brown study, his
mind already roaming on to scenes where M. Gribaud,
official candidatures, and parliamentary speeches,
played the leading parts, and whence love conse-

quently was excluded. At home he found Angélique not anxious about his absence during the whole morning, as he had rather feared she would be. His morning rides were become so regular; and so regularly did they lengthen every day, that she was resigned to them, never asked where he had been, never showed that she suspected it; but only inquired in her sweet way whether he had had a good ride, and on occasions like the present, when he returned extra-late, whether he had lunched.

Answering both questions in the affirmative this time, he kissed his young wife rather more tenderly than usual. This is a way with husbands who have faithlessness on their conscience; and try to persuade themselves that by simulating a great deal of love, they are making honourable amends for the total want of it. The only possible inconvenience of the system is that of the wife seeing through the device, which generally happens.

"Nothing new, child?" he asked, in appendix to the more than usually tender kiss, and Angélique replied that there was nothing; the remark being echoed by the Crimean Hero, who, astride upon a camp-stool, in the garden, opposite to Angélique and Aunt Dorothée, on chairs, had been reading them the morning papers.

"There has been a shocking murder. An uncle cut into small pieces by his nephew and left wrapped up in bits of newspapers on kerb-stones," ejaculated Aunt Dorothée, dismally. "I shall dream about this to-night."

"Yes, there's that in the way of news," laughed the Crimean Hero, "and amongst the electoral intelligence I see that Arcola has issued his address. You must have had a pretty serious tiff with him, Duke, to bring him up against you like this. Why, not a month ago you were hand in glove together."

"The Prince is a Bonapartist and I am not," answered Horace, uneasily, and taking up the paper.

"The address is tame," observed the Hero, as he saw Horace glancing at it.

"Very," said Horace, when he had read it through; but, perhaps, in his inmost mind he thought differently, for when he went out again to go down to the House, his brow was knit and he stepped out of his brougham, saying to himself that it would be a pretty thing if his political career was to be cut abruptly short by this Prince of Arcola.

It was the first time he had appeared at the Corps Législatif since his father's funeral, and on his crossing the threshold of the Debate Room a hush fell on the assembly, then gathered for the last time prior to the dissolution. Much curiosity was there amongst the honourable members to see how their colleague would disport himself after his famous duel; some anxiety to behold whether his ducal honours had changed him, and whether he would be as much of a Radical as before. The Ministerialists on the extreme Right, who knew no compromise with duty, but voted fearlessly before God and man as they were ordered to do, wondered how M. Gribaud would bear himself towards the new duke. They had heard that M. de Hautbourg was to be opposed by Government, but they were half prepared for some touching scene of reconciliation on this last day. A solemn recantation of errors on the one hand, a magnanimous absolution on the other;

much as on the breaking-up day at a private school,
the boy who has been unruly during the half-year
makes his humble *mea-culpa*, and promises to behave
better next term on condition of not being expelled.
Indeed, the proceedings on the closing day of session
in the Corps Législatif, closely reminded one of going-
home-day in a well-conducted academy for young gentlemen. First, the head-usher, Minister M. Gribaud,
made a speech, shortly summarizing the events of the
term, complimenting the pupils on the amount of work
they had done, and extolling the virtue of obedience,
without which no progress is possible. Then the best
pupil in the school—that is, the most prominent member
on the Right—rose, and bore grateful testimony to the
assistance received during work-hours by their much-
esteemed teacher. He hoped M. Gribaud had found
no reason to complain of the conduct of his school-
fellows, and promised on their behalf that they would
endeavour to merit his approbation, both by studious
attention to his precepts during the recess, and by
diligent practice of the same when they returned to
their work next half. Lastly, the Head-Master, President, blandly reminded everybody that they would
go back to the bosom of their families with that satisfaction which the accomplishment of duty always brings
—the *mens conscia recti* of which the poet speaks. He
had nothing more to say but to wish them pleasant
holidays, and hope that next time he and they met
again, he would see them all in the enjoyment of good
health; and so:—

Ite domum, saturæ; venit hesperus; ite, Capellæ.

Horace's arrival did not interrupt this programme,

for nothing had yet commenced. The boys were empty-
ing their desks of their contents and making convenient bundles of them to carry away. Some amused
themselves by turning the keys of their desks in the
locks, making *snap*, *snap* noises. The keys were to
be left in the desks to-day, and not carried away, so
that there was no harm in damaging them. Everybody
was more or less eccentrically attired in shooting-coats
and coloured shirts, indicative of precipitate departure
to the railway-station as soon as the school-gates
should be opened; and everybody was talking at his
loudest, until the entry of the unruly pupil produced
the lull already mentioned.

Then, just as at school when the unruly pupil appears, all the other boys who are in disgrace instinctively rally round him in order to feel less isolated in
their guiltiness; so when Horace took his seat he at
once became the centre of a group of some thirty or
forty honourable members, who, having either made
incautious speeches, or so far forgotten themselves as
once or twice to vote wrong; or been in any other way
disobedient to M. Gribaud, during the past session, were
aware that they would be left to shift for themselves at
the next elections. Amongst these were the Alsatian
count who wanted Protestant school-teachers, the Gascon
marquis who wished to have his brother made a Catholic bishop, and numbers of other worthies of the
same calibre. All these gentlemen were vehemently
opposed to the system of official candidatures. They
had been official candidates themselves; but that didn't
matter. Liberalism simmered in their patriotic souls.
They were full of the people's rights. They could no
longer conscientiously submit to see France deprived

of her just liberties. Next session when re-elected—and every one of these interesting neo-liberals made certain that he would be re-elected—they would form a constitutional-opposition party of which they trusted M. le Duc de Hautbourg would assume the leadership; and they would turn out M. Gribaud, not a doubt of it.

A peculiarity about these gentlemen was that, although each felt sure of his own return, they all struck commiserating attitudes in alluding to one another's chances.

"So Gribaud is going to oppose us? Well, I don't care for myself; in fact, I wouldn't have accepted Government assistance, if it had been offered me. But it's uncommonly hard on you—you who only got in by an ace last time, with the bishop, prefect, and two hundred mayors, all pushing you together."

Horace was favoured with condolences of this pattern by the whole of the forty.

"A crying shame, I call it, Monsieur le Duc."

"I'm proud to say Gribaud hasn't insulted *me* with any offers of patronage, else I would have cast them back in his face, after the manner in which he has behaved towards you." (This from a deputy who an hour before had told M. Gribaud that he had a wife and family, and that the loss of his seat would be beggary to him.)

"It seems, M. le Duc, that the Prince of Arcola is making himself very popular at Hautbourg. He has gone down there for a canvass, and is sowing his money broadcast." (This was a charitable fiction, invented on the spot.)

15*

"I hear he is going to build them a new church."
(Other charitable invention.)

"I despise the Government that sanctions bribery."
(This from an honourable member who, on his last
return had, under Government sanction, invested ten
thousand francs in corduroys, five thousand in felt hats,
eight thousand in new vestments for rural clergy, and
kept seventy-seven parishes drunk on the day of poll
from morn till even-tide.)

"I never felt any esteem for Gribaud. Did you
see what an insolent look he gave you, M. le Duc?"

"Ay, he would have deserved a slap on the face
for that look."

"And would have got it, if he had given it me."

Now here was another fiction. In order to reach
his place Horace was obliged to pass M. Gribaud, and,
in so doing, habitually favoured him with an inclination of the head, which the Minister, of course, returned. But his Excellency's bows were far from insolent, or even stiff. They were the cautious bobs of
a statesman who, with not much diplomacy to aid him,
had got to steer his way between excess of affability
and the counter-excess of reserve. M. Gribaud had no
desire to take up the cudgels with Horace. If the
latter would koo-too to him, he asked for nothing more.
As to his opposing him at Hautbourg, that was a trifle,
for Horace had only to make his submission any time
before the poll to be hoisted into a seat somewhere or
other—only the seat would not be Hautbourg, if M.
Gribaud could help it. It would be a seat whence
Horace could be turned out on misbehaviour—say one
of those halcyon constituencies near the Pyrenees, where
the wittiest nation under heaven went to the poll in

droves of a thousand heads, and, on a wink from their
prefect, would attach thirty thousand names to a petition, calling upon their deputy to resign his place, or
leave off making speeches against the Government. M.
Gribaud infused all these sentiments into his bow,
which would have been a very essay on Imperialist
statecraft if bows, like verbal utterances, could have
been taken down in short-hand. And the Minister did
more, for, in the usher-like speech to his pupils going
home, he held out the fold of salvation to Horace,
offered him extrication from the Radical whirlpool
where he was floundering, and a safe standing-ground
on the *terra firma* of Bonapartism.

"I cannot conclude," said he, amidst the loud,
long, and continued cheering which had greeted the
first part of his oration, commenting upon the in-
dustrious labours of the session,—"I cannot conclude
without a reference to one of our young and distinguished colleagues, whom we all rejoice to see in
his place to-day, after the recent heavy domestic
calamity which has overtaken him. (Hear, hear.) Gentlemen, I need not say that, in his bereavement, the
honourable gentleman has our most heartfelt sympathies. It was my fortunate privilege to be, at one
time, bound by ties of close friendship with the
eminent Patriot who has died upon a foreign soil, and
though we were afterwards estranged from each other
by those differences which, alas! too often divide
public men—for, in devoting ourselves to our country's
welfare, gentlemen, it is seldom that we are not compelled to sacrifice our private feelings—I can say that
no one regretted the circumstance more than myself;
that no one felt to the last more admiration for the

chivalrous illusions of the statesman, more reverence
and affection for the personal character of the man.
(Loud cheers.) I would it were possible to pass unnoticed an event with which the lamented decease of
our great countryman is in some way associated—I
mean the scene that attended that noble Patriot's
funeral; but I feel that to do so would be to miss the
occasion of deducing a moral, which I hope our
honourable colleague will lay seriously to heart. There
are political classes and political theorists with whom
no man can sympathize. (Loud and prolonged cheering.) Our honourable colleague has been able to
judge for himself what is the worth of the fraternity
which these persons preach and never practise. But
let him be assured that, in that party, such men are
not the exception: they are the rule. It is the party
of envy, calumny, and incapacity, the party where
every man thinks himself born with a soul to com-
mand, who has not even the patience, fortitude, and
modesty to obey. For men of mere honesty to ally
themselves with this faction is to risk contamination in
its most insidious forms; but for a man who is gifted
with youth, a great historical name, and surpassing
talents to lend even his fellowship to it, would be a
thing in every way sad and deplorable. It would be
the wreck of a promising career, which might shine
with a peerless lustre if devoted to the cause which
we on these benches serve—that of order, of justice,
of the prosperity, and true greatness of France."

(Enthusiastic and continued cheering from the legislators on the right. The forty malcontents, clustered
together in a lump, sneer, snigger, dig their elbows
into one another's ribs, and whisper "Gammon!")

Half-an-hour afterwards the portals had closed upon Horace's first session as a law-maker. Vehicles of every description were scurrying away from the door of the House to the four great termini. Honourable ex-deputies were bidding each other good-by and good luck; and Horace himself, ex-member for Paris, sauntered eastwards through the streets of the Circumscription which he no longer represented. There was a crowd collected without the gates of the building to watch the deputies disperse, and as every one of these gentlemen was cordially and contemptuously detested by the Radical element of the Parisian population, Horace benefited by the contrast which his relative liberalism afforded, and was cheered by about two dozen gamins. As he lifted his hat in acknowledgment of this cheap ovation, he remembered that on that same spot, many years before he himself was born, his father had been rapturously acclaimed by a countless multitude stretching as far as the eye could see. It was under the reign of Charles X. when outspoken Liberals were few, and when every parliamentary session offered a series of stirring popular triumphs to those who dared speak. How different his father's beginning from his own! Yet, the liberal cause had even greater need of champions now than under the Bourbons, and a career as distinguished as his father's had been open to him had he chosen to follow it. Why had he not?

Then came the reflections—But what had Manuel Gerold's career, what had his speeches and example profited, since France was in 1857 politically lower than in 1827? Was it worth while to preach freedom all one's days, to see it at last strangled in a night by

a crew of adventurers who, red-handed after the murder, had only to appeal to the nation to be forthwith
absolved by seven million voices!   Amongst those
seven millions there were assuredly many who, before
cheering the hero of the *coup-d'état*, had cheered
Manuel Gerold; and was it not the vanity of vanities
to endeavour to please such weathercocks?   Horace
asked himself whether his father would not have done
more for the true interests of France if, instead of advocating an ideal Republic for which men were not
yet ripe, he had accepted the forms of Government
existing, and applied himself to improve, without sub-
verting, them.   If, for instance, all the men of intellect who assailed the dynasty of Louis Philippe (and
Manuel Gerold was of the number) had joined in con-
solidating it, the senseless revolution of '48 would
never have happened, and in 1857 France would have
been in the enjoyment of one of the freest constitutional monarchies in Europe.   "My father was ahead
of his time; I will keep on a level with mine," mentally ejaculated Horace.   "If France is not Republican,
why should I be?   The majority of the country accept the Empire: they vote for it, they prefer it to
other forms of Government: I may be of a contrary
opinion, but as a citizen the most patriotic thing I can
do is to submit.   They talk to us of the prosperity of
England, but England is only prosperous and free because the minorities there have learned to obey the
majorities.   Every man does not set up a standard of
government for himself, and try and force it upon his
fellows.   Where is the inducement to the men who
rule us to give us liberties if we say: 'Whatever you
do, whether you govern us well or ill, we will combat

you?' Systematic opposition excuses systematic despotism. An Englishman in my place would manage
to be loyal and liberal at the same time:—liberal from
principal, loyal from expediency. So will I be. By
loyalty is not meant servility; I shall be no official
candidate or supporter of Gribaud's. I will struggle
to establish in France the parliamentary liberties which
our neighbours have: and if I succeed I shall have
spent my life to better purpose than as a Republican
agitator, hurrying on my countrymen by utopian doc-
trines to bootless revolutions."

He quickened his pace. There were seductions
enough in the career of French Whig, which he was
sketching out for himself: it led to honours, and
power, in the first place, to reputation in the next.
But it was indispensable that he should not lose his
seat in the House; and, here, the dispiriting prognosti-
cations of his forty malcontent colleagues of a sudden
chilled him. They had done their very utmost as
good colleagues that they were to represent his case
as desperate, and as he was in total ignorance of the
steps which M. Macrobe had taken to ensure his return (to do him justice, he would never have lent his
countenance to those steps), he saw the Prince of
Arcola in his mind's eye as already triumphant. There
was but one way— one infallible way—to prevent that
triumph, and Horace shook off the last relics of re-
pugnance which he had for it.

"I must go to Clairefontaine," murmured he resolutely. "The estate is mine. It was unjustly con-
fiscated by the ruffians of '93, and if it was bought
back with slave money, the five million francs we have
paid to charities during the last five years are a suf-

ficient expiation. There is not another family would have done so much. And besides, in my hands the estate will be an instrument of good: I shall use the influence it gives me for the welfare of France."

And he shaped his course towards the Law Courts, where he hoped to find Emile.

CHAPTER XVIII.

Manuel Gerold's Sons divide his Inheritance.

"I THINK you will find Maître Emile Gerold in the Second Chamber," said an affable Briefless, in the Pleaders' Hall.

The Second Chamber was one of the Civil Courts, and not often crowded. Horace proceeded to it, pushed the folding doors, and entered into quasi solitude. The auditory was scantily attended, the barristers' benches almost empty; but the judges were at their post,—seven of them—and, what is more they were all attentive.

Emile was speaking.

Horace subsided noiselessly into a seat, and behind him heard the following muttered dialogue between a shabby man who took snuff and an old woman who complained of rheumatics:—

The Shabby Man.—"Hark to him there, Madame Pomardier, he has made another point. His logic's close."

The Rheumatic Woman. — "Mon dieu, Monsieur Garbillaud, I knew that the young man had talent, and that's why I said to the poor young thing: 'My dear, if you *will* go to law—though, in my opinion, going to law for justice is like going to a puddle for spring-water—I'd see young M. Gerold. He won a suit for some neighbours of mine, poor bodies, that would never have had a sou to this day if it hadn't been for his taking up their case; but that, my dear, doesn't prove that he'll get you righted, for good luck doesn't come twice in one season,' said I."

The S. M.—"Hark to him again, Madame Pomardier. That last argument came pat down on the nail. Do you take a pinch?"

The R. W.—"Thank you, not any for me, M. Garbillaud. There is that Municipal Guardsman who has swung open that door again: that man can never have had the rheumatics to let in draughts of cold air as he does. Well, as I was saying, the poor young creature she would go to law for, says she: 'Madame Pomardier, there must be a God in Heaven to prevent the weak being wronged;' and said I, 'My dear, about there being a God in Heaven I don't doubt, but as to his interfering with these sort of matters I don't believe it's his way, for,' says I, 'if I was to count up on my fingers all the folk I've seen get less than they deserve, and all the other folks I've seen get more than they had a right to, I shouldn't have fingers enough, and I should be sorry to say that all was God's fault, my dear, it would be laying too much on Him.' However, good words never yet mended sore trouble. She said she had right on her side, and so far as that goes, it would be a sin to gainsay her. She was properly married to her dead husband, and for that man's family to say that she wasn't and that there was some irregularity in the wedding, owing to its having been done abroad, and for them to seize that pretext to try

and take away from her the two thousand francs a
year, that ought to be hers, and her title of wife and
widow which is what the poor young creature most
cares for, is a crying shame as I do say; and so did
M. Gerold say it when she went to him about it. And
I declare it goes to one's heart, it does, to see the
way the poor thing is looking at him, there, as he
speaks for her—see, M. Garbillaud."

Horace followed the direction of the worthy Madame Pomardier's glance, and saw a slight young
woman with a careworn face, dressed in deep black
and holding a child of three or four on her knee, and
gazing at Emile with an expression of anxiety and
yearning suspense utterly impossible to depict. She
seemed to be restraining her breath, lest the faintest
sound should prevent her defender's voice from reaching the judge's ears; and when he produced any telling
argument, looked from him to them with suppliant,
wistful inquiry to see whether they were attending and
had caught the words; and then from the judges to
her child as though to mark whether, young as he was,
he did not understand that it was his mother's honour
that was being debated. Horace turned from this
group to Emile, who was speaking as he always spoke,
unaffectedly and persuasively. His manner was not
that of some of his more eminent colleagues who pocket
an enormous fee, read your brief half through, and
plead your cause like a tired parson reading the evening lessons. There was, probably, no fee at all in
this case, but the brief had been read through, every
line; and more than read through—pondered over long
and thoughtfully, for the words in their eloquent
earnestness flowed limpid and unhesitating, coming

from a mind and heart both full of their subject. There would have been a fine opportunity for a true Radical barrister to have howled democratic platitudes, shrieked anathemas against the rich who trample down the poor, and earned the good graces of the gallery by insulting the judges. But Emile as usual neglected this mode of serving his client's interests. He was modest and respectful towards the judges; and the result was no failure, for when the Imperial Magistrates returned from their council-room, it was with a judgment for the Plaintiff, on all points.

The young woman rose with her child in her arms, tottered forward to grasp the hands of her defender and swooned at his feet.

Emile lifted her gently, committed her to the care of some friends amongst ·whom the worthy Madame Pomardier, who was blessing his name aloud; and came away, happy from his humble triumph but courting no thanks. Horace met him at the door.

It was evening and the courts were being closed, so after Emile had unrobed himself in the vestiary, the brothers set off for the Rue Ste. Geneviève, where Emile still resided notwithstanding that the retirement of M. Pochemolle had given him a new landlord. This new landlord, was also a draper and kept the name of Pochemolle with the sign of the Three Crowns over his door as of old, the privilege of doing so having been conceded to him for an increase of purchase money. This practice, by the way, is not an uncommon one in trade, and nobody ever appears to suspect that writing Pochemolle over a house where Pochemolle no longer flourishes, has the same sort of morality about it as pasting "Old Port" on a bottle that does not contain that beverage. On the way from the Law Courts, Horace did not allude to the subject which had brought him to see Emile. He talked about the trial with emotion and admiration; and was still full of the topic when he found himself seated in his old quarters in the lodgings on the third floor above. Nothing was changed there any more than downstairs, where Horace had almost expected to see Georgette seated at her counter behind the window and look up at him as he passed. At Horace's marriage, Emile had removed into his rooms, abandoning his own to a stranger, and there stood all the things as Horace had left them, books, pictures, the table where Georgette used to lay his letters; and the shelves off which she had helped him collect the prohibited writings, that day when she had come to warn him of the domiciliary visit: "Why, I declare you even use my old pen-holder," said he, glancing at the desk and smiling at Emile.

"My favourite pen-holder," answered his brother affectionately.

Horace took up a roll of paper that lay on the sofa—it looked like a music roll—and, playing with it mechanically, said: "And do you mean to cleave for ever to these rooms and to this life, old fellow? I was listening to you to-day. There is not a man in the Corps Législatif who can speak as you do, and I don't believe there are three at the Bar who can speak better. Everything would be open to you if you had any ambition. Do you remember my asking you some time ago what your day-dreams were? You surely have some visions of greatness, glory, or public usefulness?"

As if to answer Horace's question, a waiter from

a neighbouring cookshop at that moment appeared with a basket containing Emile's dinner—the fare of an anchorite; and whilst this pitifully frugal repast was being set on the table, flanked by a half-pint decanter of the commonest *vin ordinaire*, a poor-looking girl of twelve, who had come in behind the waiter, and turned suddenly shy at beholding a stranger, stammered: "Mother said you had left word I was to call for some wine, M. Gerold."

Blushing as if he were being caught in a mean act, Emile went to a cupboard and drew out two bottles with the well-known crimson seals of the *Château Lafite*, also a parcel. The girl seemed doubtful about the parcel being for her; but Emile whispered something, and the girl withdrew, thanking and curtseying. The same instant entered the concierge.

"M. Emile, there's that cripple down below who called the other day. He wanted to thank you for what you had sent him, but couldn't get through the streets fast enough to be at the door against your return. As he isn't able to climb the staircase, he asked me to come up.and say how much obliged he is to you."

"You see," said Emile to Horace, and reddening anew, "you have lighted at the hour when I sometimes receive visits." And as he was speaking the door opened before a third applicant. This time it was a young and intelligent workman in a blouse. He had some books under his arm, and had come to return them, as well as borrow others.

"Well, Denis," said Emile, when the workman had chosen the volumes he wanted—volumes of Diderot's *Encyclopédie*—"I hope you and your friends have

settled matters amicably with your employers, and that
there will be no strike?"

"We feel that we have a grievance, M. Gerold,"
answered the workman, in a frank, respectful voice.
"The profits of our employers have gone on increasing,
and so has the price of living, yet the wages in our
trade have not changed since the last ten years. But
I have told the men what you thought, and they deputed me to say that they would be guided by you,
and that if, after giving them a hearing, you were of
opinion that their present demands were not fair, they
would modify them."

Horace had not uttered a word during this succession of interviews; but whilst the workman was
speaking he opened the scroll he had taken up. It
was an address signed by five thousand mechanics of
the Tenth Circumscription, and offering Emile their
suffrages for the seat which he himself was about to
vacate. The memorialists wrote that they had been
reluctantly compelled to vote against M. Horace Gerold
at the last election, being persuaded that his views did
not tally with theirs, but they had the utmost confidence in the principles of M. Emile, and, if he would
come forward, undertook to return him free of expense. Horace laid down this document with feelings
easy to understand; and watched the workman take
his leave: which he did with the air of a man who
bows to nothing save intellect, but bends the knee before that.

When he was gone Horace took up the scroll again.

"And have you accepted this offer?" said he to
Emile.

"Accepted an offer that contains an implied slight

on you!" answered Emile sadly and a little reproach-
fully. "You could not think it. In so far as public
opinion is concerned together we stand or fall."

"Yes, we will, will we not?" exclaimed Horace in
an outburst of eagerness, laying his hand on his
brother's shoulders. "Let us stand by each other,
Emile; and we may attain fame side by side. I have
resolved upon going to Clairefontaine, and do you
come with me. Our landed interest can ensure our
being both elected in the department, and we can
labour together for the true interests of France, and
for the glory of our own family name. Whilst our
father was alive I respected his ideas about Clairefontaine, but by renouncing that estate any longer we
shall be discarding the means of doing a great good:
we shall be like soldiers throwing away their best
weapons before battle."

He spoke at length and enthusiastically, unfolding
all the plans he was forming, and revealing new ones,
as they started extemporized to his brain. The immense services that could be rendered to the Liberal
cause was the chord on which he harped most strenu-
ously, knowing that it was the one which would strike
the surest echo; and the burden of his whole discourse
was that for such an end as that any honourable means
were justifiable.

Emile listened to him without apparent surprise,
though not able to repress the shade of disappoint-
ment that stole over his face.

"I was prepared for your resolution about Clairefontaine," said he quietly. "And the moment you
differed from any of the opinions which rendered the
sacrifice imperative on our father, a like sacrifice ceased

to be binding upon you.   But it gives me some pain, dear fellow, to think of your rallying to the Second Empire; I would have heard a great deal of bad news sooner than that."

"But I don't rally in the sense of liking or respecting this régime, nor for my own profit," exclaimed Horace.   "Why, man, to take a comparison, I shall only be doing what you did this very afternoon.   Did you respect the judges before whom you pleaded? You know what kind of men the Empire has placed on the judicial bench, yet in your client's interest you silenced all your own feelings, spoke reverentially to these men, and won your cause.   Well, France will be my client; I will plead for her rights, and in order to obtain them will defer to those who hold her freedom in their keeping.   That is all."

The comparison was not inapt, but it failed to shake Emile, who answered: "We cannot always make our sentiments fit with logic; and perhaps I shall have given you the best of my reasons when I say that as our father's bones must rest in exile so long as this Empire lasts, I could never have the courage to support it.   Then, I do not believe the Empire will ever restore our liberties, for those who respect freedom do not begin by destroying it. But supposing I should be mistaken it seems to me there would still be grounds for refusing our allegiance.   The establishment of the Second Empire was one of the most wanton outrages ever perpetrated upon a peaceful community, and it is like offering a premium for such acts when honourable men lend their countenance to those who commit them."

"That is all very well," cried Horace excitedly,

"but the remark may be reduced to this: that you would rather see France fettered under the Second Empire than free from it?"

"Yes, I would," replied Emile firmly. "I think in the first place our country should learn what it costs to set up a despot; and in the next I would not let crowned desperadoes suppose that they may be left to reign in peace by restoring liberties which they have dishonestly plundered. Of a robber we ask more than restitution, we demand atonement. I would have patriots hold aloof from the authors of *coups-d'état*—leave them to themselves until they fell by their own weakness, or finished as they began, in violence."

There was a silence. Emile had spoken with perfect calm, but with a kindling light in his eye—just the light that comes of immovable purpose assailed by sharp arguments, the spark that flashes between flint and steel. Horace exclaimed dejectedly: "It is no use trying to convert you. You reason like a man who sets up an ideal world for himself, and will not see that you can benefit your species more by taking account of their foibles and errors and bearing with them, than by preaching to them a standard of political excellence that is quite beyond their reach. Progress does not fly on the wing, it plods on tediously. In a hundred years men will not yet be ripe for the republic you propose. Why then sacrifice your life to it? Look at our father's career. What was it?—a pure and generous one; but whom has it benefited?"

"Every lover of what is good," answered Emile, quickly. "Every man who proposes to his fellows a high standard of excellence in politics, art, or social conduct is a benefactor of humanity. And what does

it matter if our father's example has found few imita-
tors? Did Raphael paint his 'Transfiguration' in vain
because no picture like it has since been produced; or
did Milton write to no purpose because *Paradise Lost*
will remain unrivalled? The life of an honest man is
a beautiful poem; and every human being who reads
it will feel better, stronger, more hopeful from it. But
even if none understood the life, and if none were
found to take pattern by it, there it would still remain
—the highest, finest, and noblest work of God." He
took down from a shelf one of the early editions of a
book, then but lately published, and interdicted in
France, Victor Hugo's *Châtiments;* and pointing to a
page, said, "Read this passage. Do you think this
will be thrown away? It will redeem our character as
a people in the eyes of future generations. When
historians write that seven million Frenchmen fell down
and worshipped the man who enslaved them, it will be
remembered that there was a patriot who wrote this,
and that he found companions, our father amongst
them, and the memory of these few men will save a
whole nation from odium."

Horace read the verses. They were the immortal
lines of the poet speaking in his exile:

> Devant les trahisons et les têtes courbées
> Je croiserai les bras, indigné mais serein ;
> Sombre fidélité pour les choses tombées,
> Sois ma force et ma joie et mon pilier d'airain !
>
> Oui, tant qu'il sera là, qu'on cède ou qu'on persiste,
> O France, France aimée et qu'on pleure toujours,
> Je ne reverrai pas ta terre douce et triste ;
> Tombeau de mes aïeux et nid de mes amours !
>
> Je ne reverrai pas ta rive qui nous tente,
> France, hors le devoir, hélas ! j'oublirai tout ;
> Parmi les éprouvés je planterai ma tente ;
> Je resterai proscrit, voulant rester debout.

J'accepte l'âpre exil n'eut il ni fin, ni terme:
Sans chercher à savoir et sans considérer
Si quelqu'un a plié qu'on aurait cru plus ferme,
Et si plusieurs s'en vont qui devraient demeurer.

Si l'on n'est plus que mille, et bien j'en suis, si même
Ils ne sont plus que cent, je brave encore Sylla:
S'il en demeure dix, je serai le dixième:
Et s'il n'en reste qu'un, je serai celui-là.

"Well, I have nothing more to say," replied Horace, closing the book. "I see we must walk our separate ways. If I am wrong, let me bear the consequences; but I am acting for the best. I have no vocation for the life you would lead: to adopt it would therefore be hypocrisy. In a few days I shall start for Clairefontaine. My wife and my father-in-law both urge me to this course, and it would have given me strength and courage if your good wishes had accompanied me."

"My good wishes you have," exclaimed Emile, earnestly; "and my approval, too, if you are following the bent of your conscience—a man's best guide. Besides you are my brother, and if your opinions were ten times more opposed to mine than they are, I would still wish them success for your sake."

"And what do you mean to do with your own share of the estate?" asked Horace, a little moved; "remember half of it is yours."

"I had almost forgotten it," answered Emile, with a sigh; and he began reflecting a moment: then turning with an appealing look of affection to his brother, he faltered: "Look here, Horace: you won't think I am trying to sermonize you or put you to the blush; but don't ask me to have anything to do with this money. You say the landed influence of Clairefontaine is what you most want: well, then, let the whole estate remain yours. And as to the revenues of that part of it which would have been mine, dispose of them as you will: I give them over to you in trust for the public good— yes, for the public good."

He laid both hands on his brother's shoulders and kissed him, impulsively, fervently.

In this way they parted; but when an hour or two later the waiter from the cookshop returned to fetch his plates away, he found the dinner standing untasted as he had laid it. Emile was sitting by the open window, his arms resting on the sill and his head buried in them.

"Don't you dine, sir?" asked the waiter, coaxingly.

Emile started, and the question had to be repeated. Then he answered absently that he had no appetite. The epilogue to which was that on reaching the cookshop the waiter observed, "That poor M. Emile does take on terribly about his father's death. I found him broken down like just now, and I'll stake my head he'd been crying."

CHAPTER XIX.

Angélique's Confession.

CERTAINLY the most edifying priest in Paris was Father Glabre of the Reverend Society of Jesus. He had a voice like a sweet barrel-organ, a smile that did one good to witness, and walked the road to the Kingdom of Heaven in polished leather shoes. This holy man's church was that of St. Hyacinth, and on the Sundays when he preached there was a great tail of carriages stretching outside the church-door on both sides of the street, and footmen in plush hanging about the porch enough to make a goodly battalion. But Father Glabre was seen to greatest advantage on "Confession Mornings." Confession mornings were Wednesdays and Fridays. On those days Father Glabre gave ear to the sins of his flock, chided gently and bestowed absolution. It is to be supposed that the male element in the St. Hyacinth congregation were either singularly free from human error or lamentably blind to their own short-comings, or painfully remiss in their religious duties; anyhow no trowsered penitent was ever seen to kneel in Father Glabre's confessional and declare himself a miserable sinner. But the women made up for this. What a throng, and what devotion! What a rustling of silk-dresses, what contrite rows of six-buttoned gloves clasped daintily over velvet missals, what pretty attempts to corrupt that righteous servant of the church, the beadle, in order to secure a privileged seat whence one might dart into the tribunal of repentance out of one's turn! There were so many ladies that it was a sort of point of honour between them that none should take more than five minutes over the recital of their sins. Most of them cheated and took ten minutes, and said even then that they had not half done; which used to make M. Gousset remark, that, next to the pleasure of sinning itself, there was nothing women liked better than remembering their sins and talking about them. This M. Gousset used to make other impertinent speeches. To one lady acquaintance who told him she was about to confess herself, he had been known to say: "I protest against your going and demoralizing that good man;" and to another who had just come from confession: "And how did the poor fellow bear up against it?"

The church of St. Hyacinth was in the same quarter as the Hôtel Macrobe, and one of Father Glabre's most punctual parishioners was Angélique. She was punctual in this sense, that she and her aunt had sittings close to the chancel, and might be seen in them every Sunday morning at high mass, whether the reverend father preached or not. But she did not often attend confession, and when she did, had more than enough with the regulation five minutes. The fact is, she scarcely understood the ceremony. She had a kind of idea that those of her own sex who did not attend Father Glabre's confessional at least once in the half-year would find it disagreeable for them at some distant day of reckoning; but wherefore it should be so, why women should need this ordeal more than men, and wherefore, above all, an indispensable preliminary to salvation should consist of kneeling for ten minutes in the year in an oak box, were questions which she was content to class amongst the sublime mysteries of the holy Catholic church, not intended to be fathomed by the faithful. One day, however, it occurred to her—as a new use for some long familiar object may strike an observer—that there might, perhaps, be something more in this practice of confession than appeared in the kneeling and avowing that one had been reading good books and found them dull, which was what Angélique's disclosures generally amounted to. Might not the priest be a friend to whom one could unburden one's heart in moments of sore difficulty, and from whom one could receive advice that one dare not ask of mundane friends or relatives? That Angélique should have arrived at this thought by her own unaided self; that it should have come to her in the light of a boon; and that she should have contemplated at once availing herself of the opportunities it revealed to her, were proofs of how lonely she must have felt her life to be, and of how great a fund of trouble must have been stored up in her simple heart since she yearned to relieve herself to any one, even to a stranger.

Yes, lonely and full of trouble, though she would have been at a loss to define what was the nature of the confession she wished to make, and what sort of solace it was she hoped to obtain. Womanlike, or rather childlike, she went no farther in her reflections than beyond this point—that she was unhappy; and, with the touching confidence of those who suffer, believed that all save herself could prescribe for her pain and assuage it. So, when Father Glabre preached she listened to him with the anxious attention we bestow on those in whom we think of confiding, examined his features intently, and felt her heart flutter when he looked and spoke in her direction. And when one Sunday he announced that during the Easter season he would be at home at stated times to hear the confessions of penitents who were unable to attend at the church hours,—or those, he might have added, whose confessions necessitated developments—she took mental note of the days he had named, and waited for the first of them with a trepidation that almost counted the minutes.

It was on the day of the close of the Corps Législatif session that Angélique went to Father Glabre's. She had, of course, spoken her intention to no one,

and had even been compelled to use stratagem to rid
herself of the Crimean Hero.

Father Glabre had not been apprised beforehand
of her visit, but, on receiving the name of the Duchess
of Hautbourg, hurried out with more than his usually
unctuous welcome. Somehow he seemed agitated and
unduly pleased at her visit, as if it were a stroke of
good luck that he had not expected, but which he had
particular and private reasons for rejoicing at. The
sanctum where he led her was dim, half oratory, half
study. The furniture, scanty but rich, and prelatial,
attracted the eye by its appropriateness, and reposed
it by its good taste. There were no books, excepting
a red-leaved breviary; but—unlooked-for thing in such
a place—an open newspaper had been thrown on a
chair; and had Angélique been collected enough to
make such an observation, she might have noticed that
this was not a clerical journal, but a purely financial
organ.

However, she was not collected enough for anything; for now that she was alone with the priest, who
was to smooth her troubles away, everything she had
thought of saying seemed to have oozed completely
out of her memory. But Father Glabre was cognizant
of this symptom from having often witnessed it before;
and in his most dulcet, winning tones, set himself to
allay the nervousness. There was a comfortable softly-
cushioned fall-stool for such of the fair penitents as
held strictly to the rubric of observance, and could not
have been persuaded to recite their *mea-culpas* otherwise than in a posture of humiliation, kneeling on
thick velvet; but Father Glabre liked an unformal conversation better. He was a man of the world. He saw

with pleasure Angélique drop into the arm-chair he offered her; took another for himself, not too close, nor too far from her; and, pending the moment when she should have recovered from her shyness, spoke in an easy, reassuring way with modulated accents about nothing in particular, and more or less about everything. It was mere child's play to this consummate ecclesiastic to draw a confession from such a penitent as Angélique. He saw that at a glance, and quietly bided his time. Mon dieu, there were ladies who gave him trouble! Certain lovely but provoking sinners were quite willing to render their confession to the holy church Catholic; but they were determined, as it were, that the holy church Catholic should not get things too cheap. The reverend father had to wrestle with these, to cajole, to finesse, to extract the confession in unshapely fragments piecemeal; and, when at last it was all out, there would sometimes be nothing to show but a little bit of a sin that would not pay for the trouble of pulling up. An hysteric penitent, who looked as much overwhelmed as if she was fresh from committing 'six at least out of the seven deadly sins, had one day kept herself on her knees, and the reverend Father Glabre on tenter-hooks, for three-quarters of an hour by the onyx clock on the mantel-piece, only to avow in the end that she had eaten a ham sandwich on Ash Wednesday! Ah! all is not *couleur de rose* in the life of a confessor!

But Angélique gave none of this trouble. When Father Glabre had sufficiently laid the dust on the penitent's path by the refreshing dew of his small-talk, he began discreetly to touch upon the soothing mission of the church, in receiving secrets and giving comfort

in exchange. And then—after a last self-struggle—
Angélique confessed herself—said all she had to say,
in a low, plaintive voice, with interjection of sighs and
occasional tears; but without stopping. Women who
are habitually reticent of words will speak in exceptional moments with a quiet fluency that is astonishing.
Angélique unfolded the whole tale of her life; which
on her lips sounded a very disappointed, unhappy
story indeed. She related how she had been married;
the history of Georgette's attachment for her husband;
the comparative felicity of the first months of her
wedded life when she thought her husband perhaps
really loved her as much as he said. Then, her per-
plexities in her divided allegiance between husband
and father; her attempts to obey the latter in prevailing upon Horace to resume his estates; her powerless-
ness to influence him; and finally the certainty that he
no longer loved her, and that she had made his life
wretched by marrying him. Horace was always kind
to her, but she could see that he was weary of her.
He remained less and less with her every day; and
every day took long rides, she had no need to be told
where. She knew it was to Meudon.

Father Glabre had nothing to do but to listen in
silence. Now and then he put a short, pertinent question to help him connect all the links of the narrative,
but he made no answer, until half relieved, but bruised
and shivering after her confession, Angélique ceased
speaking and hid her face in her handkerchief.

"You could not have come to a surer fountain of
comfort than the church, dear lady," he then said in
his most assuaging tones. "Your sorrows are great,
but our sympathy is proportionate."

It was not Father Glabre's way to remind his fair votaries much that he was a priest. He preferred the character and language of friend; but his discourse was just enough garnished with ecclesiastical phrase to give it the extra force and prestige that were needed to carry it home. So his exhortations to Angélique were exactly what they should have been—benign, compassionate, hopeful; savouring a little of the pulpit, a great deal of the drawing-room, still more of the place where they were—the confidential retreat. As to the part of the narrative respecting the Clairefontaine intrigue, the Catholic priest could have but one opinion, which was shared by the man of the world and the brotherly adviser. It was a wife's duty to rescue her husband from all such contamination as would result from a long connection with the enemies of religion (read "Liberals"), and the Duke of Hautbourg should undoubtedly be urged to resume a position, where, properly guided (read, "by you, Madam, under my instruction"), he would render most signal services to the church. Coming to Angélique's domestic sorrows, Father Glabre trod lightly on the delicate ground; though he knew every inch of it, and had nothing to fear from its pitfalls. This was not, by a good many dozens, the first story of connubial woe he had been made to listen to. But his experience of such cases was that women confess their suspicions in order that the priest may dispel them; so that he carefully eschewed the blunder of admitting even by implication that there was any foundation for Angélique's fears. On the contrary, he strove to show that we often take alarm on slender proof, and that our doing so is a virtue since it only argues excess of love;

"but," added he softly, "let us not neglect probabilities," and the probabilities on which he dilated were
that the Duke of Hautbourg, being a man of taste
and culture, was not likely to prefer a person in a very
subordinate sphere of life, and no doubt uneducated,
to the gifted and accomplished lady he had before
him. There are few lines of argument more sure of
success than that which consists of proving to a woman
that her rival is not to be named in the same day with
her; and the Rev. Father Glabre said enough to dismiss a dozen ordinary women on their way with tears
dried and hearts leaping. But Angélique was not an
ordinary woman.

"Ah," said she, sadly, shaking her head, "you
don't know my husband, nor Georgette Pochemolle,
Father. She is more educated than I am, and her
rank is not lower than what mine would have been
had my father not become so rich. But I am not
jealous of her. She is worthier of him than I, and
how can I blame my husband because he has eyes to
see it? But it would have been so much better if he
had perceived this before our marriage; for, now, what
am I to do? Yet it is a terrible thing for him to be
joined all his life to a woman he does not like, when
there is another near who might make him so happy."

Unaccustomed as he was to betray astonishment at
anything—indeed there were few things surprised him
—the Rev. Father Glabre slightly opened his eyes at
this; not quite sure whether he had heard aright. Angélique caught his look and guessed the meaning of it.

"Oh, yes," continued she, with artless melancholy,
"I love my husband. I did not know at first what
love was; but when I came to feel happy at his being

near me, and sad when he looked sad, I understood
that this was love. Only I don't think it would be
love if I thought of him only for myself. Sometimes,
when he was not looking at me, I have watched him,
and seen his face darken, and I have said to myself:
'This is because of me,' and then I have felt that I
would do anything—anything on earth, to keep that
cloud from his brow. Do you know what it is to feel
this? To sit and reflect whether there is any means
by which we can take away some one's suffering and
add it to our own, and not to find any? For the
more I looked, the more dark things seemed to me;
and something like a voice in the night—yes, it was
like that, the voice of something within that only speaks
when one is alone, or when one lies awake and cannot
sleep—kept saying to me that I was guilty for this.
You see, I had only to say no when he asked me to
be his wife, and he would have gone away and soon
forgotten me; for he never really loved me—never felt
for me as I do now for him. But I was afraid. I was
afraid of my father," repeated she, with something of
shuddering terror in her accent. "He desired this
marriage, and though I did not understand why, then,
I have begun to think lately that I could guess; and
if what I suspect is true, and that the poor boy was
half inveigled into the match, then I am more guilty
than human words can tell, and all the sorrow that
overtakes me is just. But it is not just that he should
suffer because I was weak and cowardly," and she
fixed her eyes upon the priest with such a deep expression of sorrow, that he stood speechless before
this grief, of which he had never yet seen an example,
and which he could scarcely comprehend.

But sensibility was not a foible against which the reverend father was often obliged to pray Heaven to guard him. To be just, he must have been endowed at his birth with a larger share of this virtue than usually falls to one man, had he retained much of it after all he had heard in that room. A town doctor may be said to lose his illusions before his hair turns grey, a solicitor before his teeth have begun to loosen, but a town confessor loses his before the gloss has yet vanished from his first cassock. So it was not the fault of Father Glabre, but rather of the generation which had whispered its sins into his ear, if, after a moment's stupefaction, he should have darted a rather keen glance at the woman, who, for a moment, had thrown him off his impassiveness; and then fallen to musing. Imagine a man who has a new contrivance presented to him: knows there is a catch in it, and wants to discover what that catch is; and you will have before you the Reverend Father Glabre attempting to divine what could be at the bottom of the Duchess of Haut-bourg's confession, and feeling baffled.

Seeing him looking at her with benevolence—for whatever might be brewing within the reverend father's head, his countenance remained unalterably benevolent—Angélique murmured mournfully: "It has done me good, father, to confide all this to you, for I have no one at home to whom I could speak. There is my aunt, but I should only sadden her, and she could do nothing for me; and of course this is not a matter for my cousin's ears."

"Your cousin is married?" asked Father Glabre.

"It is not a lady," said Angélique. "He is staying

with us until he rejoins his regiment. He is in the Carbineers."

"Oh!" replied Father Glabre; and this "Oh!" as it was uttered by him was a thing to hear. The number of cousins in the Carbineers whom the reverend father had met lurking in the side-shifts of domestic dramas was one of the curious facts of his experience. Nevertheless, he abstained from embracing hasty conclusions, and it was well that he did so, for a few more questions answered with the naïvest candour convinced him that, whether he felt disposed to own it or no, he had come this day upon a—to him—new type of Parisian woman—one who, amidst the corruptions of the Babel City, and, though placed in circumstances where everything conspired to ensnare her, had kept the guileless innocence of a child. Then something akin to pity took possession of this priest. It was the feeling of a hard soldier who finds, wandering, in the midst of a raging battle, a young and defenceless woman. The sceptical Jesuit felt tempted to exclaim: "What are you doing amongst us, my poor child? what hope is there for you in a world like ours?" And with a perceptible shrug he reflected to himself: "Here is a fair creature who has more love for her husband than he deserves. But how will it end? A part of this affection, which he disdains, she will one day transfer to the Carbineer. *Eheu me!* what an oft-told fable this is!"

But aloud he said, with most considerate gentleness: "Dear lady, there is nothing in all you have related from which I can gather that the slightest particle of blame attaches to you. Your own conduct has been exempt from reproach; and let me persist in hoping that such is also the case with the Duke of Hautbourg.

But were it otherwise I would remind you, less as a priest than as a man who has seen much and had many opportunities of marking the courses of human weakness, that illicit passions never last long, and that the man whose affections stray for awhile from his own hearth, soon returns to it contrite, with a new craving for that peace which can only be found in domestic life. It is Heaven's will that it should be so. The satiety that cloys irregular appetites is a visible manifestation of the protection which Heaven accords to the holy institution of matrimony. Dear lady, trust in this to the healing grace of time. Your husband's heart will surely be yours again, and the sooner if you persevere in the wise and feeling course you have adopted of not letting it be seen that you have suspected him. This is but a passing trial: 'Heaviness may endure for a night, but joy cometh in the morning.'"

He gave her absolution *pro formâ*, pushing a hassock for her to kneel on during the rite; but she knelt humbly on the floor, and in accepting the assistance of his arm to rise when it was over, thanked him in a meek feeble voice for his forbearance in listening to her. He replied with a few more cheering and politic counsels, and this put an end to the clerical portion of the interview. The priest then gave way to the man of the world, or rather, in this case, to the man of business; for it was then that stood revealed the signification of the sudden look of gladness that had illumined the reverend Father's features at the sight of Angélique, and also the secret of the financial organ displayed on a chair. As he conducted Angélique out of the oratory, her black glove lightly resting on his sleeve, like a small bird, the eloquent Jesuit said, not without some anxiety in his voice: "Madame la Duchesse, have you heard that the Crédit Parisien is ailing in any way?"

"No," answered Angélique, surprised but uninterested, for the Crédit Parisien and its concerns were as so much Sanskrit to her.

"You relieve me," exclaimed the Rev. Father, who looked in truth relieved. "There were some disquieting rumours afloat, but your denial of course shows me they were unfounded. If you will permit me," said he, stopping, and running back to fetch the paper— "you will see, Madame la Duchesse"—and he pointed to the column headed "BOURSE"—"the money article adopts a certain tone of alarm. It says (excuse me for reading):—'*There was a new fall on Crédit Parisien securities this day. The closing price of the shares was one thousand two hundred and thirty francs, showing a decrease of thirty francs on yesterday's quotations, and of three hundred and twenty francs as compared with the quotations of this day a month ago.*' Not that I personally have any reason to feel unquiet at this," added the Father, with a deprecating little smile; "but I have been given to understand that sundry members of the church—some religious corporations I believe— have invested a part of their small means in the company which your eminent father governs so ably, and it was on their behalf that I experienced a little uneasiness."

Translated into French this speech meant that, the Rev. Father Glabre being not unprovided with this world's goods, and entertaining the same affection for ten per cent. as his contemporaries, had been touched by the prevailing epidemic, and bought some Crédit Parisien shares at one thousand four hundred francs.

Whence a certain degree of stupefaction, followed by doubt and distracting meditations, when these shares, after rising to one thousand five hundred and fifty francs, had suddenly begun to fall. Should he sell out at the unpleasant, but comparatively small, loss of one hundred and seventy francs per share, so as to avoid a greater sacrifice by and by; or was this merely a temporary depression from which the company would recover in a week or two? This is what he would have liked to learn of the eminent M. Macrobe's daughter, and it is this that had caused him to look upon her visit as a truly providential event.

Angélique glanced ruefully at the share-list, much as a girl of the Malay Archipelago might in trying to decipher a music-scroll.

"I have not heard that there was anything wrong," said she. "My father has not told me anything. But I will ask him, if you like."

"Oh, pray do not take that trouble," answered Father Glabre, smirking unctuously. "Only if Madame la Duchesse can gather *indirectly*" (a slight stress on this word) "from M. Macrobe what the state of the case really is, perhaps she will kindly remember that the servants of the Church resemble Lazarus more than Dives, and give me such information as may enable me to save them in time from losing their little all."

"Oh, certainly," said Angélique, with feeling, and this reminded her that she had in her pocket a purse filled with money that she never wanted, and which generally melted in instalments to beggars. She fumbled for it furtively and extracted a thousand-franc note which she pressed into the father's hand at parting: "For the poor of your parish, Father," she murmured.

But riding homewards she did not feel as though her confession had given her the relief she had sought. The palliation to her suffering had been only tem- -porary. Whilst Father Glabre spoke, she had seen a faint ray of sunshine gleaming through the clouds; but, now, the horizon on which her mind's eyes were fixed seemed as colourless, as bereft of hope, as ever. It seemed even vaguely menacing. For,—as in moments when the atmosphere is heavy,—an oppres- sive sensation stole over her spirit, an undefined presentiment of events near at hand, which would concern her, towards which she was slowly drifting and which loomed ahead of her like reefs in the hazy night of the future.

CHAPTER XX.

A Panic.

THE Reverend Vicar of St. Hyacinth's had not exaggerated matters in talking of the disquieting rumours that were bruited about the Crédit Parisien. The rumours were very disquieting indeed to those who had money in that enterprise; and amongst these, to our friend the Prince of Arcola.

Seated at his breakfast-table in travelling attire, with a British-looking tea-pot and a still more British- looking muffin before him, he read *The Times* news- paper, and thus conversed with Bateson, who, railway- tables in hand, was taking a survey of the trains that left for Hautbourg that day:—

"Bateson, have you not shares in the Crédit
Parisien?"

"Yes, my lord."

"And it is I who did counsel you to buy them.
How long ago was that, do you remember?"

"Two years ago, my lord."

"And at how much the shares were they?"

"I bought ten shares, my lord," responded the
punctilious Bateson, "at seven hundred and eighty-five
francs each."

The Prince drew out his pencil-case, scrawled a
multiplication sum on the margin of his *Times*, and
said, half-apologetically:—"Bateson, I have much fear
that this company is not what I thought. They have
made to run noises on its account, and if these noises
be true the shareholders will lose their money."

Bateson stood calmly motionless. The idea that
a French company, trading in a French land, could
presume to make him, Bateson, a British subject, lose
his money, was a thing slow to strike him as being
within the range of possibilities. There are forms of
audacity which it requires an effort to realize. At
length he asked, with imperturbable composure: "Then
the company is a swindle, my lord?" And one could
divine the unspoken corollary: "In which case, I shall
feel it my duty, on public grounds, to lodge a com-
plaint against them at Bow Street."

"Well, Bateson, one rarely knows in these mis-
adventures whom to blame," said the Prince with a
patient shrug. "What I wanted to say is, that you
must not lose by my advice. You should sell your
shares now; but, as we are going out of town to-day,
perhaps it would be difficult to see your broker in

time. Suppose, then, you pass them to me. I will take them at the day before yesterday's quotations, as given here in *The Times*,—1,275 francs."

"And yourself, my lord?"

"Oh, do not be in pain for me, I will sell yours along with mine. But you shall have what they call a clause of redemption, Bateson; that is, in the case where the shares should come to rise again, I will return them to you for what I gave. That shall be only fair."

The mind of Bateson took in the business-like aspects of this operation, and discovered that the proposal was advantageous, not to say uncommonly handsome, for whichever way the wind veered, he, Bateson, a British subject, would be the gainer.

"I am infinitely obliged to you, my lord," he said.

"Then, Bateson, it is an affair concluded. If you will give me my cheque-book, which is on that table, I will sign you a draft for the sum, twelve thousand seven hundred and fifty francs, or five hundred and ten pounds sterling, in your currency."

Which was done. Then the Prince began a second sum in pencil for his own particular behoof, and by multiplying five hundred and fifty francs (money paid for his own shares) by eight thousand (number of shares bought) arrived at the pleasant conclusion that if the Crédit Parisien were to founder he should be four million four hundred thousand francs, or one hundred and seventy-six thousand pounds sterling out of pocket. But this was not all. There were one or two other persons besides Bateson whom the Prince had advised in all good faith to invest their savings in the Crédit Parisien; and that he was morally bound

not only to guarantee these people from loss, but also
to prevent them from selling to others shares which he
now knew to be worthless, seemed to him a fact as
incontrovertible as noon-day. So Bateson was des-
patched below to make financial inquiries of, and
enter into transfer negotiations with, the coachman,
major-domo, and chef-de-cuisine, three important
functionaries who lived in clover under the princely
roof, and, by dint of occult perquisites, accumulated
salaries which allowed them to look down upon captains
of the line, country vicars, and judges of first instance
as meanly-paid officials. And the upshot of Mr. Bateson's embassy was, that before another half-hour had
sped, three more cheques on the bank of MM. Lecoq,
Roderbeim and Macrobe found their way from the
breakfast-room to the commons.

Thereupon, the Prince, rid of a double load—load
of uneasiness, and load of money—finished breakfasting, and endeavoured, with as much coolness as the
circumstances admitted, to foresee what would become
of him if he were ever ruined. He should have to
renounce his hopes of winning the English Derby, that
was clear; but he might have to renounce many other
things besides that. Perhaps this political life—which
he was now about to embrace for the sake of punish-
ing a rival—he might be compelled to cleave to from
necessity.

It would be something to have the deputy's salary
of 500*l.* on which to fall back; and then the deputy-
ships led to other things—senatorships, ambassador-
ships, Ministerial portfolios. He mentally followed
himself, pursuing the steep by-paths, the tortuous laby-
rinths, the break-neck highways that conduct one to

places such as that which M. Gribaud occupied; and, at the prospect, he winced a little, for it was not one that consorted with his ideal of an agreeable life's journey. In which predicament of mind he betook himself to reading his letters, of which a goodly heap had been brought in contemporaneously with *The Times*. There was one he had been expecting from M. Gribaud's secretary. Some days before, alarmed at the congratulations of friends, who had been assuring him that the Government was going to have the peasantry round Hautbourg marched to the poll in imposing columns, like herds of horned cattle, he had written to request that no support of that kind might be afforded him, but that he might be allowed to fight out the battle with his adversary on equal terms—a fair field, and no favour. In answer to this M. Gribaud's secretary wrote:—

"MONSIEUR LE PRINCE,—

"I AM directed by M. Gribaud to acknowledge the receipt of your letter, and to say that Government will, at your desire, abstain from taking any active part in the contest between yourself and M. le Duc de Hautbourg. At the same time, his Excellency requests me to state that it cannot be expected, neither would it be desirable, that the authorities should conceal their very sincere wishes for your success.

"I have the honour to remain,
"Monsieur le Prince,
"Your most obedient humble servant,
"C. DE BEAUFEUILLET."

The Prince had not restored this letter to its

envelope before Bateson re-appeared to say that M. Macrobe had called. Was his lordship at home?

The hour was early, but his lordship *was* at home. He had no reason to shirk seeing the financier, who was his friend as well as his banker, for conventionally, at least, the coolness with Horace was not supposed to cause any estrangement from Horace's father-in-law. Moreover, the rumours that were busy with the good name of the Crédit Parisien rendered the Prince not unnaturally anxious to sound the respected chairman as to what might definitely happen to the mammoth enterprise, erst so lusty. He was not quite naïve enough to expect that M. Macrobe would confess it if the reports were true; but he fancied he should have sagacity enough to discern, by the financier's manner, whether there were any real danger under the surface. As for M. Macrobe, the secret of his visit to the Prince might have been found in a confidential note from M. Louchard, which he carried in the breast-pocket of his coat. Here was that note:—

* "Sir,—

"The big goose has proved tough; no amount of

* "Sir,—

"The Prefect has proved incorruptible: no amount of bribing will buy him. Some of the minor officials are open to offers, but they can be of but little use to us without the Prefect. My most trusted agent has canvassed the borough electors, and those in the country districts. He is not dissatisfied with the former, but gives a poor account of the latter. The clergy will be on our side, if the Duke of Hautbourg goes to his estates; otherwise there is no reliance to be placed on them. This is the story with the rest of the constituency. Let the Duke return to Clairefontaine, or he will never win his election.

"Moïse Louchard.

"P.S.—I set the wiliest, most influential, and prettiest of the ladies in our pay to cajole the Prefect. It was of no use. He must have been promised promotion in the event of his defeating the Duke. He is working the screw with tremendous vigour."

boiling will sodden him. Some of the goslings are
tender enough, but they will not make a dish without
the goose. My farm bailiff has examined the pigs in
the sty, and those in the meadow. He is not dissatisfied with the former, but gives a poor account of the
latter. The rooks will cut up tender, if seasoned with
the patent sauce; otherwise I fear they will be uneatable. This is the story with the rest of the fowls.
The sauce, the sauce! else your friend will never be
able to digest his dinner!

"ROBERT VINCENT.

"P.S.—I put the tenderest, plumpest, and hand-
somest of our chickens into the same pot as the goose.
It was of no use. That bird must have been furiously
strong on the wing. His weight is enormous."

Coupled with the very serious complexion which
the affairs of the Crédit Parisien were assuming, and
with this circumstance that, on the preceding day—
being that on which the Corps Législatif had been
dissolved—M. Macrobe had not seen his son-in-law,
and was consequently in ignorance of the resolution
to which he had finally come, this note of M. Louchard's
was a most portentous warning. The financier was
beginning to feel that the odds were turning against
him. He had yet two cards to play, however, and
the first of these was to try and effect a reconciliation
between Horace and the Prince, in order that the latter
might be induced to retire. He did not despair of
this chance.

The two men being mutually interested in keeping
on good terms with each other, shook hands with

tolerable cordiality; and M. Macrobe at once took the
bull by the horns, by saying cheerily: "In travelling
garb I see, mon Prince. Bound for Hautbourg?"

"Yes, saddled for the road," smiled the Prince.
"The session only closed yesterday, and I believe it
is a point of etiquette not to begin canvassing until
the dissolution, in order that all the candidates may
have an equal start."

"Good practice, if well observed," returned the
financier, as cheerily as before, "but it isn't. To continue the racing metaphor, your prefect is putting all
his nags into training, and spiking the course for our
colt."

"I have heard that he has been showing too much
zeal and am sorry for it. See, I wrote to the Government on the very subject, and here is their answer"
(he handed the secretary's letter). "I have no wish to
win any victory, but such as I may be proud of."

"But come, why do you want a victory at all?"
exclaimed M. Macrobe, sinking into an arm-chair, and
looking coaxingly into the Prince's face. "Don't let
us have any mystery about this, mon Prince. I know
why you have quarrelled with my son-in-law. It is
about that little bit of a girl, Georgette Pochemolle.
But frankly, is it worth the while of two gentlemen to
fall out about such a trifle."

"It is no trifle in my eyes when a friend of mine
misconducts himself," answered the Prince drily.
"Since our quarrel is no secret to you, M. Macrobe,
you must be aware of what occasioned it. On the eve
of proposing to Mdlle. Pochemolle, I appealed to the
Duke of Hautbourg, with the utmost confidence, as to
a brother, to know whether there had ever been any-

thing between him and the woman I wished to make
my wife; and in return he deceived me. If the consequence of this behaviour had been only to entail
upon me the cruel humiliation of the refusal which
followed, I should say nothing. But my proposal
revived painful memories in Mdlle. Georgette's mind;
it distressed her; and I have a right to resent that
sorrow which I was the unwilling means of inflicting
upon a lady."

"Your proposal distressing to Mdlle. Georgette!
that I will swear it was not," replied the financier with
a coarse laugh. "As to the other points, mon Prince,
I had always imagined that where a lady's honour was
involved, gentlemen were expected to be silent—nay,
in some cases even to perjure themselves. You would
not have had the Duke of Hautbourg blight a poor
girl's reputation by too candid avowals."

"I would not have had a Duke of Hautbourg blight
a poor girl's happiness by making sport of her affections," answered the Prince, excitedly.

"Well, but, let us be reasonable, mon Prince,"
said the financier; "when Horace Gerold seduced this
shop-girl, he could not foresee that she would one day
be honoured with your love."

"Seduced her!" and the Prince looked at Prosper
Macrobe with an expression in which sudden amazement was largely blended with indignation. "What
do you mean by that, Monsieur Macrobe?"

"Well, made her his mistress, if you like the
euphemism better," answered the financier, not less
surprised. "You surely hadn't any illusions on this
head?"

"Good Heavens!" groaned the Prince turning ghastly pale.

The financier had not suspected that the Prince could be unaware of the *liaison* between Horace and Georgette. Indeed he fancied that the quarrel had been mainly caused by the Prince's intimate knowledge of what he—M. Macrobe—had only ascertained latterly. On beholding the Prince's woe-struck attitude he was for an instant disconcerted; but next moment the reflection occurred that here was an opportunity of terminating at a stroke the difference between the antagonists by proving to the Prince that Georgette was not worthy of the interest of an honest man.

"Why, don't you know?" said he, with affected concern. "Georgette Pochemolle was the mistress of my son-in-law long before his marriage, and—it is a cruel thing for me to acknowledge, but I do so to you —I have reason to fear that she is so still. I obtained evidence of this wretched fact but a few days ago; and I need not tell you what a blow it was to me. But least said soonest mended in such cases. I should only compromise my daughter's domestic peace by interfering. There is nothing for it but to let these passions wear themselves out."

The Prince was walking distractedly up and down.

"And to think I had set up this girl on a shrine in my heart," exclaimed he, in a bitter voice. "I believed in her—oh, what actresses women are! But," and he turned almost fiercely on M. Macrobe, "this does not alter my opinion as to your son-in-law's behaviour, for even this fallen girl is proved to have acted more honourably than he. He would have suffered me, his friend, to give my hand to a courtesan, to his

leman, and have polluted my hearth by-and-by by remaining my wife's paramour; but it was the courtesan
who had too much delicacy for this arrangement!"

"Softly, sir," cried the financier, nettled; "I am
sure my son-in-law had no such base design as that.
He would have respected your hearth."

"Why should he have respected mine since he
does not respect his own?" exclaimed the Prince,
laughing contemptuously. "And is it you who defend
him?" added he, surprise mingling with his disdain.
"Why, of what clay can he be moulded, this man who
not a year after his marriage, keeps a mistress whom
he has seduced and makes so little secret of the fact
that his father-in-law, and perhaps his wife, are aware
of it! A man so reckless of his good reputation, so
regardless of the decencies which even professed liber-
tines observe, can have no soul worth the name. God
forgive me! I am no Puritan, but I pity the poor lady
who has wedded her lot to his; and you, sir, whom
this marriage has made the relative of so degenerate a
nobleman. As to wishing to win a victory over him,
I desire to bar him out of the Legislature, as I would
black-ball him at a club."

"I beg you to remark, mon Prince," interposed
the financier, choler rising to his gimlet eyes, "that if
I thought my son-in-law's conduct justified any of the
stringent expressions which you use, I should not
have delayed even a day in interfering. But if I have
deemed it wise to make allowances for a young man
enthralled by a clever and designing girl, and perhaps
chained to her by that very fear of scandal, which
you accuse him of braving—for you certainly know by
what manner of threats these women are accustomed

to retain their victims by their side—I think, the least which a stranger can do is to imitate me. After all, the matter concerns me more than anybody else."

"Well, so it does," replied the Prince, wincing, but in a quiet voice; for after pacing in agitation on the hearth-rug during a moment or two, he was recollecting that M. Macrobe, as his visitor, had a claim to be spoken to undemonstratively. He resumed his seat, penned up his feelings with an effort, as a man might bottle generous, effervescing wine, and putting on a ghastly semblance of cheerfulness, said: "*Minora canamus*. I was just brooding when you came in over the chances of my having to adopt politics as a trade should the company in which both our fortunes are cast, meet with the fate that is being predicted for it."

"The Crédit Parisien is as safe as the Bank of France," said M. Macrobe, hastily, but still scowling. "Have you all your shares still?" and his tone as well as his glance quickened as he asked this question.

"All," answered the Prince, with some dolefulness. "A ten million francs' worth according to present quotations, though I had them for less than half that, as I believe you know; to-morrow, however, they may be worth less than I gave, and next year nothing at all if this fall continues."

"If you apprehend that, what is to prevent your realizing to-day?" retorted M. Macrobe, sharply.

"Just this," said the Prince, and this time it was his eyes that wore the searching expression. "I was warned the other day by somebody whose name I am not free to mention, but whose position gave almost

oracular weight to his words," (M. Macrobe seemed to
prick up his ears), "that the Crédit Parisien was tottering. If I were to sell my shares I should be obliged
to impart this bit of information to the man who
bought them; and naturally he would, then, refuse to
buy. Thus until I get sound proof that the Crédit
Parisien is not tottering, my shares are tied to my
hands."

M. Macrobe looked the Prince through and through:
"And you would sacrifice ten million francs to this
scruple?" said he.

"Please to fancy a moment that instead of so
many thousand shares I possessed a like number of
sardine boxes," answered the Prince, with good-
natured calmness: "and that these boxes, all shining
externally, were full within of rancid oil and uneatable
fish. It would scarcely be an honest transaction, I
think, to go and sell these receptacles on the market
as full of good sardines?" and he arched his eyebrows
with an air of inquiring remonstrance.

A ray as that of a dark lantern gleamed into the
dark cavern where M. Macrobe was groping, and
seemed to show him a way out.

"But what if *I* bought your shares?" he asked.

"That would be another affair," replied the Prince
with pardonable alacrity. "You are the chairman of
this company, and know all its secrets. If you buy,
it will be with your eyes open to the risks you run,
and I shall be your obliged servant."

"Then prove it," exclaimed M. Macrobe, deluded
by his own agitation into attaching an earnest sense
to these conventional words. "Yes, Prince, I have
no dearer wish than to see you and my son-in-law

reconciled. Let us put an end to this unhappy difference——"

"Oh, pardon me," interrupted the Prince, colouring, and drawing himself up with his grandest air, "this sounds like a bribe." And he added in a significant tone, to warn his interlocutor from venturing twice on the same ground: "Let us talk of something else."

. But they did not talk of something else, for, baffled and raging, M. Macrobe fled the Hôtel d'Arcole, leaving his heavy malison on it from roof to basement. It would have been better for him had he then proceeded quietly to his own house, and there seen Horace, who was waiting at home on purpose to tell him of the resolution he had formed with respect to Clairefontaine. This would at once have cleared off the clouds from his mind and set his noble soul at rest. But instead of that he drove to the offices of the Crédit Parisien, and thus came in for a day of extremely unpleasant emotions.

The offices of the Crédit Parisien were of course situated in a palatial edifice. With the same spirit of generosity as had led the promoters of the company at the outset of affairs to vote themselves a handsome salary apiece, a commission had been given to an eminent architect to build a mansion regardless of expense—out of the shareholders' money. Humble stone was too poor to carry out the elaborate designs that were projected. The Crédit Parisien must needs be treated to marble and porphyry, granite and gilt bronze, also to statues of Commerce, Industry, and Finance, very expensive and slightly clad, beaming

down on the public from sculptured frontal. And it
may be accepted as one of the characteristic symptoms
of the shareholding mind, that there was not one of
the shareholders who passed by this sculptured frontal
and scanned its semi-nude deities, and not one who
strode through its porphyry portico and noted the
fretted vermicelli work thereon, but felt the richer for
these utterly unseemly luxuries that had been dis-
trained out of his pocket. Nay, there is ground for
supposing that had the board economized at starting
the two or three million francs it had wasted in building itself a house four times larger than it wanted, the
shareholding mind would have thought meanly of that
board, and have complained of the lack of enterprise
discernible in its undertakings. Oh! shareholder, shareholder, my friend, and thou, taxpayer, his brother, what
flats on earth so flat as ye!

Often had the well-pleased chairman seen the
street in which his offices stood thronged with beatific
physiognomies serene with the pocketing of fifteen per
cent. dividends. Pretty pink faces peeping out of
broughams, and stopping him as he hurried by, crying: "Oh, dear M. Macrobe, do come here and tell
me what I am to do. See these papers, I gave seven
hundred francs for them, and they are now worth
fifteen hundred. If I were to sell them, you would let
me have some more for seven hundred, wouldn't
you?" Sleek citizens with round paunches greeting
him bareheaded: "This is better than investing in
three per cent. *rentes*, monsieur." Playful copromoters
digging him in the ribs, and chuckling: "The pot
boils, Macrobe, eh? the pot boils." But this morning
it was another story. There were plenty of broughams

18*

and no lack of greetings as he descended from his own conveyance: but what greetings! Small gloved hands, and rough ungloved ones, griping him firmly by the coat-tails; blanched, feminine features, and haggard masculine ones pressing distractedly around him; anguishful *soprano* voices and hoarse *basses* calling upon him wildly for explanations: "What are these rumours, M. Macrobe?" "Is there any truth in this report?" "Why are the shares falling in this way?" "Have you seen that article in the *Constitutionnel?*" Unceremoniously shaking off these assailants like a pack of yelping curs, the chairman shouted to them: "There's nothing the matter at all. I hold to your shares or you'll be throwing coined gold out of the window," and darted upstairs. In the board-room most of the directors were assembled, a gloomy conclave; nor were they cheered by M. Macrobe's protestations: "This is nothing but a cabal got up by Gribaud, with whom I am at loggerheads." All eyes seemed to say: "Why the devil did you fall to loggerheads with Gribaud?" And the evident impression was that the chairman's speech was tantamount to what a captain's would be who were to sing out to his crew during a gale: "This is nothing. I am only at loggerheads with the north wind. It will be over presently." Yes, indeed, it might be over presently, when the north wind had worked his will, but then where would the good ship Crédit Parisien be? In the midst of grievous cogitations on this point, and tart debates on what had best be done, and what ought to be left undone, a clerk hurried in breathless, and said: "M. Macrobe, there is a panic at the Bourse. Shares have opened with a fall of 150 francs. If you could go there it might appease the public; but it should be done at once, for they have gone mad."

How do panics occur? Like storms, their course may be prognosticated by the vigilant, but upon the vulgar they come all of a heap, unawares. From the day when the formidable M. Gribaud had begun to blow Boreas-like upon it, the Crédit Parisien had ridden in troubled waters, first encountering small ripples, then little waves; and now these waves were becoming crested, were gathering ominously in strength and height, and beyond, long lines of surf, and rolling mountains of thundering sea, were breaking into sight. The small ripples were the few influential shareholders, who had been set into motion by M. Gribaud himself; the little waves, the friends of these shareholders who had caught the alarm second-hand; the large waves were the great public, who had got wind of coming evil by seeing the richer shareholders moving. It had taken about a month for the rumours to filter down from the topmost strata of shareholders to the undermost. But the final impetus to the panic, the last drop, as it were, that caused the cup to overflow, had been furnished by the closing of the Corps Législatif session. This being the signal for everybody to desert Paris and depart into the country, all who, possessing shares, had heard any adverse reports against the company, hastened to sell out before leaving town. Hence repeated falls several days in succession, and hence also the unavoidable consequence that the great herd of small shareholders being scared by these falls, it should have been a case of *turba ruit* or *ruunt* on the day following the dissolution. We beg here to

notice another peculiarity in the shareholding idiosyn-
cracy. Your panic-stricken shareholder does not cloak
his feelings under a decent garb of exterior non-
chalance. He bolts out into the highway with his
shares in his hands and his hair on end, as who should
say a costermonger endeavouring to sell his fruit with
this cry: "Who'll buy! Who'll buy! Rotten apples!
Rotten apples!"

In the Bourse, a dozen hundred of these shareholders with their nearest kinsfolk and dependents, ·
making up an infuriated swarm of some two thousand
black hats, were bellowing like ten herds of agonized
buffaloes giving tongue in concert. In the gallery overlooking the stone-paved Exchange and running all
round it, frantic members of the gentler sex—no longer
gentle at this moment—shrieked and wept and ges-
ticulated to attract the attention of their stock-brokers
below—in defiance of the by-law which enjoins that
women visiting the Bourse should be seen and not
heard, and to this end excludes them from the body
of the hall. But who cares in such moments for by-
laws? Maybe there is a by-law forbidding individuals
to rush upon a broker twelve and twenty together, to
seize him, hustle him, rend his heart and eke his gar-
ments, and yelp orders to sell into his ears under
threats of personal violence? Maybe there is another
by-law formally interdicting one man from ramming
his fist into his neighbour's eye, under pretext that the
neighbour having selfishly cornered a broker wants to
keep him all to himself? And maybe a third by-law
lays a total ban on the hurling of one's hat at a
distant broker's physiognomy as an expedient for making him look your way? But if so nobody paid any

heed to these regulations, nor, indeed, to any others which might be adorning the notice-board. Everybody was thinking about himself, howling, pushing, fighting, and perspiring in his own interests—and what a dignified animal man looks under these auspicious circumstances! Shouts of "Crédit Parisien at ten fifty!" "Ten forty-five!" "Ten twenty, then; who'll take at ten twenty?" flew upwards like sky-rockets.— "They say Macrobe has bolted!"—"Bon Dieu! I always knew it would happen; and to think I bought only a month ago at fifteen seventy!"—"*Sacré baudet*, will you let me pass?"—"Is it me you are address-ing?"—"Yes, you; do you think I am going to stand waiting here all day until you've done jabbering."— "Take that, you unwhipped cur. Piff. Paff."—"*Sacré nom d'un chien!* Paff. Piff."—"Hullo, there's a fight down there."—"Monsieur, you must give up your umbrella at the door" (this from a policeman).—"Damn my umbrella, sir!"—"Madame, upstairs is the way for ladies."—"Monsieur, I don't care for the rules, I must see my broker, and I shall."—Policeman impedes madame, who screams, slaps his face, and sheds tears. —"Crédit Parisien, nine fifty!"—"Bah! I wouldn't take it at eight nor at seven!"—"Nine twenty!" "Nine ten!" "Nine, Crédit Parisien, nine hundred!" —"Good God! do you hear that? It's down to nine hundred!"—"Just heavens! I am father of a family, and invested all my life's savings in it when the shares were at fourteen hundred!—Mon Dieu! Mon Dieu!" (moans, yells, and tears his hair out in bunches.)— "Crédit Parisien at eight seventy!" "Eight fifty-five!" "Eight hundred!" (wildest uproar.)

At this moment somebody near the door rushed in

with eyeballs starting, and bawled: "Here is Macrobe, and HE IS COMING IN!"

"Macrobe! Macrobe!" thundered two thousand voices, and the Chairman was soon visible, hot, dishevelled, panting, struggling, being mobbed along like a deliverer entering a besieged city, or like a brigand being lynched.

But now the uproar was raised to its highest pitch by a conflict of opinions, between bears and bulls, the former gentlemen being well-satisfied at the depression of stocks, and in no way anxious to see them rise again; the latter being just of the other way of think-ing, and shouting lustily to M. Macrobe to make a speech. The scene that followed was hell let loose, Charenton in its cups, or the Zoological Gardens emptied on to the Boulevards des Italiens. Many a noble silk hat that had weathered gales and showers was doomed that day to an untimely end. Many a glossy coat, joy of its owner and object of envy to the tattered, was reft of its two skirts and converted into a mark for opprobrium and jesting; many a cambric shirt-front, rest to the eye of the beholder, was lacerated beyond the remedying of needle-craft. But, at last, the bulls, by reason of the number of their allies, proving victorious, M. Macrobe was hoisted on to the table that stood within the iron pen railed off for the brokers' use; and after the bears, most of them with noses punched and cravats twisted awry by kindly efforts made to strangulate them, had bawled them-selves hoarse during seventeen minutes and a half by the big clock in the gallery M. Macrobe contrived to obtain a hearing. He had stood firm during the tempest, like Napoleon on his rock in the well-known

picture "St. Helena." His coat was buttoned up to
his throat, one of his hands thrust into the breast of
. it, the other behind his back holding his hat; his
pointed face and weas'ly eyes contemplated the multitude with no more expression than a steel mask
might. But when he uttered his short harangue he
did so with his might; and never was speech better
appreciated. After all, the shareholding intellect desired
nothing better than to be convinced, to believe and to
go on trusting to any unlimited extent which its chairman might require. The words of the financier were
therefore picked up and swallowed like bread-crumbs
by famished poultry. When he concluded he was
tumultuously cheered; and the effect of his consoling
assurances became at once apparent in a cessation of
the panic and a rise of the stocks.

But for all that the Crédit Parisien had received a
rough shaking, and none knew it better than the chairman. Credit in finance is like the bloom on a plum
—only touch it with the finger and that's the last of
it. When M. Macrobe returned home late that afternoon he could almost have counted the number of
days which must form the utmost span of the company's life, if nothing occurred to bring a turn in the
tide. On the table in his study he found a new letter
from M. Louchard.

This one was not couched in figurative style, being
a comparatively harmless communication—at least so
M. Louchard opined:—

"(*Private and confidential*).
"Sir,—
"M. le Duc de Hautbourg has been followed,

and it seems that he has been in the habit of going to Meudon to see Mademoiselle Georgette Pochemolle every morning for this past fortnight.   He went there yesterday early, breakfasted at the restaurant with mistress's brother, and returned again in the evening. *He then admitted himself with a latch-key into the grounds and remained there more than two hours.*   His visits are matters of public notoriety at Meudon.

      "I have the honour to remain, sir,

        "Your obedient servant,

          "Moïse Louchard."

    M. Macrobe refolded this letter, and his grasp tightened over it.

    "This is my last card," said he, "my last; and I must play it."

    He went to the drawing-room, expecting to find his daughter there, and intending to ask her whether Horace had left word at what time he should be home that day.   But Horace himself was in the room; and M. Macrobe perceived at a glance that Angélique, who was seated near him, looked happier than he had seen her for many weeks past.   Horace rose, and, taking his wife's hand playfully, led her towards her father.

    "I think sir," said he, "Angélique has something to communicate to you."

    And Angélique said with glistening eyes: "Papa, Horace has just been writing to his agent to prepare Clairefontaine Castle for us.   We are going to live there for the future."

    M. Macrobe by a master effort brought his features under control, so as to reveal little or nothing of what he inwardly felt; and he threw himself on to the sofa.

But the effort must indeed have been a strong one, for he remained several moments without speaking, and during that pause the letter he was holding dropped unnoticed from his hand and fell among the sofa-cushions.

CHAPTER XXI.

Love's Calvaries.

As M. Louchard accurately wrote, Horace had returned in the evening and let himself with a latch-key into M. Pochemolle's grounds, which grounds consisted of a garden about half-an-acre in extent, and embellished at one of its extremities with a belvidere, commanding an inspiriting view of not less than half a mile of country. Knowing the indomitable passion of newly-retired tradesfolk for out-door walks on a week-day (such having been forbidden-fruit to them during their commercial existence), he had calculated that M. and Mdme. Pochemolle might perhaps be in the habit of going out visiting neighbours, and sometimes leaving Georgette—less enthusiastic about this pastime—at home. It was the season of the year when the days are just lengthening sufficiently to admit of after-dinner outings. Accordingly, he had glided into the garden, after first reconnoitring over the hedge to see that the coast was clear; and, under cover of a propitious laurel-grove, had crept to the belvidere and there ensconced himself, waiting for events. Setting aside the morality of the matter, this was a foolish thing to do; for a man who introduces himself by stealth into a garden runs the risk of being collared at a turning by a gardener, or waylaid by an unexpected watch-dog, or

descried from a top bedroom window by a housemaid,
and set down for one burglariously intent—in which
last case the usual way is noiselessly to apprise the
police, who march upon one strategically, and drag
one out of concealment triumphantly and by the scruff
of the neck. But when did lovers ever hesitate to do
a foolish thing?

Horace, however, earned no recompence for his ad-
venturousness. M. and Mdme. Pochemolle did, indeed,
go out whilst he was watching; but Georgette remained
indoors, and did not come out into the garden. Horace had not quite enough effrontery to enter into a
dwelling-house with a purloined latch-key, or it may
be that he was restrained by ignoring in what part of
the house Georgette might be. Anyhow, after two
hours' weary waiting, the draper and his wife having
meanwhile returned, he withdrew.

But withdrew only to come another time. He was
at his post again on the next night, and again on the
next, and so on three or four nights a week for well
nigh a month. Owing to his recent bereavement, he
could not tell Angélique after dinner that he was going
into society or to the opera. He was reduced to
simulating a desire for a stroll, or an appointment at
his club; and such is the proneness of marital nature
to believe in its own sagacity, that he rather con-
gratulated himself on the specious pretexts which he
invented every night to rout suspicion. If men would
but devote to worthy ends one-half the ingenuity they
bestow on evil, what a change we might live to see on
the world's surface! After the fifth night of bootless
watching, Horace's passion being increased rather than
diminished by the material obstacles it encountered, he

resolved that, come what might, on a certain night
at the end of the third week, he would see and speak
to Georgette. He was mainly driven to this resolution by the fact that the Monday of the fourth week
was the day on which he had arranged to start for
Clairefontaine, so that, unless he saw Georgette now,
he might not have the opportunity again for some
time.

Dinner over, he hinted at a headache, to which
Angélique assented with a pious falsehood, saying he
looked a little unwell, and recommending fresh air.
M. Macrobe, who, now that all his own wishes were
being crowned, would not have grudged pearls to
strew on his son-in-law's path, followed in the same
strain; as did likewise Aunt Dorothée, who, however,
suggested a wet towel round one's head as a bene-
ficent adjunct to the walk. So Horace was shortly
clearing the road to Meudon.

That evening M. Pochemolle, on rising from table,
remarked that it was a long time since he had seen
his friend Bourbatruelle, late in the crockery way, now
retired and owning a villa at Auteuil. Suppose they
were to drive over and spend the evening with Bourbatruelle? Nothing loth to show off to Mdme. Bourbatruelle a brave watered silk gown resplendent with
bugles, Mdme. Pochemolle consented; and so did M.
Alcibiade, remembering that there was a Mdlle. Bourbatruelle, mirthful and goodly to look upon. Georgette would have been happy to go, too, but being
engaged in finishing a piece of tapestry, which she
had promised the curé of Meudon against Easter to
deck one of his altars with, thought she had better remain at home, so as not to risk delay with her work.

"As you please, child," said Mdme. Pochemolle, a little tartly, for ever since that unlucky rejection of the Prince of Arcola's suit, Mdme. Pochemolle's maternal heart had borne a load of bitterness. There are filial offences which a mother never quite forgives this side of the grave, and refusal of an eligible offer is one of them.

More affectionate in his tone and look, the worthy ex-draper simply said, "Well, Georgette, we will take your love to the Bourbatruelles."

And so Georgette was left alone to finish her tapestry.

She went upstairs and sat down by the open window of her room—one that was located in a corner of the house overlooking both the garden and part of the roadway skirting it. The evening was mild and fine. On the lawns of all the villas within view, Meudonites were sipping coffee or wreathing blue clouds of cigarette smoke into the thin air, whilst their offspring crowed over gravel pies laboriously constructed, or gambolled with their little close-cropped French heads in and out of lilac-bushes. It was also a pleasant sight to see such Meudonites as had been for a stroll into the fields trudging homewards in groups down the hedge-lined roads, laden with rustic spoils, a little footsore, but contented and hungering for their *pot-au-feu.* Papa to the front, with straw-hat in one hand, and prickly branch of scented may in the other; mamma, a little behind, with more may and cowslips; hopefuls closing the procession: small girl with bunches of limp daisies and buttercups, much the worse for being plucked; small boy holding a dead dormouse by the tail, slain in single combat. Then there were red-breeched soldiers, who enlivened the road, tramping along fast, to be back in barracks in time for tatoo; a desultory knife-grinder pushing his vehicle towards Paris, and whistling *le Sieur de Framboisy* as loudly as though that melody were not interdicted by the police, for its disrespectful allusions to his Majesty; and presently came the sounds of a hurdy-gurdy, and of a voice singing sweetly an old and popular ballad to its accompaniment.

Georgette listened. It was a woman's voice; and she sang with that plaintive sadness which the instrument she was playing requires. But she seemed to be returning home after a toilsome day, for, trudging slowly, she stopped no longer before any one house than the time to repeat a single verse of her song, and then proceeded, her hurdy-gurdy droning mournfully, almost weirdly, in the meantime. In this way she reached the Pochemolle villa, and would have passed on, but, looking up, perceived Georgette at her window, and so paused in the road. Turning the handle of her instrument in measured cadence, and drawing notes so low, tender, and melancholy, that they were like the strains of a young girl's dirge, she sang this:—

Pour chasser de sa souvenance,
  L'ami secret,
On se donne tant de souffrance,
  Pour peu d'effet;
Une si douce fantaisie
  Toujours revient;
Lorsqu'on songe qu'il faut qu'on l'oublie,
  On s'en souvient.

Georgette dropped her needle. There was not a word in these lines so true to nature but might have been penned for her special case. How often had she not tried to forget Horace, and how often had not some *douce fantaisie* returned to keep his image ever present in her memory! She threw out some money to the woman, who called on the Virgin to bless her, and then she would have resumed her work, but the hands, unguided by the mind, which was just then straying far from gold and silver thread patterns, rested on the tambour-frame without moving. Of whom was she thinking? Of whom *do* women think? Of the men who love them most? Seldom. Of the men who have caused them most suffering, and whom they love the more for that reason. Georgette thought—and this was not the first time that month, that week, nor even that day—of the last time when she had seen Horace, of that short cruel interview, when she had reviled him, and he had insulted her. But she did not think with anger, or resentment, of that scene: on the contrary, Horace had cleared himself by his violent indignation. In hurling back upon her without restraint, without pity, the accusations she had launched against him, he had proved his innocence in her eyes more signally than if he had adduced innumerable arguments and circumstantial proofs. She blessed that passionate outburst which had restored again to his place in her esteem the man she loved: for the insults he had heaped upon her bore no grudge. Like a penitent kissing the rod that has lashed her she murmured that she deserved them. But she felt contrite—bitterly, unspeakably contrite—for her unfounded suspicions against him. These she magnified into crimes, and would have done penance for on bended knees. A loving woman's heart is an unfathomable abyss of humility.

"That he should love another, what more natural,

since my own heart and temper are so wicked," was
her meek self-confession. And then she accused herself for ever having hoped to be loved by a man who
was above her in everything—in mind and soul, as well
as worldly rank—accused herself for having mentally
despised Angélique, who was gentler and purer than
she—accused herself for dreaming still about Horace,
who ought to be sacred to her as if he were dead.
Yet, underlying these repentant, self-denunciations, was
a heart-felt though scarcely defined wish to see Horace,
if but once more to ask his forgiveness for having
wronged him. She deluded herself into fancying that
this expiation was a duty; she knew it would be a relief.
So these two, Horace and Georgette, were both tending
towards the same point: they desired to meet and ask
each other's pardons.

For several minutes after the minstrel-woman had
disappeared—her touching notes lingering behind her
like the trail that follows light—Georgette sat, full of
emotion, applying the words she had just heard to herself, and thrilling at the echoes of them that vibrated
in her heart. At last—it may have been after ten
minutes, perhaps after twenty—she looked up from a
particular flower in her embroidery, to which her gaze
seemed rivetted, and glanced into the garden. On
the gravel path below her window stood a man, and
that man was Horace.

He looked so sepulchral in his dark clothes—his
black gloves and his face beaming paler from the dusk
—that she started, and pressed her hand to her side,
as if she had seen an apparition.

"Mademoiselle," he said, with bated voice and in an
appealing tone, "can I speak to you—a single instant?"

She descended into the garden instinctively, having no control over her own will in the matter. She wondered, when she got there, how and why she had come down.

"Thank you," he cried fervently; then with impassioned ardour, "Oh, Georgette, can you ever forgive me for my brutality to you? I have come on purpose to crave your pardon—for no other purpose than this. Remorse has been devouring me for my heartless conduct."

Paler than himself, more troubled, and more faltering, she answered: "It is for me to beg your pardon, M. le Duc—Monsieur Horace," added she, correcting herself on seeing a disappointed look flit over his features. "What can you have thought of me? Believe me, I did not speak what I feel. I hate myself for what I said to you!" And her eyes brimmed over with tears as she glanced up into his face.

He seized one of her hands, and pressed it to his lips.

"Hear me, Georgette," said he; "I love you, love you with all the might of my heart. Like a madman, I rushed into a marriage with a woman whom I did not really care for; I was blind as well as mad, for I did not see that it was you alone whom I loved. Let us not prolong our misunderstanding. Tell me that you love me. I have heard how you refused M. d'Arcola. Let me hear from your own lips that it was for my sake you did so." And, encircling her waist with his arm, he drew her to him and lowered his face so close to hers that their lips almost touched.

She quivered from head to foot, struggled feebly, and then closed her eyes, as if to shut out the sun's rays.

"Yes, yes, I love you!" she sobbed deliriously. "I have loved you always, you know it."

This time their lips met. He covered her face, eyes, hands, with burning kisses; and her head drooped languidly, unresistingly, on his shoulder.

"We have wasted enough happiness, Georgette," whispered Horace wildly. "You know that if I were free, I would make you my wife; but human laws and conventionalities must not stand in the way of our felicity. We are wedded in the sight of heaven, for the only marriages that can be sanctioned above are those of hearts linked together by love."

He spoke with the fervid tenderness of passion; but his words seemed suddenly to revive Georgette. She tremblingly disengaged herself from his embrace, and with wistful looks and voice of entreaty, said: "Oh, M. Horace, let us not mar this one hour of happiness in our lives. I shall remember it all my days as the sweetest I have ever spent; but we can never be more to each other than we are. Never, never!"

"But, hear me, Georgette," he exclaimed, trying to retake her hand.

"No, no;" and she sank on a form, burying her face in her hands. "We are both bound by duties— you to your wife, whom it would be cruelty to betray; I to—to——" Her sobs choked her. "I wanted to say, that I, too, am engaged—or nearly."

"You engaged?" cried Horace, starting back, colourless.

She did not immediately answer. Her tears were raining fast and her frame shook with agitation.

"Do not judge me wrongly again," sobbed she at last. "You see, after I made you those—those wicked reproaches at our last meeting, accusing you of having married for money, and when you answered me that

I, too, had jilted an honest man who loved me—that
M. Filoselle—I thought that all you said was right; and
I have been reflecting ever since that perhaps M. Filoselle imagined I had refused him for bad motives."
She sighed sorrowfully. "And I would not have him
think this," added she, shaking her head, "for such
thoughts sour one's heart and make it unjust to others.
You cannot conceive how perverse and uncharitable I
was when I allowed myself to suspect ill of you. So,
as poor M. Filoselle has been sending me letters for
this last month by my brother, and as I see that he
has been really expecting all along that I would marry
him, and says that the happiness of his life depends
upon it, I told my brother to answer him to-day, that
I would keep the word my father once gave, and become his wife."

A few more tears coursed each other down her
cheeks, and her hand shook as she wiped them away.

"Good heavens! you married to that ludicrous
counter-jumper!" exclaimed Horace, frenzied. "Why
I would a million times sooner see you wedded to the
Prince of Arcola!"

"If I were to marry the Prince and pretend to love
him when I did not, I should feel as if I had sold
myself to him," murmured Georgette, reddening. "I
can pretend to love M. Filoselle, because I have nothing to gain by this marriage but the consciousness
of doing right by making a man who loves and suits
me happy."

"But have you no pity on me?" broke out Horace,
distractedly; "must this poem of our love be cut short
at the first verse? Do you not see that you are condemning me to a whole life of unhappiness; and have
I, who both love and trust and adore you, no greater

claim to your compassion than this man, Filoselle?"
He took her hands beseechingly and poured out a new
torrent of vows and adjurations: "Georgette, Georgette!
are you going to let this love rankle within me, all my
days through, unchafed?"

She hesitated: then rose, and with the light of innocence beaming from her eyes, and her hand laid
tremblingly on her lover's arm, whispered: "Horace,
our love would rankle within us if we had ever cause
to blush for it. But let us make of it something pure
and sacred, enshrine it in our hearts as a second
conscience to stimulate us to good and noble deeds,
to kindly thoughts, to generous acts of self-sacrifice.
We shall be distant from one another, we may not
meet again; but let us each feel that the other's silent
love is with him to sustain and encourage in all the
trials with which life is crossed. Then will these trials
seem lighter. Wherever you may be, whatever you do,
my heart will follow you, throbbing for all your pains,
exulting at your triumphs. I have heard, though only
lately, of your father's chivalrous honour and your own
in spurning an estate which you could not accept with
consistency; and if you knew how much I worshipped
and admired you for this act! We women, you know,
will always have our lovers heroes; and spotless honour,
honour which knows no compromise nor weakness, is
the highest form of heroism we conceive. For myself,
there is no sorrow or pang that will seem hard to me
to bear now that I have your love. And after all this
sacrifice we are embracing will not last long. What
are the few years of human life in comparison with
eternity? For beyond this, there must assuredly be a
world where those who have suffered here have their
time of joy; and there, Horace, there, if we keep

stainless in this life, we may meet never to be parted again."

She uttered these words in a quick tone with almost inspired serenity on her face, and when she had concluded she raised herself, kissed him chastely on the forehead, and said, "God bless you, and good-by."

"Georgette, stay," he exclaimed in despair, darting forward to hold her back.

But she turned with a look so loving yet so full of maidenly dignity and reliance on his honour, that he remained rooted where he stood. Before crossing the threshold of the house she turned once more and waved him a last kiss with her hand, glanced to him a last good-by with her eyes. Then it was as if all light had suddenly vanished from his presence.

He was roused by the noise of wheels, caused by the Pochemolle family returning from their excursion. Night had completely set in. He snatched up his hat from a form, and as soon as the house-door had closed upon the draper, his wife, and son, and the cab had rolled away, let himself out with his stolen latch-key, which he then threw over the gate on to the gravel path, in order that it might be found again by its owner. He would never need it again that he knew.

Then he walked towards Paris with dejected gait and a heavy weight at his heart. He despised himself; yet, man-like, endeavoured to shift some of the responsibility of his own abasement on to other and unoffending shoulders: "If I had married this girl," brooded he, "I should have been a different man. Curse my marriage, curse it!"

Whilst Horace was thus madly laying a ban on his own roof-tree, this is what was passing under it.

After Horace had sallied out on his supposed stroll to cure his fanciful headache, M. Macrobe had very soon retired to go to a party, and left Angélique to the improving society of Aunt Dorothée and the Crimean Hero. The financier, by-the-by, had become very assiduous during the last three weeks in frequenting parties, and this with the object of letting everybody who still lingered in town hear that he was going to spend his summer at Clairefontaine, and that Clairefontaine was an estate worth *two* million francs a year (a little exaggeration does no harm). He was not mistaken in supposing that these recitals would operate beneficially on Crédit Parisien stock. The shareholding mind, with its habitual sagacity, opined that if the chairman admitted his son-in-law's income to be two million francs, four millions must be accounted as nearer the true mark: for did not these functionaries systematically understate their private worth? Whence it followed, as clear as a proposition in Euclid, that M. de Hautbourg having four millions a year in no way connected with the Crédit Parisien, it behoved every shareholder of that Company to sleep in peace, and rest assured that fifteen per cent. was the stablest of institutions. But M. Macrobe did not merely succeed in dazzling the shareholder, which would have been a poor triumph. Wherever he turned, Society's smiles met him. There were not many members of the *haute fashion*, as French sporting papers call it, still in Paris; but such few as there were smiled as bountifully between them as though their numbers had been quintuple; and at one house where a "liquidation" rout was being given (*i. e.* an *omnium gatherum* of all the visiting list overlooked in previous invitations during the season), M. Gribaud, who had dropped in

to talk with the master of the house, one of his colleagues, took an early and easy opportunity of sidling up
to the financier, and striking up a sort of truce with him.

"So you have reached the goal of your hopes,
M. Macrobe?" said he, with the grim bluffness of an
unfriendly bear.

"Not quite, your Excellency, but nearly."

"And I see you have come forward to contest the
second seat in the Hautbourg department. If you
win it you will be calling yourself a Liberal, and voting
with the Opposition?"

"Heaven forbid! I shall ever be a Macrobist, and
vote for Macrobe!"

M. Gribaud was pleased to grin.

"Well, you know, we have given orders to our
people to remain neutral between Duke and Prince.
We hinted to the latter that he would do well to retire, but he declined. He seems bitter against you,
and is fighting you on his own hook."

"He is like his grandfather the field-marshal, who
feared not treble odds, and took his thrashings gallantly," replied the financier, with smooth sarcasm.
"And I, your Excellency, am I to be opposed?"

"Give us a pledge, Macrobe, give us a pledge,"
growled the Minister, button-holing the other, and
drawing him into a corner. "What the devil can
possess a man like you to make war on us? Why,
you might be a Minister yourself, if you were our ally."

"My address is Bonapartist from the exordium to
the peroration, your Excellency. It concludes with
the cry, ' *Vive l' Empereur!*'"

"Ay, but there is not a word about ' *Vive Gribaud!*'" grumbled his Excellency, wagging his head
with distrust.

"That was a terrific shaking you gave the Crédit Parisien," laughed the financier, rather sourly.

"Bygones are bygones, Macrobe," grumbled the other, though a little shamefacedly. "I serve the state. It was not our interest to see you and your son-in-law become powers; but now that you are likely to become so whether we will it or not, our interest is to be friends with you. Statesmanship is all summed up in that. It's sail with the wind."

"I have little fear about my election," said the financier with an air of half-mocking assurance, for which his Excellency would have cheerfully buffeted his weas'ly head. "But if my competitor is not supported, and if your Excellency will speak a good word or two for the Crédit Parisien in the same quarters where you have been whispering evil, your Excellency's name goes into the second edition of my address with a laudatory notice attached to it. My conditions are not hard," added the financier, his voice beginning to grate; "for whatever you may say or do, you can never repair the mischief you have done the Crédit Parisien. From the day when you drove all its official wire-pullers from it, its hours were numbered, but if you instruct the Government organs who have been abusing it by your desire to change their tune, and if you let it alone yourself, it may run on for another year or two; and this will enable me to retire from it before the crash, which is all I want."

"Well, well, I like a plain bargain: I let the Crédit Parisien alone and you let me alone, eh?" and M. Gribaud holding out his hand griped the financier's fingers between its knotty joints like filberts between a nutcracker.

So the peace seemed signed; and M. Macrobe

gadded about night after night from drawing-room to drawing-room, holding his head aloft and evincing all the good-humour of success. But we must return to Angélique.

Left alone with her aunt and her cousin after her father had gone out, she thankfully assented to the Captain's offer to read to her, and composed herself on the sofa to work—or rather to play mechanically with coloured wools—and to listen to him, or feign to do so. Reading, however, was but an amatory device of the gallant officer's. He read until he had sent Aunt Dorothée to sleep, which was never long; then he would lay down his book and talk confidentially and tenderly about himself by the hour—the only method he knew of making love. Captain Clarimon was of opinion that the French Army was to regenerate the whole civilized world by thrashing it—every nation taking its turn—the Russians had just had theirs; next would come the English, who had been wanting a thrashing for some time; then Austria and the Prussians, and lastly those miserable Spaniards and Swedes. He developed these views with no lack of fire, and was especially descriptive as to the parts he himself would take in the double work of civilizing and discomfiting, basing his predictions as to the future on his entirely satisfactory achievements in the past. Angélique always listened kindly, though sometimes venturing on some such simple question as whether it would not be possible to civilize some of the nations without thrashing them; but the Captain complained to himself that there was an absence of glow in her enthusiasm, none of that rapture, none of those effusive transports which the novels he had read had led him to believe were usual with fair women hearkening to the deeds

of heroes. To speak in military phrase, the brave warrior had been laying siege to his cousin for some time,
and he found that the fortress was a little long in
capitulating. This was so much the case that on the
particular evening in question, having kept up a close
bombardment for two hours, and having finally awaked
Aunt Dorothée with a start by his *furore* in picturing
for about the fifty-sixth time how those *pauvres diables
d'Anglais* would all have been stewed at Inkermann if
he and his men had not delivered them from the fry-
ing-pan, he retreated disheartened as he had done on
many former occasions, and went out to solace himself
with a night walk and a cigar on the Boulevards.
Then Angélique, a little wearied by this sanguino-
civilizing talk, laid aside her balls of red and yellow
worsted, and closed her eyes as if for a nap.

"That young man's conversation is most terrifying
and makes one's flesh creep," exclaimed Aunt Dorothée
lugubriously. "My dear, it's ten o'clock and your
husband is not in yet. He will make his headache
worse instead of better by walking so long."

"He will be in soon, I daresay, dear aunt," said
Angélique, patiently. She, too, had noticed how long
her husband remained absent; but she was used to it now.

"My dear, you are getting sleepy. That all comes
of the late hours we kept before we went into mourning," resumed Aunt Dorothée, with conviction; "which
mourning—Heaven forgive me for saying so!—is almost a mercy, for how people could remain out night
upon night as we did, and not get into their beds
until three or four in the morning, and sometimes not
until the milkman had come, is more than I can understand in a Christian land. You must lie down and
sleep, my dear. I won't speak."

Angélique faintly combated the impeachment of being sleepy, but, as the twinkling of her eyes belied her, she was soon fain to give in, and let her head sink back into the cushions.   In less than five minutes more her regular breathing told that she was asleep.

And in that short sleep she dreamed—dreamed that she was in a lonely spot amidst trees, whose branches were tossed about by the wind, whilst deluges of rain fell around her from a dark, thundering sky.   Seeking for shelter, she came to an oak, whose spreading canopy of foliage seemed to offer her protection, and there crouched.   But at that moment some of the mist and rain before her cleared away like a curtain, and disclosed two figures walking hand-in-hand.   They were the figures that were constantly in her thoughts day and night—her husband's and Georgette's.   She could see them distinctly, as if they were but a few yards off, and they were walking slowly; but there was this difference between their position and hers, that, whereas the storm raged in all its black fury above where she was standing, Horace and Georgette appeared to be in the sunshine, in a garden full of flowers and songs of birds.   They looked lovingly into each other's eyes, stopped and kissed each other—then parted.   And Horace, hurrying quickly away, came towards her under the oak.   And she would have fled, but her limbs refused to move: she was petrified, and could not even utter a cry.   He came rapidly and straight in her direction, but apparently without seeing her, for not until he almost touched her did he pause.   Then the love that still gleamed on his face changed suddenly to anger and menace.   He raised his hand and cursed her!

She started from her sleep, and sat upright with

blanched face and starting eyes. "Aunt, where is he? Did you hear what he said?" she asked, wildly.

"What, dear?" answered Aunt Dorothée, frightened and rising.

Angélique looked round her with horror-stricken gaze, as if the image she had just seen was still present to her there in the room.

"Oh! pity, pity," she cried at last, putting up her hands before her eyes to avert the light. "What a dream—what a frightful dream!"

Aunt Dorothée, in alarm, pressed to her, and endeavoured to comfort her. "You are agitated, child. It's those long walks this winter. I knew they could only do harm."

"It is over now, dear aunt," pleaded she, faintly and shivering.—"It was only a dream"—but at her aunt's urgent request, she agreed to go to bed.

In her affrighted start from her dream, however, she had upset one of the sofa cushions on to the floor. She picked it up, but, in restoring it to its place, and settling it with the others, she noticed an edge of white paper peeping out of the cavity, formed by the tight drawing of the satin covering of the sofa at one of its corners. Thinking it was a letter she herself had dropped, she drew it from its nook. As fate would have it, it was the letter written to the financier with respect to Horace's doings, by M. Louchard, three weeks before, and which had lain there ever since it had fallen out of M. Macrobe's hand—a mute witness to the careful way in which drawing-room furniture is dusted in great houses by well-paid servants.

The letter had no envelope. She opened it and read:—

"SIR—

"*M. le Duc de Hautbourg has been followed, and it seems that he has been in the habit of going to Meudon to see Mdlle. Georgette Pochemolle every morning for this past fortnight. He went there yesterday early, breakfasted at the restaurant with his mistress's brother, and returned again in the evening. He then admitted himself with a latch-key into the grounds, and remained there more than two hours. His visits are matters of public notoriety at Meudon.*

"MOÏSE LOUCHARD."

What passed within Angélique as she read this, none but God and herself ever knew. But the look of silent, agonizing, deadly woe and resignation that impressed itself on her face, would have moved a heart of stone. Aunt Dorothée seeing her stand lifeless as a statue exclaimed, "Gracious mercy, my dear, what is the matter with you? Your face has completely changed this minute. Speak, dear, you frighten me."

And Angélique spoke:—

"It was not a dream, aunt dear," she said plaintively.

CHAPTER XXII.

In Excelsis.

NOT since that day of glory, when the mighty Count Alaric had ridden triumphantly into his good town, after routing his excellent king in the field adjoining it, had the borough of Hautbourg been thrown into such a state of commotion as that caused by the announcement that Clairefontaine Castle was to be opened again, and that the new lord thereof was com-

ing to reside there. The oldest inhabitants affirmed
that the return of the first Duke after Waterloo and the
Restoration was nothing beside it; and that the solemn
visit paid to the Castle by King Charles X. and Court
was a paltry event in comparison. These were great
concessions for the civic Nestors to make, for deprecia-
tion of the past is not a common foible with those
who are leaning towards three-score and ten. But
then, it should be said, that the admission was, so to
speak, imposed upon the Nestors by the imperious
voice of public opinion, which would have flouted and
scorned and held up to ignominy any individual so
abandoned as to hint that the return of the young
Duke to his ancestral towers, and the consequent flow
of custom that would accrue to Hautbourg tills, was
not the most important episode in the modern annals
of France.

All our old friends of the "Hôtel de Clairefontaine"
table-d'hôte were to the front in their jubilations. M.
Ballanchu, the seedsman, in a new velveteen coat, for
had he not been sent for by M. Claude the agent to
furnish seeds to the Clairefontaine gardeners for all
their flower-beds? M. Scarpin, the bootmaker, who had
taken the measures of five grooms, three footmen, two
cooks, and the gamekeepers—all lately engaged at the
Castle, and who saw boundless avenues of future boots
unwind themselves before his imagination. M. Hochepain, the tax-gatherer, who would now resume the
quarterly calls he used to make at the Castle, and with
them the quarterly dinners in the butler's room that
were wont to solemnize these occasions; and Farmers
Toulmouche, Truchepoule, and Follavoine, who were
not contented about their crops, and wanted improve-
ments on their farms, and thought their rents ought to

be lowered, and hoped to set all these points right out of the new Duke's pocket.

As for M. Filoselle, who ran down for a day or two, and with an eye to business during the ferment of excitement, he was received with cordiality, and a generous forgiveness for past errors; but M. Ballanchu called upon him complacently to remember how thoroughly all his—M. Ballanchu's—predictions had been justified by the event, and how egregiously he, M. Filoselle, had strayed in his prophesyings.

"Do you recollect that discussion we had, M. Filoselle, when you attacked the Clairefontaine family, and I defended them? You said that the Hautbourgs would never come back among us, and I offered you to bet all my fortune that they would—knowing them, as I did, to be true noblemen."

"You did, you did," rejoined M. Filoselle, at first surprised, but then laughing, "and I remember I took the bet. It was ten sous. Here they are."

"I would never listen to any calumnies that were uttered against the Dukes of Hautbourg," exclaimed M. Scarpin, with determination.

"Noa," echoed Farmers Toulmouche and Truche-poule, with their mouths full.

"'Twarn't likely," continued Farmer Follavoine, licking some sauce off his fingers.

"Was I the only one, though, at the table who fell foul of the Duke?" asked M. Filoselle, amused. "I fancied I had some supporters round the board."

All eyes became intent upon their plates; then, the pause being awkward, rose and converged, with touching unanimity, towards M. Hochepain, who, being deaf, was not in a position to defend himself.

"So you and I minced the same meat, did we, M. Hochepain?" cried the traveller across the table.

M. Hochepain caught the words "mince-meat."

"Yes," said he, "it's not bad, but ought to be served with poached eggs and a bit of lemon."

"Allow me to send you some more of this goose, M. *de* Filoselle," exclaimed M. Duval, the host, blandly. He had not forgotten the wordy tournament between M. Filoselle and M. Ballanchu three years before, nor the fears he had entertained lest the peace and some of his plates should be broken. He was anxious to avoid a repetition.

"No goose ever appealed to me in vain, M. Duval. Madelon, my child, here is my plate. I expected to find you in the possession of a husband, Madelon, and hold the gallantry of Hautbourg cheap since I see you still a spinster."

"As if I wanted husbands!" exclaimed Mdlle. Madelon, pertly.

"Not many husbands, child, but one," suggested the traveller.

"I drink to the health of Monseigneur le Duc de Hautbourg," cried M. Ballanchu, as the sweets appeared on the table, and he filled his glass to the brim, undiluted.

"Stay," interposed M. Filoselle. "M. Duval, these gentlemen will allow me to offer them some champagne in which to drink this auspicious toast. Some of Mdme. Cliquot's vintage if you have it."

The wine was fetched, the corks popped, the long glasses foamed, and M. Filoselle, on his legs, amidst convivial rapping of knives, said: "Gentlemen, I second the toast of M. Ballanchu. This is to the health of

M. le Duc de Hautbourg, and God bless him! Gentlemen, I have the honour to inform you that I hope soon to be married (sensation), and my happiness on this occasion I shall owe greatly to the distinguished and amiable nobleman who is about to return to his estates to scatter prosperity amongst you all. It is not using a liberty to term him my friend, gentlemen, for we have lived under the same roof (renewed sensation). I have had the honour of grasping his hand (stupefaction), and he deigned to plead my cause with the very tortuous-minded person, whom I hope soon to call my mother-in-law (prolonged marks of astonishment). But this is not all, gentlemen. In the course of business I lately did myself the pleasure of forwarding to M. le Duc de Hautbourg a list of current prices of my employers, the MM. Campèche, wine-merchants, 367, Rue Lafitte, second house from the corner, and the answer I received was equally flattering and magnanimous—being an order for twelve dozen bottles of burgundy, and with it a cheque for the amount—one thousand four hundred and forty francs—not a centime less. (Emotion.) Messieurs, I contend that the nobleman who, whilst aiding the projects of true love, thus furthers the development of commerce—giving his orders on a liberal scale, cash down, and without asking questions, is—is all that can be said on the subject. (Loud and continued cheering—enthusiasm.) Gentlemen, I have but a word to add before finishing this after-dinner speech, which the Greek poet Virgil said ought to be short and sweet, like a burned almond. Last year, at the Paris elections, I voted for M. de Hautbourg—coming from Marseilles in the 7.55 mail-express for the special purpose, and this year I look to your all following my

example, in despite of prefects, curés, and all other
functionaries, whom I respect when they are of my
own way of thinking, but do not value that" (M.
Filoselle courageously snapped his fingers) "when it is
otherwise. Gentlemen, here is my toast: Long live
the ex-Member for Paris! Long live the new Member
for Hautbourg!"

M. Filoselle sat down amidst obstreperous rattling
of knives, and energetic shouts of "Long live the
Member for Hautbourg!"—M. Hochepain bawling the
loudest, though he bawled wrong, saying, "Long live
the Mayor and the Municipal Council!" under the
impression that it was these civic dignitaries who were
being toasted. Farmers Toulmouche, Truchepoule,
and Follavoine, having never before drank champagne,
gulped theirs down the wrong way, and then sneezed
in unison—a touching sight. M. Ballanchu mopped
his brow with his napkin, and then stoutly bellowed,
"Vote for M. le Duc? Of course we will. I should
like to know who wouldn't? I'd call him a cur."

"Quite right—never stick at trifles," responded M.
Filoselle. "But, by-the-by, you've not forgotten that
M. de Hautbourg is a sort of Radical, have you?"
And he grinned with good-natured malice at the seeds-
man. "Unless my memory fails me, you have set your
face against 'those vermin.'"

"What, I?" exclaimed M. Ballanchu, in the voice
of one crying: 'Just Heavens! was there ever so foul
a charge?' "Why, I have been a Radical ever since
—ever since, I don't know how long; and so are we
all Radicals at this table—every man jack of us, except Hochepain here," added he, adroitly. "It must
have been he who told you that."

20*

And the entire table, except the Hochepain afore-named, protested with one accord: "Yes, yes, it must have been Hochepain."

But it was not only at the table-d'hôte of the "Hôtel de Clairefontaine" that the resolution to vote for the Duke of Hautbourg was included in the programme of arrangements destined to celebrate his return. Everywhere the Hautbourgian conscience became penetrated with the sudden force of liberal principles; and the Prince of Arcola, who, on first coming down, had found the borough not indisposed against him, had, on the third or fourth day, seen the wind veer round completely. Nor was the prefect more fortunate. The private instructions given to this gentleman were enigmatical; and, to a less expert functionary, might have seemed distressing. He was not to oppose the Duke of Hautbourg, and he was not to let him get through if he could help it: which means, that outwardly his demeanour was to be smiles and honey; but that inwardly his soul was free to brew crafty rumours which the trusty agents of the prefecture would disseminate perfidiously on village swards, and in borough market-places, to undermine the candidature, if possible. To make matters worse these instructions came late. The prefect was in the heat of battle when he got them. Already had the four hundred mayors of the department been drilled and equipped for the fray; already had the four hundred vicars been put through their political catechism, reproved, exhorted, and taught the way they should go; already had justices of the peace, commissaries of police, and rural guards been told in no devious language wherein—and wherein alone—their hopes of promotion lay; and already had the prefectoral organ,

unique journal of Hautbourg, fired volley upon volley
of leading articles very heavy to read, but effective
nevertheless, as heavy shot is. It was rather hard that
all this labour should have been in vain. Rather hard
to disband the mayors, to un-lecture the vicars, to
enjoin the justices of the peace, policemen, and others
to remain religiously neutral; and to make the furious
artillery of the prefectoral organ vomit pretty sugar-
plums instead of bomb-shells. Still, all this had to be
done. When M. Gribaud requested one of his prefects to swallow a leek, that prefect swallowed the leek
and made no bones about it.

So Church and State, the governing and the
governed, all seemed in league to make things pleasant
for the lord of Clairefontaine. Carpenters began running up triumphal arches, painters to adorn them,
drapers to deck, and gardeners to festoon them.
Lumbering waggons were seen groaning on the road
to Clairefontaine under piles of new furniture, and the
Hautbourg upholsterer, exalted by a cubit in his stature,
communicated to all who would hear him, that it was
he who had executed the order for these goods, none
but he. Like stories told the grocer, the chinaman,
and the candlestick-maker, whose merchandise was
finding its way to the Castle in bales; and the butcher
and baker smiled, foreseeing that their turn would
come presently. Then the clergy and the mayoralty
laid their heads together to plan whether the two
should amalgamate in receiving Monsieur le Duc or
each give him a separate reception. And hereupon a
tremendous question of etiquette arose as to whether
the mayoralty should receive M. le Duc in official
capacity, *i.e.* clothed in its insignia of office, or merge
its welcome within that of the multitude. The point

was deemed so important that the united wits of the
prefect, his whole council of prefecture, and two sub-
prefects, declared themselves unable to solve it, and it
was referred to the Ministry, who in doubt submitted
it to the Tuileries, and the Tuileries, always full of
tact, decided, that as the return of the lord of Clairefontaine was an event with which his Majesty could
not but sympathize, the authorities should receive M.
le Duc in state; nay more, that as the crowd would
probably be great, and, perhaps, importunately affectionate, the ducal carriages should have a brigade of
mounted gendarmes to escort them from the station
to the Castle. Here was honour with a vengeance,
though, to be sure, there were some who hinted that
as the duke's entry had been fixed to take place on
the very day of the Hautbourg election, the gendarmes
might be intended quite as much to overawe the
population from uttering seditious shouts against his
Majesty as to swell the triumph of his Grace.

Whatever may have been the opinions of the prefect on this head, he kept them to himself, but about
this time a really transcendent expedient for satisfying
everybody, Tuileries, ministry, affectionate population,
and his own self, occurred to his great mind. It was
obviously quite unsafe and useless to spread defamatory
rumours against the duke—unsafe because these rumours
might be traced to their source, and useless because
the affectionate population could no longer be brought
to believe them. But there was a way of making the
very enthusiasm of the electoral mind act as a lever
for overturning the duke's election, as who should say
steam set to explode the engine it is propelling. The
prefectoral agents—generally much esteemed and un-
suspected members of municipal councils—began to

be lyrical and gushing about the bright young Seigneur who was coming back to his home. Only, they sighed and muttered what a pity it was he should be wanting to get into the Chamber again, for if returned he would certainly live three-fourths of the year at Paris, whereas in the contrary case they would enjoy the inestimable benefit of his society all the year round. The prefectoral organ scored the music to these laments, and came out diurnally with little insidious notes, such as, "M. le Duc, who is returning amongst us *for a few short weeks.*" "M. le Duc, who will henceforth be with us *at least a month or so every year.*" "M. le Duc, who will *soon* be absorbed again in the vortex of politics," &c. &c. These were good tactics. They allowed the prefect to turn the enemy's flank, to work havoc and to sow confusion without appearing to do it. There was no elector, however opaque, but took in this maxim: If the duke is at Paris he can't be here too. Several faces began insensibly to lengthen; sundry brows to brood; the election grew to be a less popular subject of conversation than it had been before. But nobody said anything. It was one of those under-water commotions that perform their ravages at a silent depth below the surface. Somehow, though, an observer might have fancied that people glanced often and pensively at M. Hochepain the tax-gatherer: as though, under certain contingencies not as yet definable, that personage might be turned to practical account. It would always be feasible to say: "I protest and vow that *I* voted for M. le Duc. It must have been Hochepain who did all the mischief."

At last the great day dawned.

Dawned with golden sunshine, speckless blue sky,

and pealing of bells, as if for a marriage feast. Hautbourg fluttered all over in bunting from its nethermost
street to its uppermost. The "Hôtel de Clairefontaine"
seemed one mighty laurel-bush blossoming with flags.
The statue of the Count Alaric had a crown of bays
set conspicuously on its head; and the museum of
stuffed birds—pride of the department—had displayed
a white eagle with a scroll between its claws:—

> Au Fils de ses bienfaiteurs
> La Ville de Hauthourg
> Souhaite Bienvenue.

On the pavements thronged densely, expectantly, solemnly, and palpitatingly, more suits of Sunday best
than had ever been seen gathered together in one spot
within that borough, on the same day. Peasants from
the villages in indigo blouses, and with scarlet um-
brellas under their arms; peasant women with white
cone-caps towering sprucely out of sight, smart ker-
chiefs pinned cross-wise on their bosoms, golden crosses
pendent from black velvet ribbons round their throats.
Every window was abloom with new bonnet-strings;
every doorway had its cluster of sight-seers holding on
anyhow, as it pleased Heaven, by the lintels, by the
backs of chairs placed so that those behind might see
over the heads of those to the fore, by the shop-fronts.
Now and then a wag would cry: "Here they come;"
and there would be a rocking forward, a headlong
heave, and some well-laden chairs, taken unawares,
would crash down supine, they and their cargoes.
Upon which general merriment: people are easily ex-
hilarated in such moments. Suddenly a shout, a long
murmur, and then suppressed excitement as three
splendid barouches, each drawn by four horses, and
flashing with fresh paint, armorial scutcheons, and

purple and gold liveries of postilions and outriders sweep, at a stately trot down the main street from the castle on their way to the station. Horace had left his agent to manage matters, and the agent, directed by M. Macrobe, had managed them royally. Almost immediately, new murmur, and then imposing apparition of the Mayor and Municipal Council: the former in a new hat, and with a tri-coloured scarf round his girth; the latter treading on each other's heels, clean shaved, shy at being looked at, but impressed with the gravity of the situation, and prepared, like Roman senators, to do their duty to the last. Then, triumphant march in lonely glory of Monsieur the sub-Prefect of Haulbourg, majestuous in a silver-spangled swallow-tail, a cocked-hat too big for him, and white gloves, which he cracks as he strides in trying to get into them. Next, the local clergy in cassocks, not chasubles, but headed by an archdeacon great at controversy, gaunt-eyed, and evidently pregnant of a speech. Lastly, the gendarmes, yellow-belted, pipe-clayed, prancing, and much admired by the cone-capped peasant-women. Then a lull. The tower clock of Ste. Brigitte's chimes musically the three-quarters past something. It is the hour. A moment more, and the piercing whistle of the express is heard in the distance . . . .

Then—but why describe such a sight, or how describe it? How phonograph delirium on to paper? Again and again, peal upon peal, round upon round, rose the cheers, the shouts of welcome, the benedictions. Down fell the nosegays in showers, thick, fragrant, pitiless, everywhere, on the horses' heads, under their feet, in the carriages, on the laps of the carriages' occupants, covering hoods, seats, spatterdashes, with white, red, pink, and lilac petals. Handkerchiefs, banners, scrolls, waved, flapped, tossed to and fro as if blown by a gale. The gendarmes, clearing the way, ploughed slowly through a mass of outstretched hands, uplifted children, agitated hats, like fishing-smacks steering their keels through a surf; and above this astounding din, this frantic tumult of a city in a fever, rose the riot of the belfries and the crashing strains of brass bands drawn up under the triumphal arches.

Horace moved his hat off and on, very pale, and bowed without respite during three miles. He was startled and dazzled, but if ever man felt himself master of a town and king of it thenceforth, assuredly that man was he. And his heart beat fast, and his temples throbbed as he thought that this ovation was but the prelude to others, the first step in a long vista of power and fame then opening before him. In the second barouche, M. Macrobe, by no means overcome, but beaming, smiled and bowed to the crowd as General Monk may have done, to whom M. Gribaud had not inaptly compared him. But it was General Monk become Duke of Albemarle, knowing what was what, and saying within himself: "All those cheers of yours, my friends, are of my manufacture—don't let's have any mistake about it." Beside the financier sat Aunt Dorothée, but the worthy lady could scarcely be compared to the Duke of Albemarle's sister, if that illustrious man possessed such a relative. Scared, in an utter state of collapse, and ready to cry, she whimpered her orisons beneath her breath, and dismally expected to meet the end of the world at the termination of all this. And ever and anon in her bewilderment she gazed stupefied at the bunting, reflecting that there was enough there to clothe ten villages; and at the purple vestments of the outriders, and the satin linings of the carriages, and at the prodigal waste of flowers, with disjointed thoughts as to what all these things must have cost. In the third vehicle was another scene. There the delighted Mr. Drydust, self-invited, held forth to Jean Kerjou, come as special reporter to the *Gazette des Boulevards*, to M. Gousset and to the Crimean Hero, about the marriage of his Pomeranian friend, Count Trinkgeld, of which the present festivities reminded him. The coming of age of his other friend, Lord Wildoats, had also been very remarkable. But he was inclined to award the palm to French solemnities of this kind. To begin with, they were rarer, and then the people shouted more and weren't ashamed to shed tears at the sight of one: "Which is what I like," said Mr. Drydust.

And so saluting and full of emotion, or radiant and quietly chuckling, or terrified and miserable, or agreeably anecdotical and loquacious, according to the mood and temper of its individual members, the cortége moved on its way: until the park-gates of Clairefontaine were passed, and all other feelings became immersed in one dominant, though voiceless, burst of admiration for the lordly castle, over whose towers the standard of the Hautbourgs was now waving for the first time after such a long period of mourning.

The tenantry were marshalled in respectful rows; on the marble staircase the dependents had arrayed themselves to do obeisance; and as the carriages stopped, the bare-headed steward stepped forward to assist the Duke and Duchess to alight and said: "Welcome to Clairefontaine, Madame; welcome to your home, Monseigneur."

* * * *

It was mellow evening before Angélique could

withdraw from the feasting, and toasting, and speech-making, which, under the form of a breakfast to local magnates, officials, tenants and guests, took up the whole afternoon from midday till six.   Then she con-trived to glide out into the park with Aunt Dorothée, whilst a good many of the gentlemen sped Hautbourg-wards to be present at the close of the poll and bring back the result early.

She wanted to be alone, and to think.

With the letter she had found a day or two before pressing on her bosom like a cilice, with the memory of her short, frightful dream glaring before her eyes like a fixed vision, how wonder, that during the re-joicings of the morning, her own spirit should have been as heavy as that of one bereaved, amidst a banquet?

Bereaved, indeed!   Bereaved of all that made life worth living for.   Confidence, hope, the sense of being loved, and of having a blessed part to perform in effect-ing the happiness of a loved heart.

All this was gone now.   All washed away by one black tide.   *Omnes fluctus tui et omnes gurgites tui super me transierunt.*

She had not had the thought of destroying the letter.   She had kept it next her heart.   Why, she scarcely knew.   But there was a vague idea, a trust that it might help her to take a resolution and ac-complish it.   Early Christians going to martyrdom hung amulets about their necks to give them fortitude.

On the way through Hautbourg the women had been moved by the pale, young, and beautiful duchess, who smiled to them so softly, yet with such wistful melancholy as she bowed.   "She was a little dazed, poor thing," said they, and the men, not less compassionate, remarked: "It seemed to frighten her, poor lady."

Angélique was feeling all the way as if she was usurping the place she held, as if the cheers and welcomes she received were not hers. She entered Clairefontaine like a stranger. She had heard of those death's-heads put on the table at feasts. She was as one of these. What right had she to a place in her husband's castle, she who had no room in his heart?

"Where shall we go to, dear," asked Aunt Dorothée. "Gracious mercy! it is a boon to be out in the fresh air alone again. How people can go through all we have this day and not be struck ill in their beds is more than I know, my dear."

Angélique looked round and saw a sheet of water glancing under distant trees in the golden light of the setting sun.

"Let us go that way, aunt dear," she murmured.

The lake was a broad and deep one, with a leafy island of willows in the middle; and an ornamental grotto or two dotting its margin. These grottoes had been used as boat-houses, or arbors in which to picnic in summer weather; but deserted for years, they were now carpeted with velvet moss, and drops of crystal water fell like stalactites from their roofs.

To the largest of these grottoes went Angélique and her aunt. The evening was fairy-like, and the herds of red and fallow deer trooping away affrighted at the approach of footsteps, lent an air of sylvan beauty to the noiseless scene. The grotto stood in a retired bend of the lake, and nature was so still around it, the water so profound, the foliage so dark and clustering, that Aunt Dorothée, a little awe-struck, whispered: "My dear, how death-like this is. It makes one think of graves."

"Let us go into the grotto," said Angélique.

This grotto had two chambers, one below and the other above. They were connected by a winding staircase of rocks and shells, and from the upper room, which, like the lower, had only three walls, the fourth side being open over the lake, a wide view of the surrounding park could be had. Both women stood gazing at the lake during a minute, and then Angélique, with a strange expression in her eyes, which her aunt called to mind later, suddenly kissed her—once, twice—silently.

"Aunt, dear, I am going to ascend the staircase to see the view," she then said.

"Oh, my dear, we shall never be able to get up those stairs."

"No, don't you follow me, aunt; it will be too steep. I shall not be a minute."

And she began her ascent; but half-way she stopped, turned, and again looked at her aunt. There was that same strange look in her eyes, only deeper and moistened. She kissed her hand to the good woman who had been all her life as a mother to her, and the next instant was in the upper grotto.

Then she looked round. There was nobody in sight. The air was so still that the willow-branches scarce touched the water with their green lips; the water was calm, deep, and clear—one could see the white bed of sand some twelve feet below the surface.

"It must be a gentle death," said Angélique, gazing at that white bed,—"like sleep."

Then she looked once more around her, and at the corners of the grotto, and below her feet at the slippery ledge overlooking the lake.

"It will free *Him*," she murmured, "and I shall make him happy, which I could not do by living.

But he must never know that it was done on purpose.
They will think it was an accident—that I slipped. I
will scream as I fall."

She unfastened her dress, took out the letter, and
threw it into the lake, with a little stone in it, so that
it might sink.

"You will not punish me for this, Almighty God!"
she said, dropping on her knees on the brink, and
clasping her hands humbly; then, raising her hands
aloft at the precise moment when the sun sunk out of
sight, she uttered a wailing cry, and allowed herself to
fall forward.

   *   *   *   *   *

It was not till almost an hour afterwards that the
crowd reached the spot—appalled, hurrying, bringing
drags, ropes, and restoratives. Aunt Dorothée had at
first fainted, and could not tell how long she had remained senseless, before strength returned to her to
crawl away, and summon help; but when she reached
the Castle she found it already dismayed. A startling
piece of news had just been brought in by reluctant
messengers. The new lord of Clairefontaine and his
father-in-law had both missed their elections, and
simultaneously a telegram from Paris had brought the
news that M. Emile Gerold had been elected, in spite
of himself, in the Tenth Circumscription of the Seine.
The Duke had made no remark, but he had bit his lips,
and turned ashy white. As for Monseigneur's father-
in-law, he looked like to have a stroke of apoplexy.

This is what the servants were whispering to one
another in the quadrangle of the Castle when Aunt
Dorothée appeared amongst them, like a ghost, and
shrieked, "Help! help!—my child—the Duchess—your
mistress—has fallen into the lake!"

But the crowd might have spared itself its haste, its efforts, its well-meant ministrations; for when they drew the fair young body from the water, it had sunk into that last sleep from which no restoratives can revive us. A great circle was made, and every head was uncovered, as, whiter than a marble image in the moonlight, Angélique was laid on a hurdle-bier covered with soft branches.

"Poor child, poor child!" cried some. "She slipped off the grotto."

"Monseigneur," said a diver, reeking wet, and approaching Horace, who was holding his wife's head whilst the men were lifting the bier; "I found this paper close to the poor lady so to say, near her hand."

Horace unfolded the paper with trembling hand. It was M. Louchard's letter. Then those who watched him saw his knees shake and his body stagger forward heavily. He fell prostrate with his face to the earth, and his lips sealed on the hem of his wife's garment.

The great circle standing around respected this grief and remained motionless waiting till he should rise; but as his position did not change, somebody advanced and said: "Monseigneur," and laid a hand gently on his shoulder. Then he swayed a little to his left and rolled over by his wife's side, her hand falling softly on his in that motion, in silent token of forgiveness.

He was dead.

THE END.

www.ingramcontent.com/pod-product-compliance
Lightning Source LLC
Chambersburg PA
CBHW021220270326
41929CB00010B/1202